OCTOPUS

CHILDREN'S
ENCYCLOPEDIA

OCTOPUS

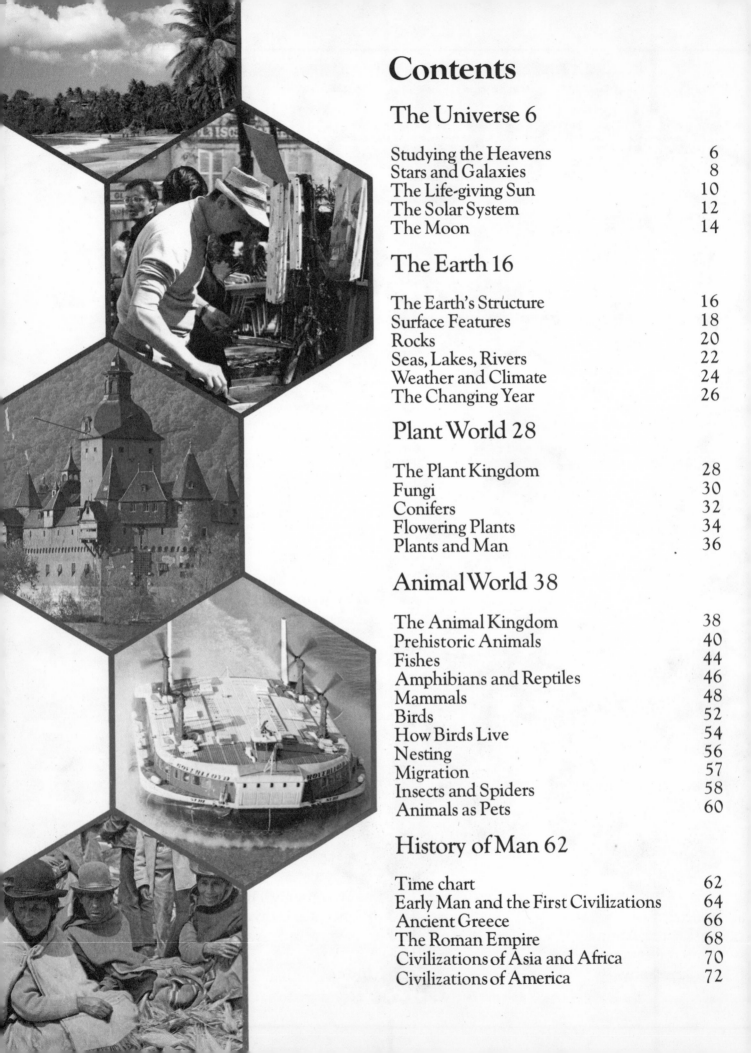

Contents

1 THE UNIVERSE

The universe stretches as far as the most powerful telescopes can see—and farther. It contains countless millions of galaxies, and each galaxy contains countless millions of stars. Our Sun is just one of these stars.

Studying the Heavens

People who study the heavens are called astronomers. They practise the science of astronomy. Astronomy is also a popular hobby. Thousands of amateur astronomers, young and old, enjoy gazing at the night skies with simple telescopes or through binoculars.

Early Astronomers
Astronomy is perhaps the oldest science of all. The Chaldeans and the Babylonians were skilled observers of the heavens

Below right: Some telescopes use curved mirrors to gather light rays. They are called reflectors. Others, called refractors, use lenses. The diagram shows how a refractor works. It has two sets of lenses held in a tube. The object lens collects the light. The eye-piece lens can be moved in and out for focusing.

Below and left: Astronomers pass starlight through a prism in an instrument called a spectroscope. The prism splits the starlight into a spectrum, or band of colour crossed by dark lines. These tell them many things, such as how hot the star is. Sirius, for example, is a hotter star than the Sun.

Words Used in Astronomy

eclipse The partial or complete 'hiding' of one heavenly body by another.

galaxy A large group of stars.

light-year A unit of distance used in astronomy. It is the distance travelled by light in one year—9.5 million million kilometres (5.9 million million miles).

moon A natural body that orbits a planet.

orbit The path of one heavenly body as it travels round another.

satellite Any body—natural or man-made—that orbits a heavenly body.

solar system A star and its satellites.

star A heavenly body that produces its own heat and light. Our Sun is a star.

universe Everything that exists. The universe appears to be expanding like a balloon being blown up.

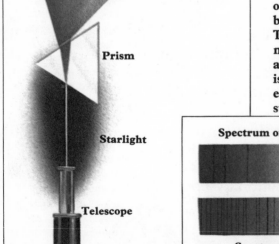

Spectrum

Prism

Starlight

Telescope

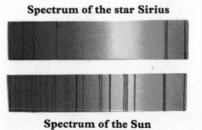

Spectrum of the star Sirius

Spectrum of the Sun

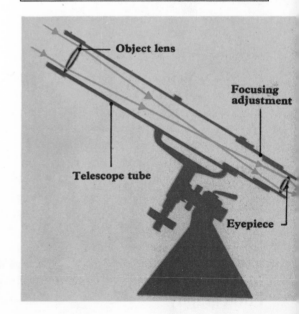

Object lens

Focusing adjustment

Telescope tube

Eyepiece

more than 5,000 years ago. Without the help of telescopes, they were able to make up a calendar from their observations.

The ancient Greeks mapped the stars over 2,000 years ago. Later, the Greek astronomer Ptolemy wrote the first books on the subject. He believed that the Earth was the centre of the universe, and all the other bodies revolved around it. This belief was widely held until the year 1543, when a Polish astronomer, Nicolas Copernicus, suggested that the Earth and the other planets revolved around the Sun.

The first simple telescopes were invented in the early 1600s. By studying the heavens through a telescope, the great Italian astronomer Galileo Galilei (1564-1642) was able to show that Copernicus had been correct. Later, other astronomers confirmed this.

Astronomy Today

Professional astronomers today work in observatories. These are large dome-topped buildings that house the giant telescopes used to observe the night sky. But astronomers seldom look through their telescopes. They use them as cameras to take pictures. By exposing film for long periods, they can spot some of the faintest stars.

Other modern 'tools' of the astronomer include the great dish-like radio telescopes which are used to study radio waves given out by stars. Since the start of the Space Age, astronomers have been able to send telescopes into space, where viewing conditions are ideal. They have also sent telescopes and cameras on space-craft to the Moon and the planets to study these at close quarters and send back information.

Many stars give off radio waves as well as light. Astronomers study them with huge radio telescopes. The Arecibo tele-scope, above, in Puerto Rico, is built over a natural bowl in the mountains. Its dish, which is 305 metres (1,000 feet) across, collects radio waves from distant stars. The more common types use metal mesh dishes, as shown at the bottom right.

7

Stars and Galaxies

The stars you can see in the night sky are many billions of miles away. Even the Sun, which is a star, is 150 million kilometres (93 million miles) away. Some stars seem to be much brighter than others because they are nearer, and some are bright because they are very big.

Distances in space are so enormous that it is easier to measure them in light-years than in kilometres or miles. One light-year is the distance that light travels in one year, about 10 million million kilometres (6 million million miles). The nearest star to Earth, beyond the Sun, is more than 40 million million kilometres (25 million million miles) away. The light from this star takes 4·3 years to reach us, so you can say that it is 4·3 light-years away.

Our Sun is an average-sized star, about 1,400,000 kilometres (865,000 miles) across, but there are stars called giant stars that are several times bigger, and supergiant stars which are hundreds of millions of kilometres across. There are also stars called white dwarfs that are very much smaller than the Sun.

Stars seem to twinkle as you look at them, but this is because the Earth's atmosphere is bending the light. The stars normally shine very brightly, but some, called variable stars, periodically change in brightness. Stars called novae flare up and then fade in brightness and supernovae flare up so much that they blow themselves apart.

Pictures in the Sky

The bright stars in the sky seem to form patterns in groups. These groups of stars are called constellations. When the first astronomers noticed these groups, they imagined that they formed pictures in the sky. Constellations are named in Latin after the sort of picture that they form. For example, Ursa Major (the Great Bear), Leo (the Lion) and Orion (the hunter).

The stars that you can see in the constellations look close together, but they are sometimes light-years apart. They only seem

Below: On a clear night it is sometimes possible to see a faint band of light arcing across the sky. This is called the Milky Way and it represents a slice through our galaxy. It consists of millions of stars which you can see if you look through binoculars.

The constellations we can see depend on where we are on Earth. The best place to be is near the Equator where, over the year, we can see almost all the constellations.

Constellations of the Southern Hemisphere

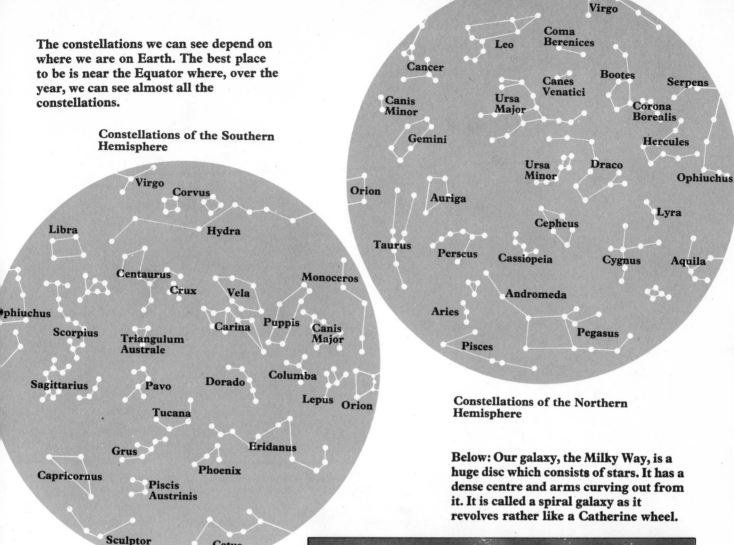

Constellations of the Northern Hemisphere

Below: Our galaxy, the Milky Way, is a huge disc which consists of stars. It has a dense centre and arms curving out from it. It is called a spiral galaxy as it revolves rather like a Catherine wheel.

close together because they are behind one another as we look at them. Some stars travel through space alone, but most stars group together to form star clusters and galaxies. When two stars revolve around each other they are called a binary star system, and when there are more than two they are called a multiple star system. Sometimes stars group together in clusters of hundreds, known as open clusters, or even in clusters of many thousands which are known as globular clusters.

All the many constellations that we can see with the naked eye form a huge disc of stars that revolves in space. This is the Milky Way. The Milky Way is a galaxy, which is a huge group of millions of stars. Our galaxy is about 100,000 light-years from edge to edge and contains about 100,000 million stars. It is spiral shaped, with bands of stars curving out from the centre. Other galaxies are elliptical, or oval, and some are irregular in shape.

The Life-giving Sun

The Sun is a star, just like thousands of other stars you can see in the night sky. The reason it seems so much bigger and brighter than all the other stars is because it is so much nearer to us. But it is an average-sized star with a diameter of about 1,400,000 kilometres (865,000 miles).

The Sun was formed many thousands of millions of years ago. A cloud of gas and dust in space gradually began to spin until it became a huge disc. The centre of the disc was thicker than the edges and soon became a hot ball in the centre. This ball got hotter and smaller and detached itself from the disc to form the Sun. The planets of the solar system formed from the rest of the disc, and still revolve round their parent star, the Sun.

Like all stars, it will not shine forever. It will probably continue to shine for another 5,000 million years before it changes very much. After that time it will get bigger and bigger until it has become a giant red star many times its present size when it will scorch all life from Earth. Then it will begin to shrink again until it is very much smaller than it is now and will become first a white dwarf star, then end its life as a black dwarf.

A Nuclear Furnace

The Sun shines in the same way as all other stars. It is a huge ball of plasma that is white-hot on the surface. At the centre there is an enormous atomic reaction which 'burns' hydrogen. The process of nuclear reaction in the Sun is the same as in a hydrogen bomb. The very centre is the hottest part of the Sun where the temperature is several million degrees Centigrade. This nuclear reaction fuses atoms of hydrogen together to form atoms of helium and the energy produced in this natural nuclear reactor is given out as heat and light. At the surface of the Sun the temperature is very much less, about 6,000 degrees Centigrade, but is still extremely hot.

Scientists have studied the Sun's surface with special instruments and found that it is a huge sea of gas. Until recently it has been difficult to study the Sun because looking at it, especially through telescopes, damages

Above: Eclipses of the Sun were feared in ancient times. The Chinese believed that a dragon was trying to swallow the Sun. They would make a great noise to frighten it away, which, of course, always worked.

Bottom: The Moon is eclipsed when it moves into the shadow cast by the Earth, and the Sun, Earth and Moon are in a straight line. It takes the Moon up to two and a half hours to move through this shadow.

Below: An eclipse of the Sun occurs when the Moon comes between the Sun and the Earth. A total eclipse is when the Moon's disc covers the Sun's disc exactly. Day turns into night for about seven minutes.

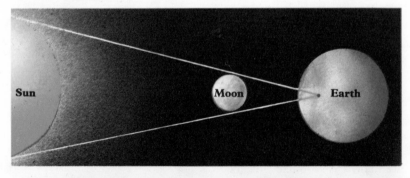

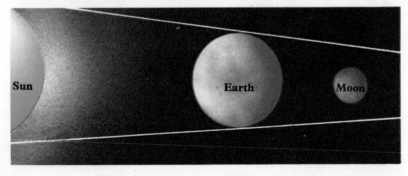

the eyes. Astronomers now use special equipment to tell them about the Sun. You should *never* look at the Sun, except through darkened glass.

Life-giving Energy

The energy that the Sun gives out is essential to life on Earth. It provides us with both heat and light. Plants need light to grow, and they are an essential part of our food chain. We eat plant food ourselves, but we also eat animals that live on plants. Some of the rays that the Sun sends out are very harmful to life, but these are filtered out by our atmosphere.

Changes in the Sun, or in the amount of energy reaching Earth, can affect conditions here. For example, scientists have observed dark sunspots which are cooler than the rest of the Sun's surface. Sunspots vary in size and sometimes they disappear altogether. Over a period of time, an absence of sunspots seems to make the weather on Earth generally colder. Some scientists believe this could have caused the great ice ages.

Eclipses of the Sun and Moon

Eclipses happen in our solar system when two planetary bodies are directly in line with the Sun. The planet farther away from the Sun is then in the shadow of the nearer body. An eclipse of the Sun happens when the Moon comes between the Earth and the Sun. In a partial eclipse, the Moon cuts out some of the light from the Sun, and in a total eclipse, the Moon appears to cover the Sun completely. Although the Moon is very much smaller than the Sun, because it is closer it almost exactly covers the Sun as we see it on Earth.

Another kind of eclipse is an eclipse of the Moon. This happens when the Earth comes between the Sun and the Moon. The Moon is then in the shadow of the Earth and is in darkness. An eclipse of the Moon can last for up to two and a half hours because the Earth's shadow is so large, but an eclipse of the Sun only lasts for a few minutes. When the Moon is eclipsed there is no light falling on its surface, but even in a total eclipse of the Sun, only a small part of the Earth's surface is in shadow.

A total eclipse of the Sun is a very strange event. Primitive people thought that it was some kind of sign from the gods, or even that the world was coming to an end. It is still a very peculiar sensation being at a total eclipse when, locally, day very quickly becomes night. Because the Sun played such a large part in ancient religions, many superstitions and myths have grown up about eclipses of the Sun.

Above: Huge flames shoot out from the surface of the Sun like fountains. These are called flares. Sometimes there are fountains of flaming gas thousands of kilometres high called prominences. In other places on the surface there are areas that are relatively cool. They look darker than the rest of the Sun and are called sunspots.

11

The Solar System

The solar system is the name given to our Sun and its planets. The word solar comes from the Latin name for the Sun, *sol*. The Sun is a star, and it is quite likely that many other stars have planets circling them, but so far no other system of planets has been discovered.

There are nine planets circling the Sun in huge oval paths called orbits. People of the ancient world observed the movements of the planets and thought they were wandering stars. They were frightened by the idea that stars could move about and gave them the names of powerful gods— Mercury, Venus, Mars, Jupiter, Saturn. They did not know that the Earth was one of these 'wandering stars'. The nearest planet to the Sun is Mercury, and it is probably the smallest planet in the solar system. It has a diameter of about 4,850 kilometres (3,015 miles) and is about the same size as Pluto, the planet farthest from the Sun. No one knows exactly how big Pluto is and it is thought by some scientists to be smaller than Mercury.

The second nearest planet to the Sun is Venus. It is only slightly smaller than the Earth. Venus is sometimes known as the 'evening star' although it is not a star at all. Stars shine because they are burning and produce their own light, but planets only reflect the Sun's rays. It is called the evening star because at certain times of the year it shines brightly in the sky just after sunset. Venus and Mercury are nearer to the Sun than the Earth and are very hot planets. It would be impossible for any life as we know it to survive on these planets because of the heat. Venus is also covered with thick clouds of carbon dioxide and sulphuric acid.

Our Sun is a very ordinary star. It is just one of millions in our galaxy. But it is more than a million times larger than the Earth. The planets move anti-clockwise around the Sun. It takes Mercury 88 days to orbit the Sun, Earth 365 days, and Pluto as long as 247 years.

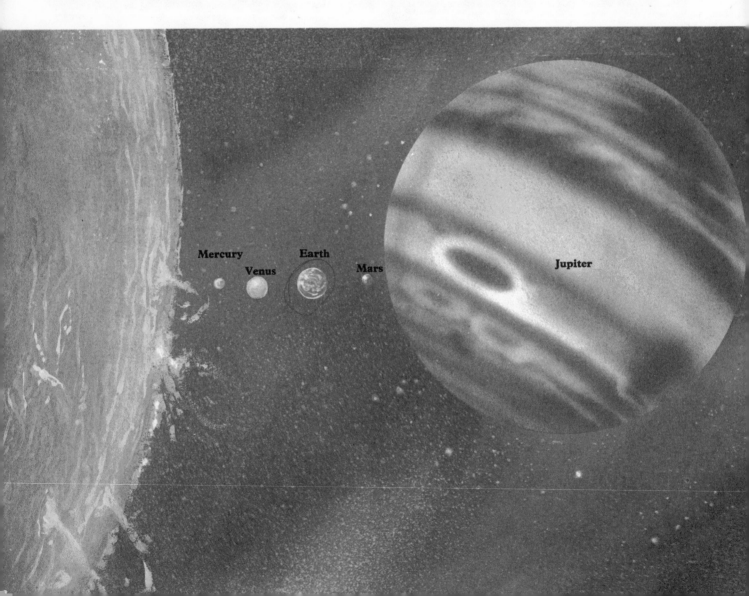

Mercury Venus Earth Mars Jupiter

The planet next distant from the Sun is our own planet, Earth, and next comes Mars. Mars is a little smaller than Venus and is often known as the red planet. The dust on its surface is red, and when it reflects light from the Sun, Mars appears to shine with a red light. When the Italian astronomer Schiaparelli observed Mars in 1877, he noticed straight lines across its surface which he called 'canals'. People thought that these canals had been made by animals or people who lived on Mars, but space probes have now indicated that there is probably no life on Mars. The surface of Mars is like a huge dusty desert covered with volcanoes and craters, and the atmosphere of carbon dioxide is very thin.

The Giant Planets

Jupiter, the fifth planet away from the Sun, is huge. It has a diameter of 142,600 kilometres (88,600 miles) and is more than a thousand times bigger than the Earth. When astronomers look at Jupiter through a telescope they can see that it has bands of different colours. There is a red spot on the planet. This may be a huge and violent storm that has been raging on the surface of the planet for centuries.

Saturn is almost as big as Jupiter. It is about 120,200 kilometres (74,700 miles) across and is the planet which has a set of rings around its equator. There are four rings, probably made of ice and dust, and they can be seen from the Earth at certain times, with the aid of a powerful telescope. When the angle of the rings means that they are edge-on to the Earth, it is very difficult to see them because they are so thin.

Beyond Saturn, Uranus and Neptune orbit the Sun. They are about the same size. Uranus is about 46,500 kilometres (28,900 miles) across and Neptune is about 48,000 kilometres (30,000 miles). Beyond them is the planet farthest from the Sun, Pluto. Not very much is known about these planets as they are so far away. Even when it is at its closest to the Earth, Pluto is about 5,000 million kilometres (3,000 million miles) away, well beyond the reach of space probes.

The idea that the planets revolved round the Sun, rather than around the Earth, was first suggested by the Greek philosopher Aristarchos in about 290 BC. But nobody would accept this idea until it was reintroduced by a Polish doctor called Nicolas Copernicus (below) in 1543.

Pluto

Neptune

Uranus

Saturn

The Moon

The Moon is Earth's nearest neighbour in space. It is close enough for us to see surface details. The bright regions are highlands covered with craters, and the dark regions are flat plains called 'maria'. The Apollo astronauts visited the Moon. They found that it is a lifeless wasteland covered with dust.

Several planets have smaller bodies circling them. These small planets are called satellites or moons. The Earth has only one satellite (which we call the Moon), and Mars and Neptune have two moons each. Uranus has five moons, and the two giant planets, Saturn and Jupiter, have several more. Saturn has ten, and Jupiter has 14.

The Earth's moon is only about 385,000 kilometres (240,000 miles) away. Because it is so close, scientists have discovered a great deal about it. Men have walked on the Moon and brought back samples of its rocks.

The Moon is very small compared with the Earth. Its diameter is about a quarter that of the Earth's, which means the Earth is about 50 times the size of the Moon. Because it is so small, it does not have a strong gravity. Things weigh far less on the Moon than they do here, and it is possible for a man to jump about six times as high as he can on Earth. The Moon's gravity, nevertheless, is strong enough to influence the tides on Earth.

Astronomers have examined the Moon's surface with telescopes for hundreds of years. They have now made maps of the surface and discovered mountain ranges and craters. They also found that many of the dark areas on the Moon are flat plains. Early astronomers thought that these plains were seas and called them 'maria' (the Latin for 'seas'), but we now know that there is no water on the Moon.

Before men invented rockets, it was

Moon Myths

The ancient Romans and Greeks thought that the stars and planets they could see were gods living in the sky. They gave these heavenly bodies the names of their gods and goddesses and the Moon was known as Diana, who was also goddess of the hunts.

Because of the colour of the Moon's surface and the dark patches on it, people used to think that it was made of green cheese! People also thought that the dark patches formed a kind of face which they called the Man in the Moon. We now know that these different colours are caused by the mountains, plains and circular craters on the Moon's surface.

Many people still believe that the Moon affects our lives here on Earth. Astrologers say that the different phases of the Moon are important when they are working out a person's horoscope.

The word 'lunatic' comes from the Latin word 'luna' which means 'moon'. People used to believe that anybody who was mad had been affected in some way by the Moon. Lunatics were supposed to be more mad at the time of the full moon.

Werewolves are also said to be affected by the Moon. In some areas people still think that some people change into wolves at the time of the full moon. Like vampires, werewolves only exist in horror films and books!

There are many superstitions connected with the Moon. It is said to be unlucky to look at a new moon through glass, but the full moon is the time to make wishes or choose a husband.

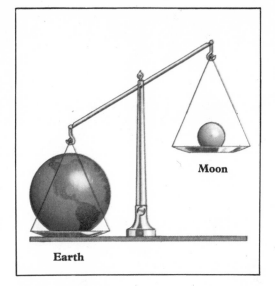

Moon

Earth

Left: The Moon is considerably smaller than the Earth. Its diameter is about a quarter of that of the Earth. If the Earth was hollow nearly 50 Moons could fit into it. But even though there is a big difference in size, the Moon and the Earth are still closer in size than the other planets and their satellites or moons.

Below and bottom right: The light of the Moon is not given out by the Moon itself. It is reflected from the Sun. As the Moon circles the Earth different parts of it are lit up by the Sun. It looks as if the Moon is changing shape. These different shapes are called the phases of the Moon. These two diagrams together show how the phases occur.

impossible to know what the other side of the Moon looked like. As the Moon circles the Earth, it rotates so that it keeps the same face towards us. Pictures taken from rockets circling the Moon have now shown us that the far side of the Moon has a much smoother surface than the one we can see.

The Moon reflects sunlight on to the Earth. It shines at certain times. Each month, the Moon appears to change shape as only part of it is lit up by the Sun. The full moon can be seen when the Sun shines directly on to the Moon, and the new moon when the Sun lights up the opposite side. There are several phases or stages of the Moon between the full moon and the new moon, when it has a semicircular or crescent shape.

Moon's phases

1   2   3   4   5   6   7   8

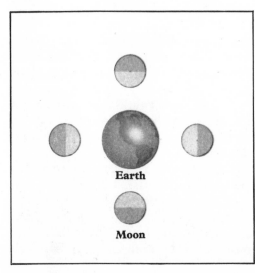

Earth

Moon

Left: Whenever there is a full moon you will always see the same face of the Moon. This does not mean that the Moon doesn't move, but that as it circles the Earth it spins on its own axis. It takes the same time to spin once on its axis as it does to circle once round the Earth. Rockets have enabled us to study the far side of the Moon for the first time.

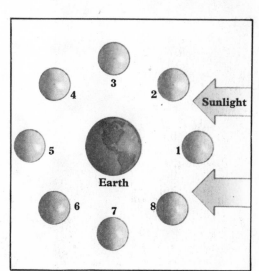

Sunlight

Earth

2 THE EARTH

Our planet, the Earth, is about 4,600 million years old. It was probably formed, along with the Sun and the planets in our solar system, from a massive cloud of gas and dust. It is the fifth largest planet in the solar system.

The Earth's Structure

How the Earth was Formed

Scientists do not know how the Earth was formed, and several theories have been put forward. The theory most generally accepted today is that the Sun and its planets were formed at about the same time from a huge cloud of gas and dust. The Sun was probably the centre of this cloud. As the dust swirled around the centre it flattened out, like a huge wheel, and a number of eddies or whirlpools formed in it. In time, the Sun became smaller and very hot and separated from the disc. Each of the eddies drew more dust and gas into it, and gradually they contracted to form the Earth and the other planets.

It is thought that as the mass of dust and gas shrank in upon itself it produced great heat—the heat we know is present today under the Earth's surface. The heat led to a number of chemical reactions, which in due course produced the water of which the oceans are made, and the mixture of nitrogen, oxygen and other gases which forms the Earth's atmosphere.

Earth's partner, the Moon, was formed at the same time as the Sun. One theory is that the Moon was originally another, smaller planet which was 'captured' by the Earth's gravitational pull.

The Earth's Cross-section

If you could cut a wedge out of the Earth you would find a very dense, heavy inner core. As the Earth was forming, heavy materials, such as iron and nickel, formed this solid core. Around this is the outer core. Scientists believe that the materials in this layer are hot and liquid. The diameter of the whole core is about 6,920 kilometres (4,300 miles). The next layer is the mantle, about 2,900 kilometres (1,800 miles) thick and around this is the outermost layer or crust. The crust varies between 8 and 32 kilometres (5 and 20 miles) in thickness and is formed from lighter materials, mostly granite and basalt. The mantle beneath it consists of heavier rocks. You would not be able to see exactly where one layer ends and another begins, because they all blend into each other.

Unlike prehistoric man, we now know that the world is not flat. But it is not completely round either. The constant rotation of the Earth pulls out the Equator. So the diameter of the Earth at the Equator is greater than the diameter from pole to pole.

The Earth is not a true sphere. The diameter at the Equator is 12,756 km (7,926 miles), while from pole to pole it is 12,713 km (7,899 miles). The Earth's mass is 5,976 million million million tonnes (5,882 million million million tons).

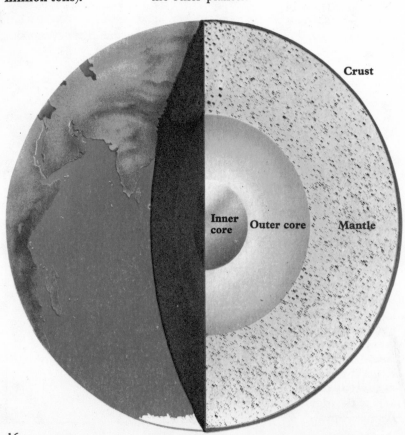

Crust

Inner core   Outer core   Mantle

Dictionary

abyss The deepest part of the ocean.

atmosphere The layer of gases that surrounds the Earth. It consists mainly of nitrogen and oxygen and smaller amounts of other gases and water vapour.

continent A large land mass and the islands around its coast.

continental drift The gradual movements of the continents to their present positions from those that they occupied in the distant past.

continental plate A large area of the Earth's crust that lies under oceans and land areas of the surface.

continental shelf The part of a continent that is under the sea.

continental slope The steep slope which goes from the continental shelf to the abyss. The continental slope is the true edge of the continent.

core The centre of the Earth. The inner core is solid and is surrounded by an outer core of liquid rock.

crust The outer shell of the Earth.

delta The area formed at the mouth of a river by the deposit of sediment.

equinox The days on which the Earth's position in relation to the Sun allows equal hours of daylight and darkness.

erosion The way that the land is worn away by wind and water.

fault A crack between two continental plates which forms an unstable line in the Earth's crust, along which earthquakes and volcanoes may occur.

glacier A slow-moving 'river' of ice.

igneous rocks Rocks made of solidified magma.

lava Molten rock that comes to the Earth's surface.

magma The liquid rock under the Earth's surface.

mantle The layer of the Earth between the core and the crust.

metamorphic rocks Rocks that have changed because of the effects of heat, pressure, and chemical action.

Pangaea The name given to the land mass formed when all the continents were joined together 200 million years ago.

sedimentary rocks Rocks formed from fragments of older rocks, which were suspended in water and settled down to the bottom of the sea in layers that have become compressed.

solstice The days on which the Earth is tilted at such an angle to the Sun to allow the most or the fewest hours of daylight.

water cycle The circulation of water from the sea to the clouds, on to the land as rain and back to the sea in rivers.

water table The level below which the land is saturated with water. It may vary according to the amount of rainfall.

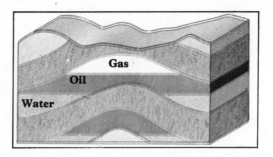

Left: Natural gas and oil are often found in layers of porous rock in an upfold or anticline. The porous rocks are trapped between layers of solid rock.

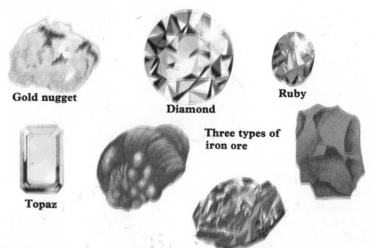

Gold nugget

Diamond

Ruby

Topaz

Three types of iron ore

Natural Resources

The Earth's crust is full of valuable substances that we use in everyday life. These include many minerals, and the fuels coal, oil and natural gas. These are called fossil fuels because they were formed from the remains of prehistoric forest trees and smaller plants. To get these substances we either dig them up (mine them) or extract them from the crust. Solid materials such as coal are mined and gold and precious stones are also found by mining deep into the Earth. Oil and natural gas are often trapped between layers of rocks. We drill through the rock to release the oil or gas.

Many of the Earth's most important minerals and fuels are becoming scarce. As natural resources dwindle, the difficulty and expense of mining them increase and scientists seek alternative materials.

Above: The Earth's crust contains many metals. Gold is a rare metal—that is why it is so expensive. There are also precious stones like diamonds which are cut to make jewellery.

Below: This diagram shows how long we can expect the resources of various fuels and metals that we currently know about to last at our present rate of consumption.

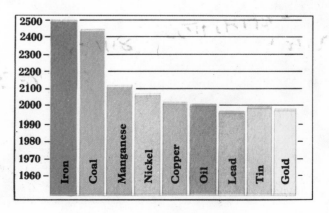

Surface Features

The Earth's surface features can be divided into three parts. Although we think of the Earth as a solid object, the atmosphere, or air, and the hydrosphere, the water areas, are as much a part of the Earth as the land. The land areas are sometimes called the lithosphere.

The surface of the Earth's crust is very irregular and varies a great deal in height. It consists of two thin layers: the continental or outer layer and the subcontinental or inner layer. The continents, or large land masses, are constantly moving very slowly

Right: Kilimanjaro is the highest mountain in Africa. Despite being very close to the Equator it always has snow at its summit.

Below: Volcanoes erupt when molten magma forces its way to the vent. Magma sometimes solidifies underground forming batholiths.

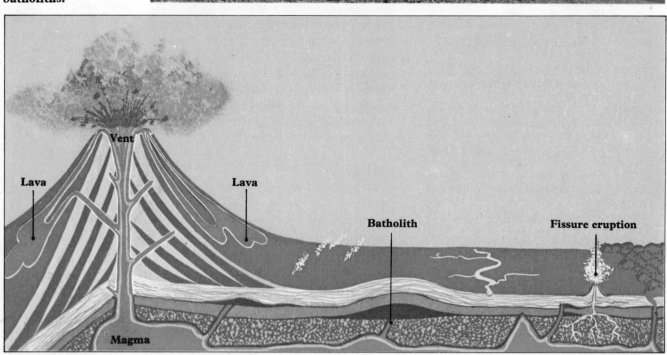

18

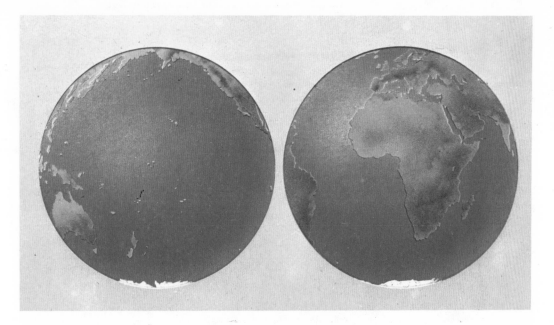

and this movement is called continental drift. The true edges of the continents are not the coasts you can see. Beneath the water is a sloping shelf and then a steep slope down to the depths of the ocean, called the abyss.

The continents of the world sit on large blocks of the Earth's crust which are called plates. These plates drift away from and towards each other. The areas near the edges of the plates are very unstable. This means that volcanoes and earthquakes can happen there. Volcanoes form when the magma or molten rock inside the Earth forces its way to the Earth's surface. It then appears as either ash or lava. Lava is the name used to describe the liquid rock that pours out of some volcanoes. When volcanoes erupt on land, they can, in time, form high mountains. In the ocean, a volcanic eruption can create islands. The Hawaiian Islands were formed in this way.

Earthquakes happen when continental plates move suddenly. This causes an earthquake along the fault or crack.

Below: This oasis in the south of Morocco has a good supply of water. Rainfall in desert areas is unreliable. It often falls in fierce storms and disappears rapidly.

The Continents

Africa The second largest continent. It contains the longest river in the world, the River Nile.

Antarctica Antarctica is a continent. The Arctic is a frozen ocean.

Asia Asia is the largest of the continents.

Australia Australia is the smallest continent.

Europe Europe's eastern edge is joined on to Asia. Together they form the Eurasian plate.

North America Reaching from the Arctic ice to the tropics, the terrain of North America contains forest and mountains, deserts, plains and jungles.

South America Scientists believe that North and South America were once connected to Europe and Africa until continental drift separated them. Now these two continents separate the two largest oceans, the Atlantic and Pacific.

Rocks

The Earth beneath our feet is moving, slowly but surely, all the time. Apart from continental drift, the rocks in the Earth's crust are changing all the time too.

Rocks are made of different kinds of minerals and are formed in three main ways. First there are igneous (or firelike) rocks formed from magma. Magma is hot, molten rock from the Earth's interior which solidifies as it cools, forming igneous rocks. Lava from volcanoes is magma that is still hot and flowing.

Sedimentary (or settled) rocks are formed from worn fragments of other rocks. Tiny particles, or sediments, are collected by water as it travels through rock and soil to the sea. Layers of this sediment gradually build up on the sea bed to form rocks, such as sandstone and shale. Sedimentary rocks are the most common rocks found on the surface of the Earth.

Lastly, as the Earth's crust moves, some rocks are changed by heat, pressure or chemical action. They become new kinds of rock called metamorphic (or changed) rocks. not the coasts you can see. Beneath the In this way, the sedimentary rock known as shale becomes another, metamorphic rock, called slate; and limestone is turned into marble.

Some Important Minerals

Asbestos A heat-resistant mineral. It is often used to make fireproof materials.

Calcite The mineral that makes up the chalk and limestone you can see in cliffs.

China Clay (kaolin) Used for making pottery and fine paper.

Diamond A form of carbon. Diamond is the hardest substance known.

Fluorspar (fluorite) Some kinds of fluorspar can glow in the dark. It is used in the steel industry.

Graphite The 'lead' of pencils is made of graphite. Like diamond, it is another form of carbon.

Gypsum 'Chalk' used on blackboards and 'Plaster of Paris' are made of gypsum.

Haematite An ore of iron. It is a deep blood-red colour.

Halite This is used in the home as salt for cooking and in industry to make soda and chlorine.

Quartz The mineral that makes up sand and gravel. It is used in making electrical instruments.

Talc The softest mineral. It is sometimes called soapstone. Talcum powder is made from talc.

Below: In the top 16 km (10 miles) of the Earth's crust 95 per cent of the rocks are either igneous or metamorphic. Only 5 per cent are sedimentary, although they are the most common on the surface. Basalt and granite are igneous rocks. Heat and pressure turn shale and limestone (sedimentary rocks) into slate and marble (metamorphic rocks). Coal is a sedimentary rocks but many other rocks of this type consist of fragments of sand, silt and pebbles, called sandstones and conglomerates.

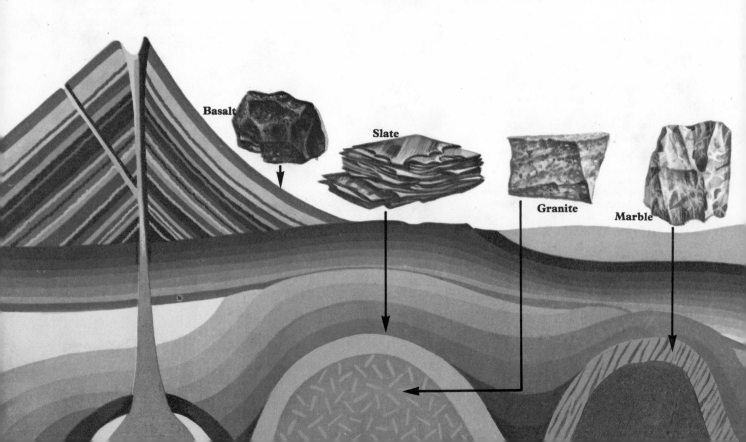

Basalt

Slate

Granite

Marble

Sedimentary rocks and lava flow are usually laid down in horizontal layers. But there are such tremendous forces at work within the Earth's crust that the rocks are pushed into great folds. When the rocks are folded into an arched shape it is called an anticline, and when they form a basin it is a syncline.

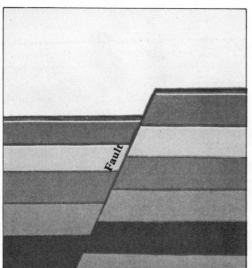

Rocks on the Earth's crust are subjected to great strain and occasionally they fracture. When the two rock masses move in relation to each other the fracture is called a fault. The rock layers on either side of the fault no longer match. The most famous fault is the San Andreas fault in California in the United States.

The Changing Face of the Earth

Erosion, the wearing away of the land, is happening all the time and is one of the main forces that changes the appearance of the Earth. Water is one of the main causes of rock erosion. If you watch waves pounding on a beach, or a river roaring down from a mountain, you can understand how rocks can be worn away after millions of years. Frozen water, in the form of glaciers, or great ice rivers, has also carved through rock, and wind, too, can gradually erode rock faces. The desert winds drive sand along, and this wears away the surface of rocks like sandpaper.

How Mountains are Formed

Some mountains begin as volcanoes with steep cones of ash and layers of hardened lava. Japan's Mt. Fuji is a volcanic mountain. Other mountains are made by the movements in the Earth's crust. When the moving plates push sideways against each other, flat layers of rocks are squeezed into folds. These are called fold mountains. Block mountains are blocks of land that have been pushed up between faults, or cracks, in the Earth's crust. Lastly, pressure inside the Earth sometimes pushes up blister-like mounds, called dome mountains. A mountain range can include two or more types of mountains. The Alps, for example are fold mountains that have also known some volcanic activity in the past.

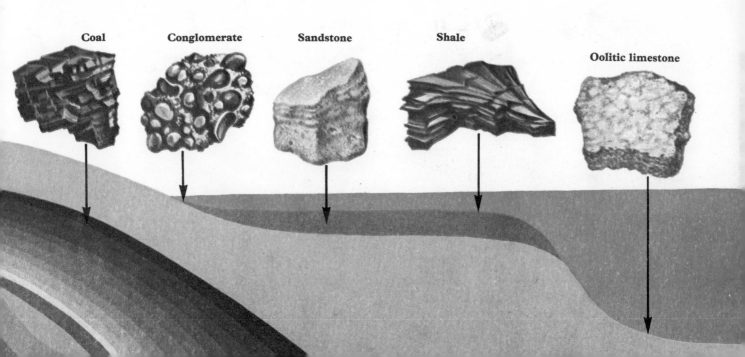

Coal   Conglomerate   Sandstone   Shale   Oolitic limestone

Seas, Lakes, Rivers

It is surprising how little of the Earth's surface is covered by land. In fact, 70.8 per cent of the Earth is covered by water.

The sea is moving all the time. The wind blows currents of water round the Earth and they constantly mix the oceans' waters. Much of the sea rises and falls twice daily and we call these movements *tides*. They are caused by the pull of gravity from the Moon and Sun.

The Sun also makes water circulate constantly from sea to land. It heats and evaporates sea water into vapour, which rises to form clouds. These clouds of vapour are now fresh water because salt from the sea does not evaporate. When the clouds become cool, this vapour turns into drops of water, which fall as rain. As rainwater falls over land, it seeps down through the soil and rocks until every tiny space and crack in the rocks is saturated or filled with water. Above this level of saturation is the 'water table'. Often the water table is underground but where it meets the land surface, lakes and swamps form.

Below: Rivers flow through three stages. In its old age a river flows slowly across flat plains in wide meanders. It slowly changes course and eventually meanders may be by-passed by the river. The portion that is cut off is called an ox-bow lake.

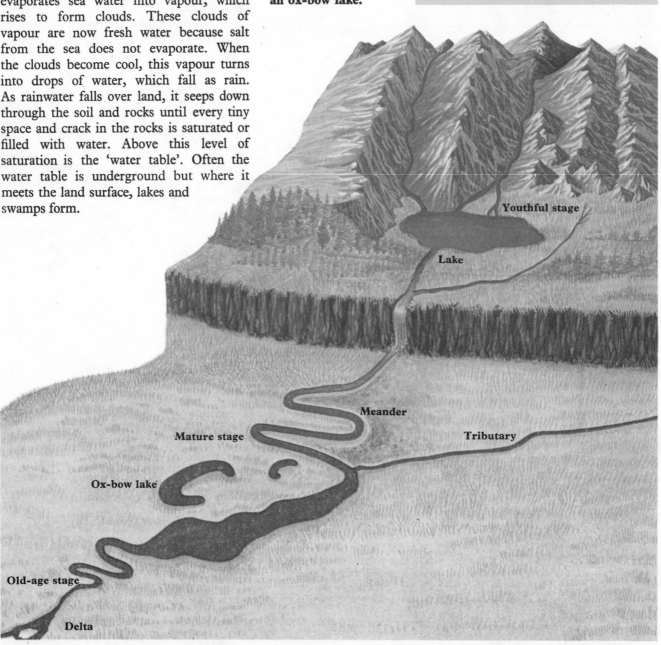

Youthful stage

Lake

Meander

Tributary

Mature stage

Ox-bow lake

Old-age stage

Delta

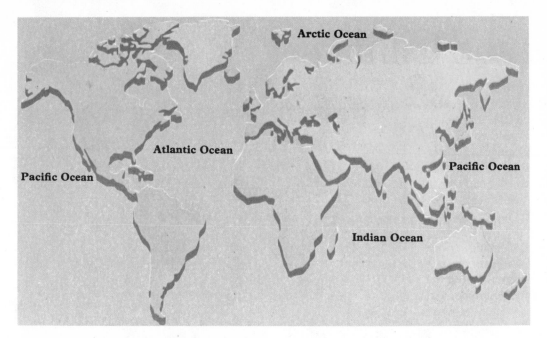

Left: This map shows the position of the world's great oceans. They cover an extraordinary amount of the Earth's surface—nearly 71%. The Pacific is by far the largest ocean. The Arctic is mostly frozen over.

Oceans

Arctic Ocean Most of the Arctic Ocean is frozen over.

Atlantic Ocean There is a huge chain of mountains under the surface of the Atlantic Ocean.

Indian Ocean The Indian Ocean is almost as large as the Atlantic.

Pacific Ocean The Pacific is the largest of the oceans. It covers more than 165 million square kilometres (63½ million square miles) and reaches a depth of 11,000 metres (36,000 feet).

Left: Rivers are of great use to people as a means of transporting goods from the centre of a country to its sea ports. Large cities grow up on the banks of rivers, like Paris on the River Seine in France.

The Life of a River

Rivers form in quite different ways. Some flow from inland lakes or melting glaciers. (A glacier is a slow-moving river of ice.) But others grow from small mountain springs. When a river starts its life as a spring in the mountains it is small and very fast-moving. This stage in a river's life is called the 'youthful' stage. As the youthful river makes its way to the sea several things can happen to it. Sometimes it flows into a lake and reappears at the other end.

Sometimes small rivers and streams flow into a river. The smaller rivers are called tributaries. They add more water to the main river and this is why rivers get wider and deeper as they flow away from the mountains.

After the youthful stage, as the river gets older, it usually gets slower. This is because it is flowing down a gentler slope than before. This stage is known as the mature stage.

Very often, after the river has flowed down from the hills, it has to cross a large flat plain to the sea. It is now in its 'old age'. Rivers in the last part of their lives flow slowly in huge curves and bends called meanders. Meandering is a common feature of old rivers. It means that the river 'wanders about'.

Once the river reaches the sea, it spreads out into a delta, a 'V' shaped area where the river deposits the solid particles it has been carrying as a sediment. It then flows slowly into the sea.

The water cycle is then repeated, with the Sun evaporating water from the sea and returning it to land in the form of vapour which becomes rain.

Weather and Climate

Different regions of the world have very different weather. At the North and South Poles, for example, the weather is very different from that at the Equator. Because the weather at the poles is always very cold, we say it is a cold climate. The climate of an area is the average weather, or the sort of weather you would expect in that region most of the time.

There are many different climatic regions in the world, but there are five main types of climate. The polar climates are found in the icy regions of the Arctic and Antarctic, and the area either side of the Equator (between the Tropics of Cancer and Capricorn) has tropical rainy climates with no cool seasons. Between these two areas are cold forest climates, temperate climates and desert climates.

The reason that it is generally cooler farther away from the Equator is because of the shape of the Earth. When the Sun shines on to the equatorial regions its rays do not have to pass through so much air as

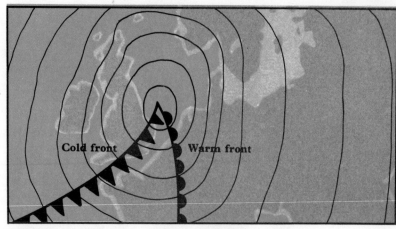

Above: A meteorologist's map has lines, or isobars, joining all areas of the same atmospheric pressure. Warm fronts and cold fronts are usually associated with rain.

Below: The five main climatic types—polar climates (white), cold forest climates (yellow), temperate (green), desert (brown) and tropical rainy climates (red).

The Beaufort Scale

Beaufort Number	(km/h)	Wind
0	below 1·6	Calm
(Smoke rises straight up)		
1	1·6—4·8	Light air
(Movement of smoke shows wind direction)		
2	6·4—11·2	Light breeze
(Enough to rustle the leaves in the trees)		
3	12·8—19·2	Gentle breeze
(Enough to hold out a small flag)		
4	20·8—28·8	Moderate breeze
(Small branches move)		
5	30·4—38·4	Fresh breeze
(Small trees sway in the wind)		
6	40—49·6	Strong breeze
(Telegraph wires whistle)		
7	51·2—60·8	Moderate gale
(Large trees sway in the wind)		
8	62·4—73·6	Fresh gale
(Twigs and leaves blow off trees)		
9	75·2—86·4	Strong gale
(Can damage roofs of houses)		
10	88—100·8	Whole gale
(Trees blow over and houses are damaged)		
11	102·4—120	Storm
(Causes great damage to buildings)		
12	Above 120	Hurricane
(Only found in tropical storms)		

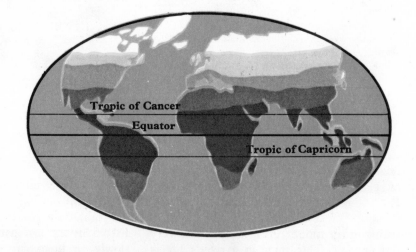

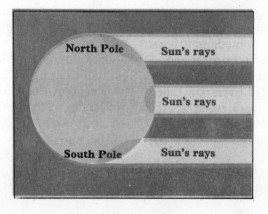

Left: The spherical shape of the Earth explains why temperatures are hotter at the Equator. The rays of the Sun are concentrated in a much smaller area near the Equator. Near the poles the rays are spread over a wider area.

they do at the two poles.

Climate is also strongly affected by the sea. Areas in the middle of large continents are often very dry, but along the coast there is more rainfall. This is because rain and snow come from the sea in the process called the water cycle. The clouds of water blow on to the land, then cool and fall as rain or snow. This happens more frequently in coastal areas near the sea as the clouds cool before they have the chance to reach areas far inland.

So that we can forecast weather accurately, it is necessary to measure the different elements of the weather. Scientists called meteorologists measure the force of the wind with anemometers and its direction with wind vanes. They use a scale to measure the speed strength of the wind. This is called the Beaufort Scale after the British naval officer who developed it in 1805.

Meteorologists also use rain gauges and sunshine recorders, and thermometers to measure air temperature. It is also important to measure the pressure of the air and this can be done by using an instrument called a barometer.

Nowadays, meteorologists have satellites out in space which send back pictures of the clouds over the Earth's surface. These pictures also tell them a lot about the wind and rain in different places and about the movement of weather from one area to another all over the world. Meteorologists keep a record of the day-to-day weather and this shows them the sort of weather that we can expect at different times of the year and helps to predict future weather.

The photographs below illustrate the two extremes of climate on the Earth. Polar climates are very cold all the year round and only small hardy plants like mosses or lichens can survive, where there is no snow. In tropical rainy climates the temperature is hot all the year round and the very high rainfall produces dense forests of vegetation.

The Changing Year

Imaginary Lines on the Earth

North and South Poles The poles are the points round which the Earth rotates.

Equator The Equator is the line that runs round the middle of the Earth, halfway between the poles. It divides the Earth into the Northern and Southern Hemispheres. At the equinoxes, 21 March and 23 September, the Sun is directly overhead at the Equator.

Lines of Latitude The lines of latitude are parallel to the Equator. They are measured in degrees north and south of the Equator. This refers to the angle that is formed by imaginary lines from the line of latitude and the Equator to the centre of the Earth.

Lines of Longitude The lines of longitude are at right angles to the Equator and lines of latitude. They are lines that run across the surface of the Earth from pole to pole and are measured in degrees east or west of Greenwich, in England. This means the angle formed by imaginary lines from the line of longitude and the line that runs through Greenwich to the centre of the Earth.

Axis The Earth's axis is a line through the middle of the Earth between the North and South Poles. The Earth rotates round this axis avery 24 hours.

Tropics of Cancer and Capricorn The lines of latitude 23°28′N and 23°28′S. On 21 June the sun is above the Tropic of Cancer (north of the Equator) and on 21 December it is above the Tropic of Capricorn (south of the Equator). These dates are the solstices.

Arctic and Antarctic Circles The areas inside these two circles have either continuous night or continuous day at the solstices. In summer they always face the Sun and in winter they always face away from it. On the Arctic and Antarctic Circles this continuous day or night lasts only a few days, but at the poles it lasts several months.

Although to us the Earth seems to be quite still, it is moving all the time. It is moving in three different ways. First, it is spinning like a top. It is also going round and round the Sun, with all the other planets of the solar system, and the whole solar system is moving through space too.

The spinning motion of the Earth, which is called its rotation, causes night and day. It takes about 24 hours for the Earth to rotate once. The side of the Earth which is facing the Sun is in daylight, while the other half is in darkness. The Earth spins round two points, the North and South Poles. The imaginary line between the poles is called the Earth's axis. The axis tilts a little bit away from the Earth's path around the Sun, and this tilt is what causes the seasons.

The Earth revolves around the Sun once every 365 days. So once each year our planet is back at the same point in its orbit around the Sun. Because the Earth's axis is tilted, the Sun's rays shine at a different angle to the Earth's surface at different times of the year, creating the different seasons of the year.

On about 21 December, the North Pole is tilted as far away from the Sun as it can be and the Northern Hemisphere (the northern half of the world) is in winter. The South Pole, however, is tilted towards the Sun, and the Southern Hemisphere is in summer. This is why the seasons are reversed in the two Hemispheres. On about 21 June, the situation is exactly the opposite. The Earth's axis is tilted the other way and the Northern Hemisphere has summer, while in the South it is winter. These two

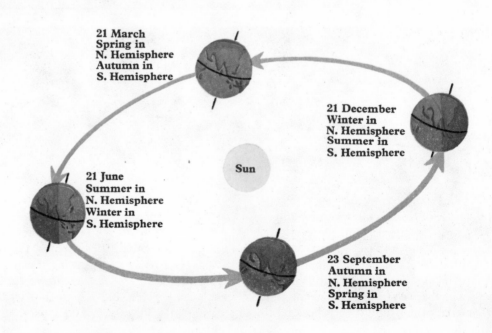

This diagram shows how the Earth's axis is tilted in relation to its path around the Sun. The results of this are the regular changes of climate which we call the seasons. Places that are closer to the Sun are warmer than those that are farther away. This means that the Southern Hemisphere has summer when it is winter in the Northern Hemisphere.

21 March
Spring in
N. Hemisphere
Autumn in
S. Hemisphere

21 December
Winter in
N. Hemisphere
Summer in
S. Hemisphere

Sun

21 June
Summer in
N. Hemisphere
Winter in
S. Hemisphere

23 September
Autumn in
N. Hemisphere
Spring in
S. Hemisphere

dates are the solstices. At the summer solstice it is the longest day of the year, and the winter solstice is the shortest day.

On 21 March and 23 September the days and nights are the same length. These are called the equinoxes. The vernal equinox is the beginning of spring and the autumnal equinox the beginning of autumn.

When the Northern Hemisphere is tilted towards the Sun and is in summer, the weather is generally warmer than in the winter. At the Equator the tilt has little effect, and the weather is hot all the time. In the polar regions, however, the axial tilt has a very strange effect. In mid-winter, the Earth tilts so much that there is no daylight at all. In mid-summer, the polar regions have no night. These areas inside the Arctic and Antarctic circles are sometimes called the 'lands of the midnight sun'.

In the temperate zones between the tropics and the polar circles, the seasons have always had special meaning for farmers who plant their crops to take advantage of the warm, growing seasons in spring and summer. From ancient times, people have celebrated the passing of the seasons at the solstices and equinoxes.

Above: These pictures were taken in England. They show the effect of the tilting of the Earth's axis. When the Northern Hemisphere is tilted towards the Sun it is warm and plants grow. It is summer. When the Northern Hemisphere is tilted away from the Sun it is much colder.

27

PLANT WORLD

Without the plants no life would exist on Earth. Animals rely on plants for their food, or eat other animals that feed on plants. Only the plants themselves can make their own food—by the process called photosynthesis.

The Plant Kingdom

The countryside is mostly green in colour, due to the presence of plants. There are familiar plants, such as grasses, flowers and trees. But there is also an enormous number of other kinds of plants, some of which are so small that they can only be seen through a microscope.

Scientists divide the plant kingdom into a number of groups. The simplest plants are the fungi (see page 30), including moulds, toadstools and mushrooms. They are not green and have no leaves.

The tiniest green plants belong to a group called the algae. There are single-celled algae, some of which can move about by using whip-like organs called flagella. There are also larger, many-celled algae. Some of these have their cells in long threads or filaments. Others are made up of larger masses of cells. The largest algae of all are the seaweeds, such as the wracks and kelps.

Most algae live and reproduce in water, but liverworts and mosses live on land. Liverworts are small plants that live in wet places. Nearly all liverworts have flat plant bodies. Mosses have stems and leaves and they generally grow in mats or cushions on moist soil.

Liverworts and mosses have to remain moist; most of them cannot tolerate living in dry places. But, more importantly, they need moisture for reproduction. They produce male sex cells which have to swim to the female sex cells.

Ferns do not dry out so easily and can therefore live in dry places, although most kinds of fern, including large tree ferns, are found in steamy tropical forests. They also produce swimming cells during reproduction, but these are not produced by the adult plants. Instead, adult plants produce

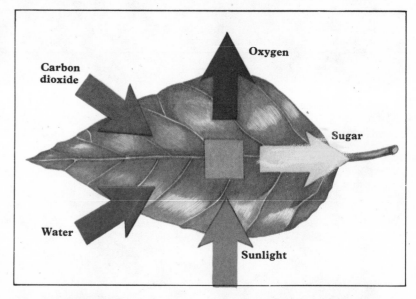

Above: The process of photosynthesis—how plants make food.

Right: All plants fall into the six main groups shown here.

Prehistoric Plants

From fossil evidence we know that very simple algae existed on Earth 3,100 millions years ago. But we know little of how the higher groups of plants evolved. About 420 million years ago there was a group of marsh plants, known as psilophytes, that produced spores at the tips of their leafless, branching stems. These plants appear to have become extinct by about 340 million years ago. But between 400 and 250 million years ago many land plants appeared. There were vast, steamy swamp forests. After these forest plants died, they eventually formed coal and many fossils have been preserved in the coal. There were ferns and tree-sized clubmosses, such as *Lepidodendron*, and quillworts, such as *Calamites*. There were also tall, conifer-like plants, known as the Cordaitales, which in fact were the ancestors of modern conifers and their relatives. Another group, the pteridosperms, looked like ferns but produced seeds. These seed ferns were the ancestors of modern flowering plants. About 150 million years ago several interesting groups of plants were flourishing. Among these were the cycads, of which only a few remain, and the ginkgos, of which there is only one survivor—the Maidenhair Tree. The cycads and the Maidenhair Tree, like the conifers, belong to the plant group known as gymnosperms. Gymnosperms produce naked seeds which are not enclosed in fruits.

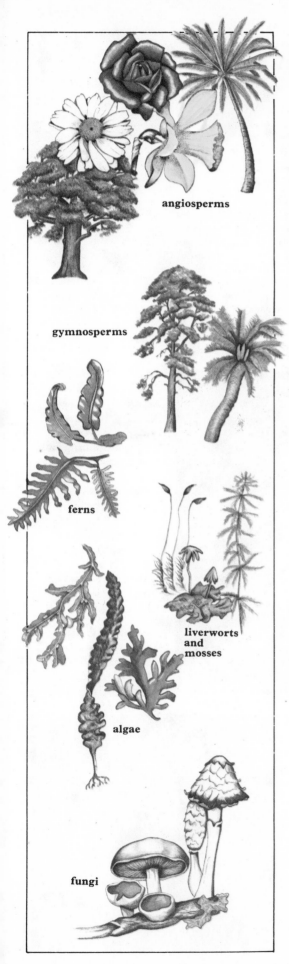

angiosperms

gymnosperms

ferns

liverworts and mosses

algae

fungi

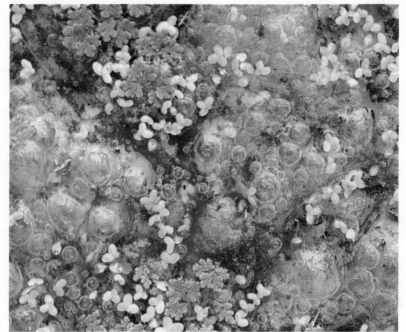

spores, which develop into tiny heart-shaped plants containing the sex organs.

Conifers (see page 32) and flowering plants (see page 34) have succeeded in doing away with the need for water during reproduction. The male sex cells are carried in grains of pollen and these plants produce tough seeds that can withstand dry conditions.

Photosynthesis

Plants make their food by taking carbon dioxide from the air and using it, together with water, to produce sugar and oxygen. This is done with the aid of sunlight and chlorophyll, the green pigment in the leaves of plants. Chlorophyll absorbs the light energy from the Sun and converts it into chemical energy, which enables the water to react with the carbon dioxide. The sugar that is produced is either used to provide energy for other plant processes or it is stored as starch.

Above: Spirogyra is an alga made up of long threads, one cell thick. It is seen here with the red-tinged water-fern, Azolla.

Below: Mosses can survive almost anywhere provided there is moisture. There are about 14,000 species in the world. They rarely grow more than a few centimetres high.

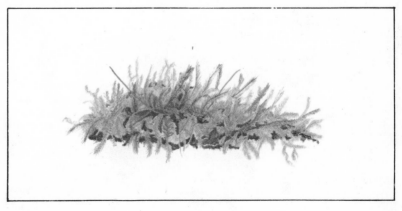

Fungi

The fungi are an unusual group of plants. Some people do not regard them as plants at all, but place them in a separate kingdom. However, fungi are usually regarded as specialized plants that do not contain chlorophyll.

Without chlorophyll fungi cannot make their own food, and so have to obtain food from other sources. Fungi which live on decaying plants and animal material are called *saprophytes*. They produce enzymes which break down the chemicals of the material they are living on into a form that the fungi can absorb. This function plays a very important role in sustaining life because plants and animals depend on constant recycling of the elements carbon, oxygen and nitrogen through the decay of organic matter. Fungi that feed in this way include the pin moulds and yeasts.

Other fungi are *parasites*; that is, they live on the tissues of living plants or animals, without being useful in return. Fungal parasites often cause disease. Powdery mildews, rusts, smuts and the ergot of rye are all plant parasites. Ringworm and athlete's foot in humans are also caused by fungal infections. Dutch elm disease and potato blight are serious diseases which result in the destruction of infected plants.

The plant body of a fungus consists of a mass of tiny threads or hyphae, known as the mycelium. Simple fungi reproduce both asexually and sexually. When a pin mould reproduces asexually it puts up special hyphae with tiny round spore-containers at the tips, hence the name 'pin

Useful Fungi

In addition to edible fungi, such as the field mushroom, horse mushroom, chanterelle, cèpe and fairy ring champignon, there is a number of useful fungi. Among the most useful are the yeasts. These are unusual fungi because they consist of single cells instead of threads. There are several different kinds of yeast. Some are used in baking and in brewing.

Baker's yeast has been used for making bread and cakes since the time of the ancient Egyptians. The yeast is left in warm dough for some time before cooking. It ferments some of the dough, producing carbon dioxide and alcohol. Bubbles of carbon dioxide gas cause the dough to rise. When the dough is cooked, the yeast is killed and the alcohol evaporates. Brewer's yeast is used to produce beers, wines and spirits. In this case the alcohol remains as part of the final product.

Fungi are also used in scientific research, medicine and the production of food. A species of red bread mould, *Neurospora*, was used to study laws of heredity. The antibiotic drug penicillin comes from the fungus *Penicillium notatum*, and two other species, *Penicillium roquefortii* and *Penicillium camembertii*, are used in the making of Roquefort and Camembert cheeses. A related fungus, *Aspergillus niger*, is used in the production of soy sauce.

Left: The fruiting body of the Earth Star fungus releases its spores through a small raised opening at its top.

Below: The antibiotic drug, penicillin, comes from the fungus *Penicillium notatum*. It was discovered in 1928 by Alexander Fleming.

Below left: Mould that forms on bread is a fungus. The black dots are the fruiting bodies.

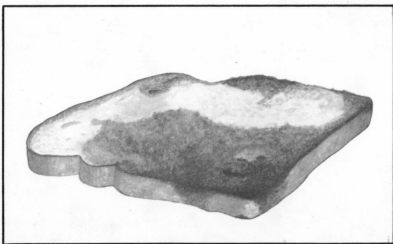

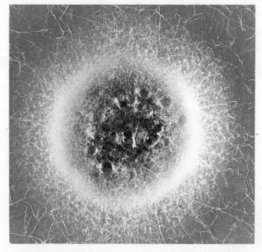

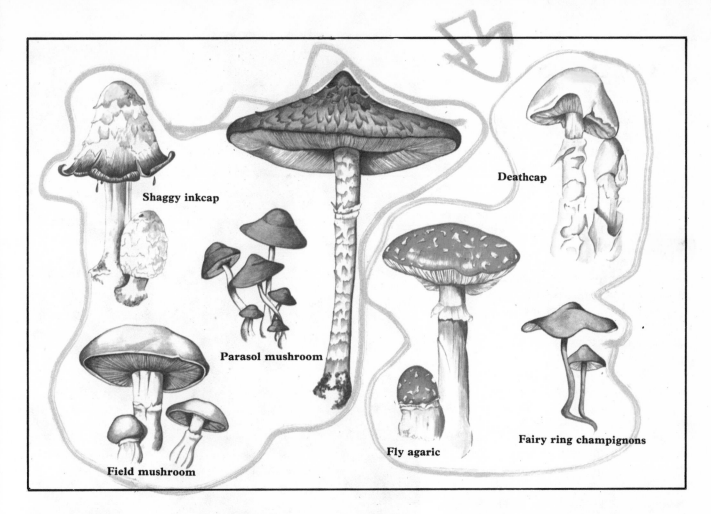

Shaggy inkcap

Parasol mushroom

Deathcap

Field mushroom

Fly agaric

Fairy ring champignons

mould'. When the pin mould reproduces sexually, two hyphae come together to produce a tough spore called a zygospore. This germinates to produce a new mycelium.

As a result of sexual reproduction fungi produce vast numbers of spores to be scattered by the wind. These spores are produced in fruiting bodies, of which there are a number of types. Some are too small to see with the naked eye, but a cup-fungus produces spores inside a large cup-shaped fruiting body. A morel produces spores on the head of its sponge-like fruiting body.

Mushrooms and Toadstools

The most familiar fruiting bodies are the mushrooms and toadstools. The well-known 'fairy ring' is evidence of a large, circular fungus colony growing just below the surface of the ground. At intervals, the hyphae on the ends of the mycelium develop into mushrooms above ground.

A toadstool consists of a stalk and a flattish cap. The spores are usually produced on gills on the underneath of the cap, but in some cases there are pores or spines instead of gills. Bracket fungi, attached to trees, have similar caps, but no stalks.

As in other groups of fungi there are both parasites and saprophytes among the toadstools. The honey fungus, which can severely damage fruit trees, is an example of a parasite. However, most toadstool fungi are saprophytes. Some can be found in woods, often near particular kinds of tree. Others are more commonly found in fields.

In addition to the well-known and delicious field mushroom, there is a number of edible toadstools. However, many are inedible and some are poisonous. Great care must be taken to identify any toadstool correctly before eating it.

Conifers

Conifers are cone-bearing trees and shrubs that belong to a group of plants known as the gymnosperms. This name literally means 'naked seed' and refers to the fact that the seeds of gymnosperms are not enclosed and protected in fruits, like those of flowering plants (see page 34). The seeds of conifers lie exposed to the air on the scales of their cones.

Many conifer trees themselves are shaped like cones or pyramids. Conifers include pines, spruces, firs, redwoods, cedars and cypresses. Most conifers are found in the northern hemisphere. There is a broad band of coniferous forest that stretches round the world just below the Arctic Circle. Some conifers are found in warmer northern areas, such as the Mediterranean and North Africa, but very few are found in the southern hemisphere.

Most conifers are evergreens. This does not mean that their leaves never fall off. In fact each leaf of a conifer lives for about three or four years. Dead leaves are continuously dropping off and being replaced with new ones. But the conifer always has a large number of living leaves. Two kinds of conifer, larches and the Swamp Cypress,

Largest and Oldest Trees

Among the conifers are the largest and oldest trees in the world. The coast redwoods that grow on the coastal plains of California, USA, are the world's tallest trees. Many of them live for about 1,800 years and grow to a height of 60-80 metres (196-262 feet).

The world's most massive trees are the giant redwoods. Also called Giant Sequoias, California Big Trees or Wellingtonias, they grow to a height of 75-80 metres (245-262 feet) with a girth of about 23 metres (75 feet) near the base.

The oldest trees in the world are the Bristlecone pines. These short, rather twisted, mountain trees live for over 4,000 years. The oldest living specimen is named 'Methuselah' and is over 4,600 years old. It is in California.

Right: A giant redwood tree in the Sequoia National Park in California. Visitors are dwarfed by the trees.

Left: A branch of the Chile pine tree, also known as the monkey puzzle tree because it is so difficult to climb.

Below: A selection of cones. The largest cone is that of the sugar pine.

Bottom: Conifers covered by snow in the Black Forest.

are deciduous; that is they lose all their leaves in autumn.

The leaves of conifers are like long needles and are tough and leathery. This helps to reduce the amount of water lost through the leaves and so conifers can survive in drier and colder places than broad-leaved trees.

Conifers can also live on poorer soils than broad-leaved trees. This, and the fact that they grow quickly, makes them popular trees to grow for their timber. Conifers are called softwoods because their wood is softer and easier to work than the wood of most broad-leaved trees. Conifer wood is much in demand for making paper, chipboard and plywood, as well as for telegraph poles, fence posts and some furniture. Conifers supply around 75 per cent of all timber used for commercial purposes.

A conifer also contains resin, the purpose of which is to protect wounds in the tree from attack by fungi and insects. It consists of a wax-like material called rosin dissolved in a fluid known as turpentine. Resin is used to make paints and varnishes.

Because these trees are so valuable, experts have developed ways of ensuring that the conifer forests will not be depleted. This science is called forest management and it involves planting new trees and cutting old ones when they have reached a certain stage of development.

Cedar

Scots pine

Larch

Douglas fir

Flowering Plants

The most successful and advanced group of plants are the angiosperms, or flowering plants. They are successful because of their efficient method of reproduction. The flowers give rise to fruits that contain seeds. The seeds have their own food supply and a protective coat. They can survive away from the parent flower for many months until conditions are right for them to germinate. This group of plants has colonized almost every part of the world's land surface and there is a vast range of different types. As well as the more familiar flowers of the hedgerows and gardens, such very different plants as trees, grasses and cacti are all flowering plants.

Herbaceous plants are those which do not form woody tissues, but have green stems. Some live for only one or two years (annuals and biennials), but others, known as perennials, may live for many years, dying down in the autumn and producing new shoots in the spring. Shrubs are low-growing, woody plants. They are perennials that do not have a single, large trunk, but branch repeatedly from a point near the ground. Trees are tall, woody plants with large trunks. Most trees that live in temperate climates are deciduous; that is, they lose their leaves in autumn.

Flowering Plant Reproduction

In a flowering plant, the flower is very important because it contains the repro-ductive organs. The male organs are called *stamens*, and the female organs are called *carpels*. Pollen from the stamens of the flower is transferred to the *stigma* (part of the carpel) so that seeds may develop. When this happens in the same flower it is called *self-pollination*. But most plants transfer the pollen to the stigma of another flower of the same species. This is called *cross-pollination*, and usually results in stronger and healthier plants.

Some flowers, such as those of grasses, are small and green. These are wind-

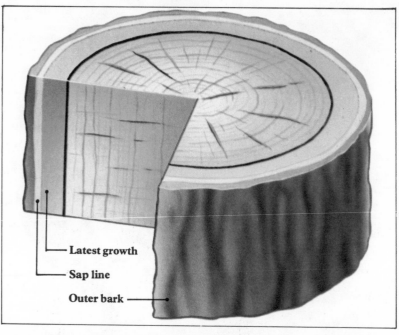

Latest growth

Sap line

Outer bark

Above: A cross-section of a tree trunk with its pattern of growth shown by the rings in the wood.

Below: The hairs and pollen sacs of the honeybee make it a very efficient distributor of pollen.

Plant Adaptations

Many flowering plants are specially adapted to life in places where conditions are harsh or otherwise unusual. Water plants, for example, have to survive the battering they receive from currents or waves. River plants, therefore, tend to have long narrow leaves and very supple stems.

Desert plants are among the most spectacular of flowering plants. Cacti are plants that use their stems as water storage organs. Their leaves are often reduced to spines, which may deter animals in search of a juicy meal. Pebble plants use their leaves as storage organs. Plants that store water in this way are called succulents.

A few plants that live in poor soil conditions have become carnivores, which means that they derive their food from insects. The Venus fly-trap and the bladderwort have ingenious insect traps. Sundews have sticky leaves that attract insects, then hold them fast, like adhesive tape.

Some plants live on other plants. Dodder and mistletoe, for example, are parasites that draw their nutrients from the plant on which they are living. Epiphytes grow on other plants but are not parasitic. They make their own food and take in water through aerial roots.

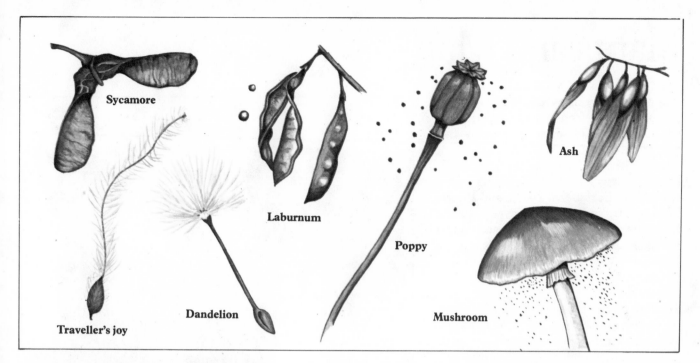

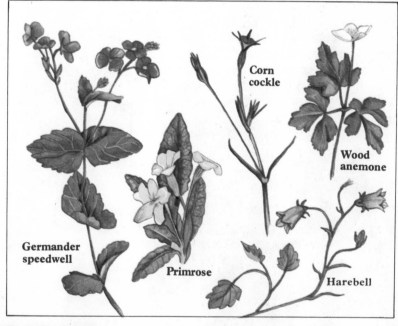

pollinated flowers. The stamens produce vast amounts of light pollen that is blown to other flowers. In order to prevent self-pollination, the male and female parts of some wind-pollinated flowers ripen at different times. Other plants may have separate male and female flowers or even separate male and female plants.

Flowers that are pollinated by insects are generally brightly coloured to attract the insects. In addition they produce nectar, and the insects fly from plant to plant carrying pollen with them.

Seed Dispersal

After pollination, seeds develop, usually within a fruit. To avoid overcrowding, the seeds are dispersed as far from the parent plant as possible. Some single-seeded fruits have parachutes or wings, so that they are carried by the wind. Other fruits open explosively, scattering their seeds over several metres. Fruits with hooks may get caught in the fur of animals and juicy fruits are eaten by animals. When the seeds have passed through their stomachs they are deposited elsewhere unharmed.

Right: The main parts of a flower, which all grow from the stem, are shown in this diagram. The ovary (containing ovules), style, stigma and stamens are all concerned with reproduction and seed formation. The petals attract insects who transfer pollen from one flower to another. The sepals protect the inner parts of the flowers.

Top: Seeds are usually dispersed by four methods: wind, animals, water and explosion of the fruit.

Above: The variety of form and colours of flowering plants is enormous. The plants shown here are native to the woods, meadows and hedgerows of northern temperate regions.

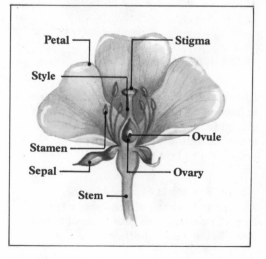

Plants and Man

Plants have very many uses for man. They provide us with food and shelter, with fuel and chemicals. But most importantly they supply the oxygen in the air that people and animals breathe. During the process of photosynthesis (see page 28) plants take in the carbon dioxide that people and animals breathe out, and give out oxygen, so that the amounts of carbon dioxide and oxygen in the air are always constant. This is a vital function.

Plants as Food

All the parts of a plant are represented in our food. We eat roots (turnips and radishes), stems (potatoes, which are modified underground stems, and asparagus), leaves (spinach and watercress), flowers (cauliflower and broccoli), fruits (plums, oranges, runner beans and tomatoes) and seeds (cereals and broadbeans) for examples. The oils that cook and flavour our food come from corn, olives and sunflowers.

Plants also provide us with many different

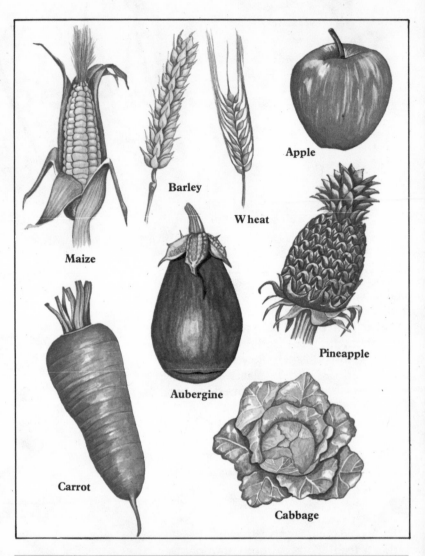

Maize

Barley

Wheat

Apple

Aubergine

Pineapple

Carrot

Cabbage

Above right: Plants are very important to humans. They provide us with nearly all the food we eat. Even when we eat meat the animals have usually been fed on plant products.

Above: Rubber is obtained by the process of slitting the bark of the rubber tree. Liquid rubber flows into a small cup fixed below and solidifies.

Endangered Plants

The world's rarest plants include the rose purple Alpine coltsfoot, the adder's tongue spearwort and the lady's slipper orchid. Man's activities around the world have caused many plants to become rare or extinct. The reasons for this vary. In some cases man has destroyed the habitats of plants in order to provide more farming or building land. This is going on today in the tropical forests of Borneo, the Philippines and the Amazon basin. Many plants that we do not even know of are probably being wiped out. In other cases man has introduced plants that take over the habitats of the native plants and make them die out. Man has also introduced grazing animals, such as goats. Grazing has prevented many plants from successfully reproducing and overgrazing has led to the formation of barren deserts.

We should all be more concerned about this. Plants are very necessary for supplying the air with its vital oxygen. Many people believe that the removal of vast areas of tropical rain forest will cause undesirable changes in the climate of the world. Also, many of the plants that are becoming extinct may have undiscovered uses as food or drugs.

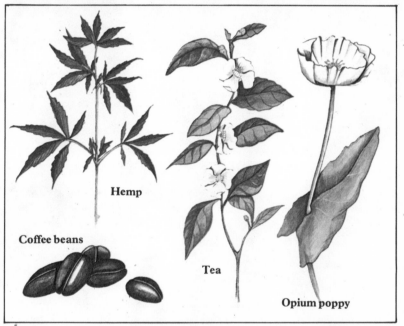

drinks. Coffee and cocoa are made from the seeds of small trees, and tea is made from the leaves of small bushes. Oranges and lemons are squeezed to give us juice, and apples are pressed to make cider. Wine is made from grapes, and many other alcoholic drinks come from cereals and roots.

Plants for Materials

Trees are valuable for their wood, or timber, of which there are two main types. Softwoods come from conifers. Hardwoods are broad-leaved trees, such as oak, beech, ash and walnut. The hardest woods include mahogany, teak, ebony and rosewood.

Softwoods are mostly used to make paper. The wood is pulped by using chemicals or a machine, and squeezed between rollers to emerge as a thin, flat sheet of paper. Different treatments during the manufacturing process produce different kinds of paper, such as fine writing paper, brown wrapping paper, newspaper, cardboard or blotting paper.

Hardwoods are used in a variety of ways. A considerable amount of timber is used for building houses. Some woods, such as mahogany and teak, are prized for making furniture.

Trees also provide other useful materials. Cork is the bark of the cork oak. Rubber is made from the milky white latex that oozes from a cut made in the bark of a rubber tree. Wax from the leaves of the carnauba palm is used in making polishes, crayons, carbon paper and cosmetics.

We also use the fibres of several plants. Cotton fibres come from the seed pods of the cotton plant. Fibres from the stems of flax are used to make linen. Hemp fibres are used to make rope and sisal fibres are leaf fibres used to make string.

Today plants are not the important source of fuel they once were, but wood and peat are still burned for domestic heating and for industrial purposes. And it was prehistoric vegetation which formed the basis for the coal and oil that fuel modern life.

Some plants contain useful drugs. The foxglove contains poisonous digitalis, which is used, in small quantities, in the treatment of heart disease. Opium, from the unripe seed capules of the opium poppy, is used to make pain-killing medicines such as codeine and morphine.

Top left: Orchids are among the exotic flowers which are becoming extinct through over-picking.

Top: Sisal fibres come from the large spiky leaves of the sisal agave. The leaves are crushed by machines to free the fibres.

Above: Many plants contain drugs. Tea and coffee contain the drug caffeine and the pain-killer opium comes from the poppy.

4 ANIMAL WORLD

Life on earth began more than 600 million years ago and today there are well over a million different kinds of animals. They live everywhere, except in the frozen wastes of Antarctica. Some are enormous, others so tiny you need a microscope to see them.

The Animal Kingdom

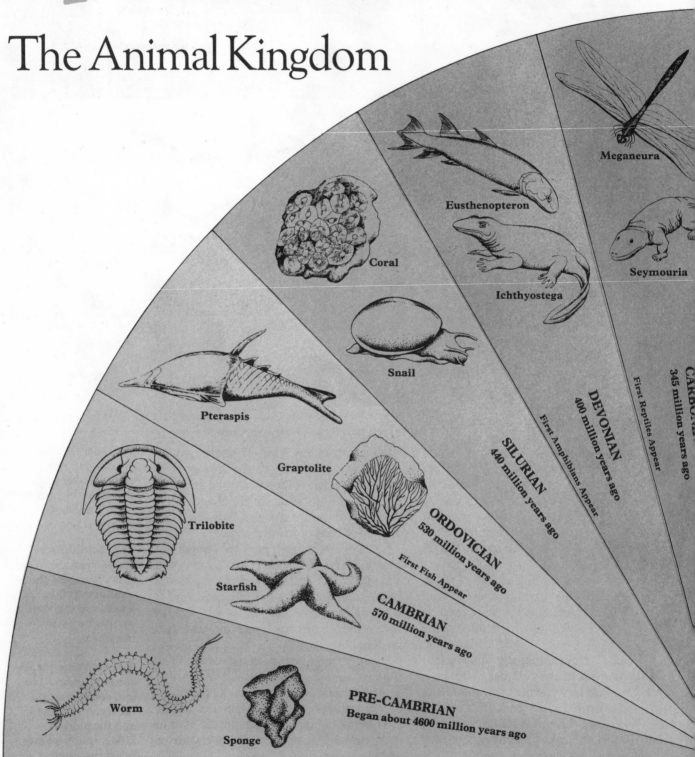

Meganeura

Eusthenopteron

Coral

Ichthyostega

Seymouria

Snail

Pteraspis

CARBONIFEROUS
345 million years ago

First Reptiles Appear

DEVONIAN
400 million years ago

First Amphibians Appear

Graptolite

SILURIAN
440 million years ago

Trilobite

ORDOVICIAN
530 million years ago

First Fish Appear

Starfish

CAMBRIAN
570 million years ago

Worm

Sponge

PRE-CAMBRIAN
Began about 4600 million years ago

Below: A chart showing the development of the animal kingdom from the first traces of life in the Pre-Cambrian period to the appearance of Man.

Animal Facts

Longest animal: the blue whale. It can grow up to 30 metres (100 feet).

Fastest animals: On land, the cheetah, which can run at speeds up to 105 kph (65 mph); in the air, common swifts, which can fly at 160 kph (100 mph).

Tallest land animal: The giraffe, at 5.5 metres (18 feet).

There are today two main groups of animals: those which have backbones, which are known as vertebrates, and those which have no backbones, and are called invertebrates. The vast majority of creatures in the world belong to the invertebrate group, but it is the vertebrates that are usually of more interest to us. This is because vertebrates include human beings and all the animals with which we are familiar, for example cats, dogs, horses and birds.

The basic differences between animals and plants, which are also living things, are: most animals can move freely about, while plants cannot; green plants can make their own food from oxygen in the air, chemicals in the soil, and water, using sunlight as energy, while animals have to eat plants or other animals as food. Animals that eat plants are called herbivores, and those which eat flesh are carnivores.

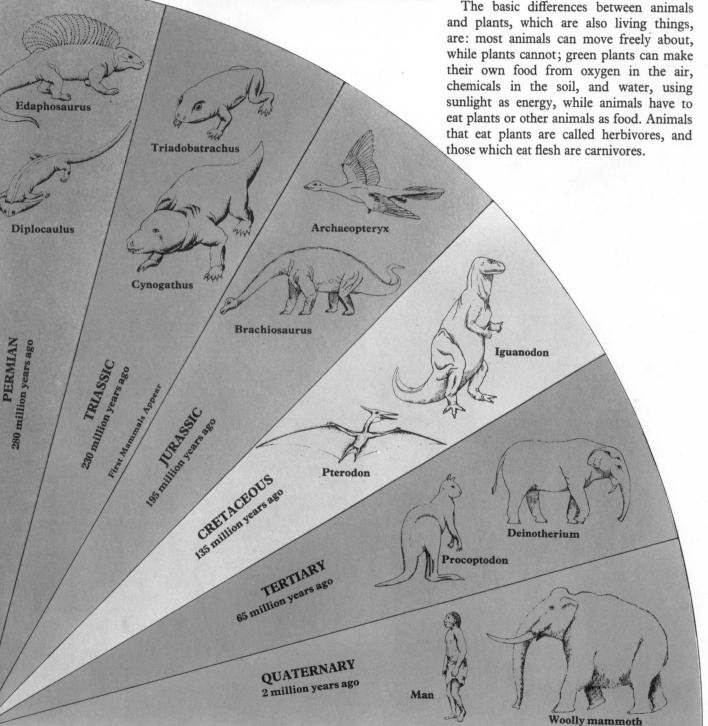

Edaphosaurus

Diplocaulus

Triadobatrachus

Cynogathus

Brachiosaurus

Archaeopteryx

Iguanodon

Pterodon

Deinotherium

Procoptodon

Man

Woolly mammoth

PERMIAN
280 million years ago

TRIASSIC
230 million years ago
First Mammals Appear

JURASSIC
195 million years ago

CRETACEOUS
135 million years ago

TERTIARY
65 million years ago

QUATERNARY
2 million years ago

Prehistoric Animals

When we use the word 'prehistoric' we mean anything that existed before history was written down—that is, about 5,000 years ago. Although we have no pictures or written records of what prehistoric animals looked like, we can find out in many ways: from fossils—bones preserved in rock—cave paintings, or mammoths preserved whole as frozen specimens (in Siberia, for example).

The first animals appeared over 600 million years ago, and were tiny water creatures that slowly developed more complex bodies and lifestyles. The earliest animals with backbones were types of fishes. One of the earliest kinds of fish we know of, because of its fossilized remains, is the *Dinichthys*.

Gradually, over millions of years, some fish began to emerge from the water and develop the ability to live on land and breed in water. These new animals were the amphibians. Some of the amphibians evolved into land animals called reptiles.

The biggest reptiles, the dinosaurs, were the rulers of the world about 225 million years ago. Dinosaurs were, like all reptiles, cold-blooded. That means that they depended on the sun for warmth to heat their bodies. The first dinosaur was probably *Ornithosuchus*, a kangaroo-shaped reptile that hopped on its hing legs. Like all carnivores (flesh-eaters) it lived on herbivorous (plant-eating) animals.

Carnivorous Dinosaurs

Some herbivores' size made them slow and clumsy, so they could easily be caught by the swift carnivores. Although four-legged, some of the carnivorous dinosaurs walked on their hind legs in an erect position, which meant they could move more quickly to catch their prey. The largest of these was the *Tyrannosaurus*. 'Rex' is often added to its name because it means 'king', and it certainly seemed to be the king of the dinosaurs.

Many other reptiles that lived in prehistoric times are now extinct (which means

Dinosaurs were the most common animals on Earth for about 150 million years. Some of the larger dinosaurs were as tall as a three-storey building whilst others were only the size of hens. Regardless of their size, all of the dinosaurs were reptiles that evolved from the same amphibious ancestors. The word 'dinosaur' means 'terrible lizard' although many of them were not terrible at all.

A Dinosaur Dictionary

Apatosaurus A giant sauropod which lived in the swamp lands. It was about 25 metres (80 feet) long. It was also called the *Brontosaurus*.

Brachiosaurus Another sauropod. It was the biggest land animal ever—14 metres (45 feet) tall and weighed up to 100 tonnes.

Carnosaur A kind of dinosaur that ate meat. It walked on its hind legs.

Ceratopsian A horned animal, one of the ornithischian dinosaurs.

Compsognathus One of the smaller dinosaurs.

Dinosaur The name given to reptiles that lived between 225 million and 65 million years ago.

Diplodocus The longest dinosaur.

Hypsilophodon ('high ridge tooth'). Probably the fastest dinosaur.

Iguanodon ('iguana tooth'). An ornithopod that stood on its hind legs.

Ornithischian ('bird-hipped dinosaur'). One of the two biggest groups of dinosaurs. They include ankylosaurs, ceratopsians, ornithopods and stegosaurs. The other main group was the saurischians.

Ornithosuchus One of the first flesh-eating dinosaurs.

Pterosaur ('flying lizards'). These were the first backboned animals to fly.

Saurischian The 'lizard-hipped' dinosaurs, one of the two main groups of dinosaurs. The include sauropods (plant-eaters) and theropods (meat-eaters). The other main group was ornithischians.

Sauropod ('reptile feet'). One of the groups of saurischians.

Stegosaurus ('roof lizard'). A dinosaur which had two rows of armour-like plates sticking out along its back.

Theropod ('beast feet'). One of the groups of saurischians.

Triceratops ('three-horned face'). A ceratopsian dinosaur with three horns on its face—one on its nose and two above its eyes.

Tyrannosaurus ('tyrant lizard'). The fiercest and largest carnivorous dinosaur.

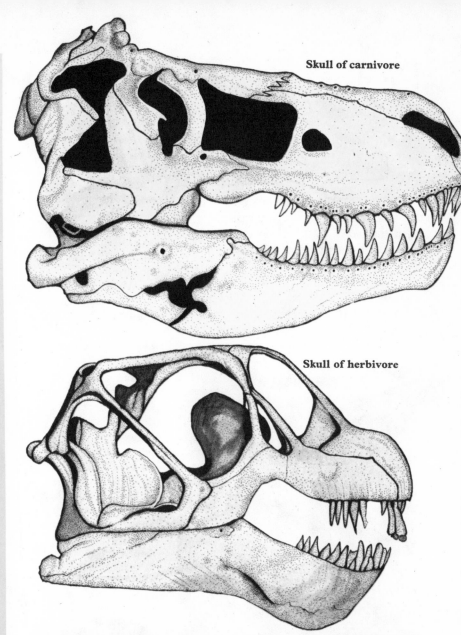

Skull of carnivore

Skull of herbivore

that they no longer exist). They include the flying reptiles, called pterosaurs. The ancestors of the pterosaurs were probably reptiles that lived in trees, and gradually developed webs of skin attached to the forelimbs. Some of the pterosaurs were small, the size of modern thrushes, and others were huge. One of the biggest was the *Pteranodon*, which had a wingspan of eight metres (25 feet). Another pterosaur with a wingspan of more than 16 metres (50 feet) has recently been discovered.

Some reptiles spent their lives in the sea. Ichthyosaurs evolved fish-like bodies, similar to those of whales, and, like the whales, they had to surface to breathe air. As they evolved they stopped laying eggs and gave birth to live young. Nothosaurs were more like lizards, and laid their eggs on land, although they were basically true marine animals that lived on fish.

Carnivorous dinosaurs, those that ate meat, had well-developed jaws to tear flesh from their prey and chew it. They were either very speedy and could catch their prey easily or else they were strong with vicious claws. Herbivorous dinosaurs, which ate plants, usually had teeth adapted to grinding food. The jaw of some herbivorous dinosaurs was projected in a horny beak.

Prehistoric Animals (2)

The time in which the dinosaurs existed is known by scientists as the Mesozoic Era. It is divided into three periods: the Triassic Period, the Jurassic Period and the Cretaceous Period. Although some people think the dinosaurs died out very quickly, they ruled the world for much of the Mesozoic Era. Man has only existed for about 40,000 years so far, and the dinosaurs lived for over 150 million years!

During this time, the dinosaurs were not the only members of the animal kingdom. There were many different insects that had developed a long time before the first

Below left: The *Triconodon*, a primitive carnivorous mammal with a hairy coat that evolved at the end of the Triassic Period. It was barely larger than the egg of a dinosaur but its relatives were able to survive where the dinosaurs could not.

Below: The *Dimetrodon* belonged to a strange-looking group of carnivores called the pelycosaurs. They carried a large 'sail' of skin over bony projections on their backs which absorbed heat from the sun to help maintain body heat for these cold-blooded reptiles.

reptiles. The early insects did not have wings but by the time that dinosaurs appeared, flying insects such as flies and bees had evolved.

During the Mesozoic Era, other kinds of animals began to evolve. About 150 million years ago, the first bird appeared. It was called *Archaeopteryx*, and was probably descended from small dinosaurs such as *Compsognathus*. The early birds did not fly very well, but by the end of the age of the dinosaurs they had developed into the kinds of birds that we could recognize today.

Mammals Evolve

Another kind of animal that developed at the same time was the first mammal. Mammals first appeared in the Triassic Period, about 200 million years ago. They were very small, furry animals and were only active at night when the dinosaurs were sleeping. Until the dinosaurs became extinct (died out), mammals were not very important animals, but after the dinosaurs they ruled the world.

The dinosaurs became extinct about 65 million years ago. There are many ideas about why this happened, but the most likely one is that their end was caused by a great change in the Earth's climate. About that time, the Earth became a lot colder, and so there was not enough heat to warm their huge bodies. They would have become

sluggish with the cold and too weak to eat. So the dinosaurs probably died of cold and starvation. The small mammals survived because they could hide from the cold in small burrows, and because they could manufacture their own heat from the food they ate.

Animals that lived in the water avoided the cold to some extent. In this way, some reptiles such as snakes, lizards and crocodiles have survived to the present day when their enormous, land-living relatives, the dinosaurs, died out.

Dinosaur Records

The biggest dinosaur was the *Brachiosaurus*. It was the largest land animal ever. It weighed up to 100 tonnes and stood about 14 metres (45 feet) tall. Fossils of the *Brachiosaurus* have been found in Africa and North America.

The longest dinosaur was the *Diplodocus*. It lived in swampland and measured up to 30 metres (100 feet) long.

The smallest dinosaur was the *Compsognathus*. It was only about 300 millimetres (12 inches) long, and looked rather like a bird without wings or feathers.

The first dinosaur was probably *Ornithosuchus*. It lived almost 300 million years ago, and was the ancestor of the carnosaurs (flesh-eating dinosaurs).

Pterosaurs, flying lizards, were the first vertebrates to fly. Some were only about 150 millimetres (6 inches) long.

The *Pteranodon* was one of the largest flying animals ever. Its wingspan was about 8 metres (25 feet).

The fiercest dinosaur was probably *Tyrannosaurus*. It had enormous teeth and sharp claws which it used to catch and kill its food.

Above: During the Earth's history thousands of creatures have flourished for periods of time and died out. The bird known as the dodo became extinct in 1861.

Left: A fossil and illustration of the earliest bird known to man called *Archaeopteryx*, which appeared in the Jurassic Period. It was about the size of a pigeon and evolved from reptilian ancestors. It had sharp teeth and a bony tail, much like that of a lizard. Clawed toes on its wings helped the bird to climb trees.

Fishes

The first true fishes evolved about 400 million years ago and they were jawless. Later, some fish developed thick, scaled fins and vicious teeth which many fish today still have. They all had well-developed fins.

At this time, a big division into two groups occurred. These two main groups still exist today. The fish in one group lost nearly all their bony skeletons, although they still had a backbone. They developed bodies made of cartilage, a softer, lighter and more elastic substance. Modern relatives of this group are sharks and rays. Sharks swim by snake-like movements of of their bodies and by thrashing their

powerful tails. Two side fins act like airplane wings to stop the shark diving down. A shark must swim non-stop or it will sink. Rays and skates live on or near the sea bed. Their bodies are specially flattened to suit this lifestyle.

The second group of fish kept their bony skeletons and are now the largest group. Perch, salmon, herring and flatfish, like plaice and sole, are all bony fishes.

Above: A perch is a common type of bony fish that is very popular with anglers. It lives in lakes, ponds and slow-moving rivers. In spring and summer it can be seen in shallow water.

Left: The shark is also a fish. Like the perch it has a backbone and fins, but it does not have a gill cover and its tail is not symmetrical. Its body is made of cartilage. The large blue shark is ferocious—it even eats small specimens of its own species.

Far left: Sticklebacks are among the few fishes that make nests. The throat of the male goes red during courtship.
Left: Female tilapia hatch their eggs in their mouths.

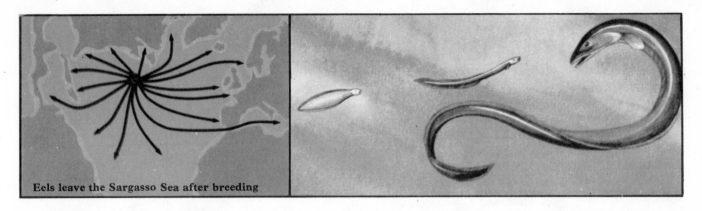

Eels leave the Sargasso Sea after breeding

How a Fish Breathes

All fish breathe through gills, tissues under covers at each side of the head. The fish takes in water when the gill covers are closed. Then the water flows out over the gills. Oxygen from the water passes into the blood in the gills and at the same time the water rids the body of waste carbon dioxide.

Bony fish have an extra way of breathing. Many of their ancestors lived in warm, shallow lakes where it was difficult to get enough oxygen. They began to rise to the surface to take gulps of fresh air. This air goes down into a pouch called a swim bladder. The air helps the fish to float without having to beat its tail all the time.

Some amazing fish can spend a long time out of water. Lungfish breathe air so they can survive when rivers dry up. They burrow deep into a muddy river bed and surround themselves with slime. Some fish can even walk or balance on their fins on land. Climbing perch and mudskippers can do this.

Fish spawn (lay eggs). Some species leave the eggs to develop by themselves, so they have to lay thousands for enough to survive. Many other animals, including Man, like to eat fish eggs. Certain fish, such as the salmon, swim long distances to lay their eggs where they themselves were spawned.

Above: Eels swim thousands of kilometres from the rivers of Europe and the eastern USA to spawn in the Atlantic near the Sargasso Sea. The young larvae then swim back. It takes them about three years.

Left: Fish are a valuable source of protein for human beings. They are found in greatest numbers in the shallow waters of the continental shelves. They are caught by trawlers dragging huge trawl nets behind them.

Left: Bony fish come in many different shapes, sizes and colours. These bright blue and yellow fishes live among the coral reefs in the Indian Ocean. Bright colours help fish to identify others of the same type and also those that are dangerous to them.

Amphibians and Reptiles

Amphibians evolved from fish-like animals. They spend part of their lives on land but they have to return to the water to breed. Only three of the eleven major groups that existed in prehistoric times still remain. They are frogs and toads; newts and salamanders; and caecilians. They all lay eggs. Frogs lay them in large masses to form spawn. Tree frogs lay their eggs in foam nests. The male rhinoderma, for example, a tiny South American frog, seems to eat its eggs, which the female has laid on damp ground. In fact, he takes them into his vocal sac inside his body. The young then develop and jump out of their father's mouth as little frogs.

Toads also produce spawn, but unlike frog spawn it is produced in long strings. The eggs are embedded in threads of jelly that may be up to 4·5 metres (15 feet) long. Toads can live in drier places than frogs. They have very rough brownish skin and usually walk about rather than jump.

Watching the development of baby frogs

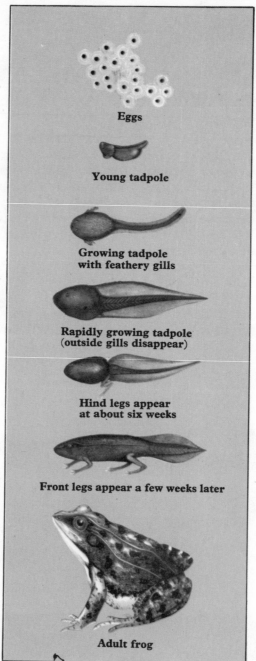

Eggs

Young tadpole

Growing tadpole with feathery gills

Rapidly growing tadpole (outside gills disappear)

Hind legs appear at about six weeks

Front legs appear a few weeks later

Adult frog

Left: It takes a frog or toad about six weeks to develop from an egg to an adult. As a tadpole it looks rather like a fish with gills and tail, but first hind legs and then front legs appear and replace the tail. The adult can then hop on to land.

Above: The male midwife toad wraps strings of eggs around his hind legs and carries them there for about three weeks while the tadpoles grow inside the eggs. He then places them in water to finish their development and hatch.

Below: Newts and salamanders are amphibians. The crested newt grows up to 15 cm (six inches) long. The axolotl breathes through the feathery gills on the sides of its head. The mud-puppy gets its name from the barking sound it makes.

Crested newt

Axolotl

Mud-puppy

Lizards have striking colour patterns, and many kinds are able to change colour. Chameleons have become known as masters of disguise as they stalk their prey. Their scaly skin has the unusual ability to change colour to blend into the environment. This lizard can assume the look of a rock or a piece of tree bark as the occasion requires. Like all lizards, the chameleon's eyes are set so that they can move independently of each other. They also have very long tongues for catching food. The chameleon gives birth to living young which are able to care for themselves.

is quite interesting. When the frog's eggs first hatch, the young are called tadpoles and they look very much like small fish. Tadpoles breathe through gills like fish and live only in the water. Legs begin to grow when the tadpoles are about six weeks old and soon replace their tails. They then begin to come on land and breathe with lungs.

Newts and salamanders still have their tails as adults. Caecilians are legless, worm-like, burrowing creatures.

Reptiles

Reptiles were the first true land animals. Although turtles live in water, they have to breed on land. Reptiles are cold-blooded animals. Only four groups survive today from the 16 groups of prehistoric times. These are lizards and snakes; turtles, tortoises and terrapins; crocodiles and alligators; and the New Zealand tuatara. The tuatara is a large lizard-like creature with a row of spines along its body.

There are about 3,000 species of lizard. Geckos, agamids, iguanas and monitors are some of the most common. Monitors can be as big and powerful as crocodiles. Some lizards can actually grow up to 3·75 metres (12 feet) long. Some have long bodies and are legless, and so look like snakes. The difference between these lizards and snakes is that lizards have movable eyelids and

Left: The cobra is one of the most dangerous snakes alive. It kills by injecting venom into its victim through fangs. It eats rodents, frogs and toads.

Below: Crocodiles are now the sole survivors of the group of reptiles that included the dinosaurs.

Left: Turtles live in water but always return to the land to breed. They lay their eggs in holes which they dig in the sand.

Left: Lizards are among the most common reptiles. They live in many types of habitat including trees, swamps and rivers.

fixed jaws, while snakes do not.

Snakes' jaws are joined together by an elastic ligament, so they can open very wide to swallow food whole. Snakes have forked tongues and kill by poisoning, i.e., biting and injecting poison into their victims. Boas and pythons are constrictors. They coil themselves around animals and crush them to death.

Tortoises, terrapins and turtles have large, horny shells on their backs and bellies. The limbs of sea-dwelling turtles have evolved into flippers.

Mammals

What do the horse, whale and Man have in common? Believe it or not, we all belong to the same group of animals: mammals. Mammals are the largest group of animals and have two main characteristics. They all have hair or fur, and suckle (feed) their young on milk. This milk comes from the mother's mammary (milk-producing) glands.

There is a huge variety of mammals, including bats (the only flying mammals), dogs, cats, horses, elephants and the giant blue whale. But we can divide them into three main groups: egg-laying mammals, marsupials (pouched mammals) and placental mammals.

The strange-looking duck-billed platypus from Australia lays eggs. Most other mammals give birth to their young. This usually means that the egg stays inside the female's body until it is fertilized by a male. It then grows inside the mother. Young marsupials only stay there for a short time and then develop fully in the mother's pouch. The eggs of reptiles and birds are also fertilized internally by male sperm.

Placental Mammals

Most mammals are placentals. The young stay inside their mother's body (in her womb, also called a uterus) for a longer time, until they are more developed. They can do this because of the placenta, a structure attached to the wall of the uterus. Food and oxygen pass through this placenta from the mother's blood. The food goes along the umbilical cord to the unborn young (the foetus). After birth the cord is broken, which leaves us with a stump where it once was: our navels.

The young of different mammals grow inside their mother for different lengths of time. The period of waiting for the young

Marsupials

Some mammals have a pouch for their young to develop in, and are called marsupials. The vast majority live in Australia and New Guinea and some live in South America. Kangaroos are the best-known. A baby kangaroo is only a few centimetres long when it is born. This little worm-like creature crawls into its mother's pouch and attaches itself to her teat. It stays there for two months, feeding and growing. By the third month it can wander about. Other well-known marsupials are the koala and the opossum.

Above: Koalas, also known as native bears, are marsupials found only in Australia. They eat only the leaves of the eucalyptus tree.

Far left: The duck-billed platypus, an egg-laying mammal which forages for food with its duck-like bill. The word 'platypus' means web-footed.

Left: There are about 2,000 varieties of bats—the only mammals that can fly. They are nocturnal— appearing at twilight and sleeping by day.

to be born is called pregnancy or gestation. For example, the gestation period for shrews is only 13 to 20 days, but for Man it is nine-months and for elephants 20 to 22 months. Mammals also look after their young for some time after they are born. They suckle and often carry them too, and so develop strong family groups. This way of producing young protects them for a longer time, so they are strong by the time they have to fend for themselves. That is one of the reasons why mammals survive so well all over the world.

Insect-eating Mammals

Many of the smaller mammals such as moles, hedgehogs and shrews, are insect-eaters. They have sharp teeth, and eat molluscs, worms and sometimes reptiles, as well as insects. Moles have specialized feelers to help them move around in their underground burrows. The flying lemur, in spite of its name, is more a glider than a true flyer. The only true flying mammal is the bat, which has wings made of skin stretched between its legs and supported by very long fingers.

Many bats are nocturnal (active at night) so have a very advanced sense of hearing. They find their way in the dark by using a kind of sonar (sound detection) system. Although they eat insects, there are also fruit-eating and blood-sucking bats.

Rodents are gnawing mammals which include mice, rats and squirrels. They feed mainly on fruit, seeds and nuts. The beaver is an interesting member of the rodent family. Like many rodents, it has highly developed front teeth. Its broad, flat tail and webbed hind feet are adapted to life in the streams and rivers where the beaver builds its dams and 'lodges'.

Left: Elephants are the survivors of a once mighty group which lived all over the world with the exception of Australia. They are now the largest and most powerful living land mammals. To maintain their weight and strength, they need a quarter of a tonne of food per day.

Left: The hedgehog belongs to the order of insect-eating mammals. It cannot move quickly and when under attack from its enemies, it will roll itself into a ball, using its spines for protection. New-born hedgehogs are blind and are covered with white spines which harden in three weeks.

Left: Squirrels are medium-sized rodents with long bushy tails, short rounded ears and sharp, hooked claws which they need for climbing. The tail is most important as it corrects the balance of the squirrel as it flies from tree to tree or along ledges and branches.

Mammals (2)

Many large mammals are carnivorous, which means that they eat flesh. There are two main groups with various sub-groups in each. Firstly, there are cats, dogs, weasels and bears. They are all strong, athletic hunters with very powerful limbs. Cats have retractable claws. This means that they can draw their sharp claws into their paws when they are not hunting, and this keeps them sharp for when they want to attack. Carnivores have specially long canine teeth that form fangs for tearing meat. Wild dogs, such as wolves and hyenas, often hunt in packs (groups). Man often uses tame dogs to help him hunt, too.

The second group of carnivores are sea animals. They are seals, sea-lions and walruses and they feed on fish, shellfish and sometimes even on penguins.

Whales are among the most interesting of the marine (sea) mammals. They are found in all seas of the world, and they never leave the water. They have long, tapering bodies and grow to vast sizes although many of them feed on tiny creatures called plankton. Some whales can survive

Man

Modern Man, *Homo sapiens*, now dominates the world. Ten thousand years ago there were only about 10 million of us, but today there are over 4,000 million people alive on Earth.

Fossils (bones preserved in rocks) show us that our early ancestors were ape-men. When the naturalist Charles Darwin first suggested this in 1859, in his book *The Origin of Species*, people were shocked. People hated to think of themselves as animals. Many believed that the Bible story of Adam and Eve was the real beginning of Man.

So why did human beings come to rule the world? Five million years ago ape-men began to leave the forests and colonize (make their homes) on the plains. They began to stand upright (which helped them to see longer distances) so we call them Upright Man. They became great hunters, they invented tools and, most important, learned to speak and communicate. Many people believe that communication is the real reason why we now rule the world. Through talking and writing we can learn from the experience of others, and in turn we can pass on our learning to others.

Top: The whale is the largest known mammal. It breathes air but cannot survive on dry land. It provides many items useful to man but is in danger of extinction.

Above: Leopards are ferocious mammals which can strike faster than any other cat. They will prey on any animal, including man.

Right: The horse is a domesticated mammal which has been bred and trained by man, usually for transportation, for thousands of years. It has strength and speed as well as a high degree of intelligence.

under water for as long as an hour and can dive to depths of 1.1 km (4,000 feet). Marine mammals look rather like huge fish, but they give birth to their live young and then suckle them. Porpoises and dolphins are close relatives of the whales. The hearing of dolphins is very acute, and they use echoes to locate their prey.

The Primate Group

Primates are the order (group) to which Man belongs. They have large, complicated brains and supple, movable hands. Primates include monkeys, which have long limbs and grasping hands and feet, and so can move quickly through the trees. They also have long tails for balance. But apes are our nearest relatives. They are the gibbons and orang-utans of Asia, and gorillas and chimpanzees of Africa. Apes have no tails, walk more or less upright and have highly-developed brains. Their arms are longer than their legs. Chimpanzees are great imitators and can often be taught tricks, because they are so intelligent. They have good memories, too, and are capable of solving quite complex problems.

Above left: An orang-utan in a zoo. Out of captivity it lives almost entirely in the trees and rarely comes down to the ground. Its arms are so long that they almost reach the ground when the animal stands up.

Left: There are only two species of camel—the Arabian, or dromedary, which has one hump and is used for riding, and the Bactrian camel which has two humps and is used for carrying goods. Camels also provide meat, milk and hair for weaving cloth.

Birds

It is easy to identify the type of animal known as a bird. Birds are the only animals that have feathers and beaks. There are almost 8,000 species of bird living today, all of them warm-blooded, two-legged animals with backbones. Birds evolved from reptiles as the scales on their feet and legs show.

Feathers

Feathers are composed of the same substance as reptilian scales (and mammalian hair). There are two kinds of feathers. Down is soft and fluffy and acts like a woolly undervest to keep birds warm. Over the down, and especially on the wings, there are quill feathers. These are much harder and stronger than down feathers and have a stiff stem.

Feathers are often very beautiful colours, and some birds have many different coloured feathers arranged in special patterns. Parrots, birds of paradise and kingfishers are particularly colourful. Very often the male bird of a species has a colourful plumage in order to attract the female who, in contrast, may be a dull colour.

Beaks

Beaks are all shapes and sizes. Birds use their beaks, or bills, for many different purposes. Most wading birds need long, slim beaks to reach deep into mud and water for their food.

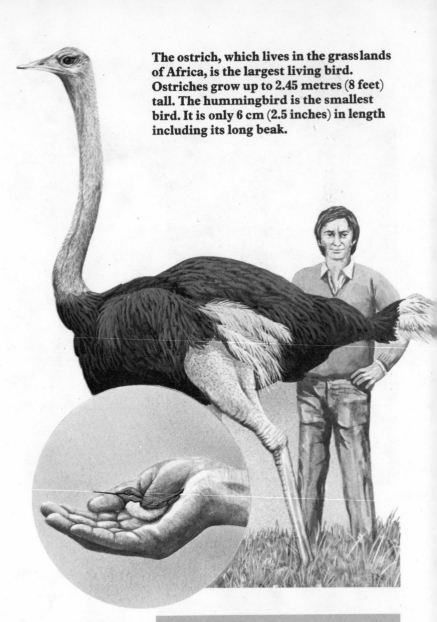

The ostrich, which lives in the grasslands of Africa, is the largest living bird. Ostriches grow up to 2.45 metres (8 feet) tall. The hummingbird is the smallest bird. It is only 6 cm (2.5 inches) in length including its long beak.

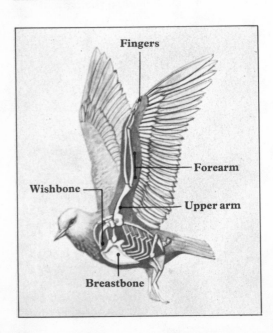

Left: The skeleton of a bird is like that of a human being, but the bones are of different proportions. The ribs are very similar to our ribs, but the breastbone is much larger because it must act as an anchor for the powerful flight muscles. A bird's knee is close to its body and most birds have four toes on each foot. The arm bones carry the wing feathers.

Fingers

Forearm

Wishbone

Upper arm

Breastbone

Cleaning Time

Feathers, like hairs on humans, do not grow evenly all over a bird's body. If you look at a plucked chicken ready for the oven you can see that the feathers grow on less than two-thirds of the skin area. To keep the feathers even, birds must rearrange them regularly. This is called preening and for the bird it serves the same purpose as brushing your hair or straightening your clothes.

Birds also have to groom and clean themselves regularly to get rid of pests and keep their feathers in good condition so that they can fly efficiently. Many birds bathe in water or roll in dust and then preen themselves. In preening the bird transfers oil from a gland at the base of its tail to its feathers to keep them waterproof. If you have a basin of water in your garden you may see birds bathing, but we do not see birds preening themselves very often. They prefer to do this alone, out of sight, in case an enemy should take them off their guard.

Extinct Birds

Many species (kinds) of birds have become extinct and some have been killed off by Man. Among them was the dodo, a flightless bird which was about the size of a turkey, which lived on the island of Mauritius. Sailors visiting the island used to kill the birds for food, and rats which came to the island on the ships ate the eggs. The last dodo died about 1681.

There were only comparatively few dodos, but the passenger pigeon of North America lived in incredibly huge flocks. There were literally thousands of millions of them in the early 1800s. But hunters shot them for food, and sadly the last passenger pigeon died in a zoo in 1914.

The moa was a huge flightless bird that lived peacefully in New Zealand. It reached a height of almost 4 metres (13 feet). But it did not long survive the coming of Man, who hunted it for food.

Right: During the breeding season birds come together to produce young. Many birds live on their own at other times of the year and the male has to persuade a female to be his mate. The peacock does this by displaying his fine tail feathers.

Hummingbirds have long, tubular beaks specially developed for drinking nectar from deep inside flowers. The pelican has a large beak with an expanding pouch which it uses to store the fish it catches.

Birds of prey, like eagles and hawks, have strong, hooked beaks which they use to tear the meat off their prey. Another bird with a strong, hard beak is the parrot. This bird can crack nuts easily in its powerful mouth. The woodpecker's beak is specially adapted for drilling into trees to find insects.

Feet and Legs

Birds also have specially adapted feet and legs which suit their ways of life. Perching birds need only short legs and strong feet to grasp the branches of trees, but other birds need more specialized limbs. The group of birds known as waders have very long legs so that they can stand in water. Storks, herons and flamingoes are a good example of this group. The eagles, hawks and other birds of prey have strong, sharp claws or talons to catch hold of their food. Other birds have webbed feet to help them swim and dive. Swans and ducks are members of this group.

Right: Toucans live in the rain forests of Central and South America. They use their large beaks to grasp the tree fruits they live on. Although the beak looks heavy it is very light.

Herons stand motionless in shallow water for long periods of time waiting to catch their prey.

How Birds Live

Birds fly by using their wings. All birds have wings, but not all of them are able to fly. The ostrich, which is the largest bird in the world, never leaves the ground. Nor do emus, kiwis, cassowaries, or penguins.

The turkey and the chicken sometimes make 'flights' that are really only big jumps. Other birds, particularly some sea birds, spend most of their time in the air. And many birds can fly with amazing speed and accuracy. The swift, one of the fastest flyers, can race at full speed through a hole scarcely as big as itself, and is said to fly at speeds of over 96 kilometres (60 miles).

How Birds Fly

A bird can fly for the same reason that an airplane can. The air pressure on the upper surface of its wings is less than the pressure on the lower surface. The reason for this is that the upper surface is *convex* (curved outwards) and the lower is *concave* (curved inwards). As the bird flies forward, the air passing across the upper surface has to travel farther than the air passing across the lower. This creates a force that lifts the bird into the air and keeps it there.

But the lifting force exists only while the bird is moving forward. To move forward, the bird glides on an air current or else flaps its wings up and down. On the downstroke, the feathers are pressed together so that no air can pass through them. The wing pushes the air down and back, and the bird moves forward. On the upstroke, the feathers part and let the air through. Then the wing comes down again and moves the bird forward.

Bird Territories

Nearly all birds have a territory—an area that they look on as their own. They attack other birds entering their territories, but only birds they consider a danger. Usually, a strange bird is felt to be a danger or a threat if it is searching for exactly the same kind of food, or is likely to interfere with life in some other way.

The size of a bird's territory depends on the way it lives. It may cover several square kilometres, or else it could simply be the ground that can be touched from the nest.

Social Birds and Lone Birds

Some birds prefer to live on their own. Usually, the reason is that there is not enough suitable food in their area to feed more than one of them.

Below: As a bird moves its wings downwards, the feathers press tightly together. The wings push the air down and back, and the bird moves forward. As the wings move up again, the feathers part and let the air through.

Downstroke

Primary feathers used for forward movement

Covert feathers give the wings a smooth surface

Secondary feathers help to give lift

Tail feathers used for steering and slowing down

Upstroke

A golden eagle soars through the air above its territory. Its sharp eyes search the ground for the small animals that it eats. Hunting birds generally live alone, and form pairs only to breed. But many birds, including goldfinches, live in busy, noisy flocks.

Goldfinches

Left: Before a bird can land on the ground or on a perch, it has to slow down. To do so, it spreads its wings and tail to catch the wind and act as a type of parachute.

However, even lone birds come together in the breeding season. Many birds form pairs to mate and rear their young. When the young leave the nest they resume their solitary life. Some birds, such as swans and storks, mate for life.

Other birds live in flocks all the year round. A flock is a group of birds that live, travel and feed together. Many species of birds form flocks for at least part of the year. They seem to need each other's company. When food becomes scarce in the place where they are living, the whole flock moves somewhere else. Other social birds come together only at night, in order to roost in a safe and favourite spot. Such birds are a familiar sight in city centres. Thousands of them meet together at dusk. Then they settle down for the night on sheltered window ledges or on trees in a city square.

Nesting

Birds choose many different places to lay their eggs and bring up their young. Eggs need to be kept warm to hatch, so most birds construct some sort of nest. The materials they use and the locations they choose can vary widely.

Some nests are built in convenient places like the fork of a branch or a rocky ledge. These nests can look untidy but are quite strong and comfortable. Some eagles use the same nest (eyrie) year after year.

Swallows and martins make their nests out of mud and clay, so they have to construct them in a sheltered place away from the rain. The tailor bird sews leaves together to make its nest. Others weave their nests from grass.

Hollows in the ground and small burrows are also used as nests. Flightless birds, such as the ostrich, dig holes in the ground to hatch and protect their young, and the kingfisher cuts a tunnel into the river bank.

Parrots, doves and some owls do not bother to build a nest at all. They try to find one ready-made to take over. And the cuckoo simply lays its egg in another bird's nest and leaves it there for the other bird to rear.

Left: A nest is usually made with several different types of material. Coarse twigs or leaves make up the outer layer. There are finer plant fibres inside and many perching birds line their nest with feathers and down. Most birds' nests are made by the female of the species, and she guards the eggs until they hatch.

Right: Woodpeckers use their powerful bill to make a hollow in a tree for their nest. It only takes the great spotted woodpecker ten days to hatch its eggs.

Below: Adélie penguins breed on the coast of the Antarctic in large colonies. They lay their egg on a nest made of stones. Emperor penguins do not make a nest. They sit their egg on their feet and cover it with a fold of skin. The parents take turns to keep it warm.

Below: The mallee fowl of Australia buries its eggs in a mound of rotting plants and warm sand. The heat in the mound hatches the eggs.

Migration

Many birds do not stay in the same country all year round. They lay their eggs and raise their young in the temperate parts of the world, where in summer insect food is plentiful and the climate is not too hot. They fly to warmer lands in the winter when food becomes scarce.

Birds which breed in the northern hemisphere fly south in winter. Some go only a few hundred kilometres to where the climate is warmer. Others go right across the Equator. For similar reasons, birds in the south fly north.

Migrating birds may fly enormous distances, sometimes more than 10,000 kilometres (6,000 miles). The Arctic tern makes the longest journey of all. Each year it flies from the Arctic region right down to the Antarctic and back.

Choosing a Route

Birds that normally live on land like to migrate over land. In this way they can stop and rest on their journey. Seabirds are happier over the oceans.

Migratory birds have a very good sense of direction and often return to the same local area each year. Nobody really knows how they find their way on these long journeys. Even young birds migrating for the first time without adults do not get lost. Like sailors, they may be able to navigate by the Sun and stars.

Many birds migrate in huge flocks. They gather together in the summer or autumn and all take off together. Some ducks and geese also migrate. They fly in smaller groups, usually either in a line or in a V-shaped formation.

Birds that Cannot Fly

There are several species of birds which have wings but cannot fly. Some, such as the African ostrich and the Australian emu, have adapted to a life on the ground, and are fast, powerful runners. The cassowary, another large flightless bird, lives in the forests of Australia and New Guinea, and the kiwi, a smaller flightless bird, is found in New Zealand. Other flightless birds, the penguins, are strong swimmers and their wings are more like flippers.

Top: Waxwings roam out of their own area in flocks during the winter to find berries.
Above: Swallows avoid flying far over the Mediterranean as they migrate south. They fly overland and cross at the Strait of Gibraltar or the Bosporus.
Right: Wheatears migrate from Greenland to Europe for the winter.

Insects and Spiders

Insects are a large group of animals which include flies, beetles, butterflies, bees and ants.

An insect does not have bones, but it has a hard outer shell rather like a suit of armour. These shells are built in sections with joints to let the insect bend its body freely. All adult insects have six legs and a body divided into three parts, the head, thorax and abdomen. The middle part, the thorax, often has wings attached to it, and many adult insects can fly. Insects usually have one pair of wings but some, such as dragonflies, have two pairs. Sometimes these wings are wide and brightly coloured like those of butterflies, or they can be very thin and delicate, like those of lacewings. The rear end of an insect's body, the abdomen, is often divided into sections so that the insect can bend it.

Insects have very strange eyes. They are made up of many tiny lenses. Each eye is in fact a collection of many eyes—sometimes up to 30,000.

Like many other animals, insects lay eggs.

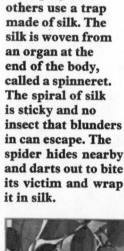

Some spiders hunt their prey but others use a trap made of silk. The silk is woven from an organ at the end of the body, called a spinneret. The spiral of silk is sticky and no insect that blunders in can escape. The spider hides nearby and darts out to bite its victim and wrap it in silk.

But these eggs do not usually hatch into the familiar insects. What come out of the eggs of most insects is a little worm-like animal called a larva. The larva of a butterfly is called a caterpillar. It grows bigger and fatter all the time until it forms a casing round itself. At this stage the young butterfly is known as a pupa or chrysalis. Inside the casing, the insect is changing its shape completely and when it is ready it will burst out as a fully grown butterfly.

Some other insects, such as grasshoppers and dragonflies, produce not a larva but a nymph—which looks like a miniature, wingless version of its parents, until it becomes adult.

Social Insects

Many insects live together in large groups or colonies. Ants, termites, bees and wasps are good examples of these social insects. They build large nests rather like insect 'towns'. The insects in these colonies have many jobs to do. Some are builders, some collect food, some defend the colony and others just breed more insects. These social insects all work together to look after each

Spider

Fly

Above: The main difference between a spider and an insect is the number of legs that each has. A spider has eight, while an insect has six. The spider's body has two main parts but the insect's body has three, and the hind part of the insect's body is made up of sections to allow it to bend, and the spider's is not. The make-up of their eyes is also different, and unlike many insects, spiders do not have wings.

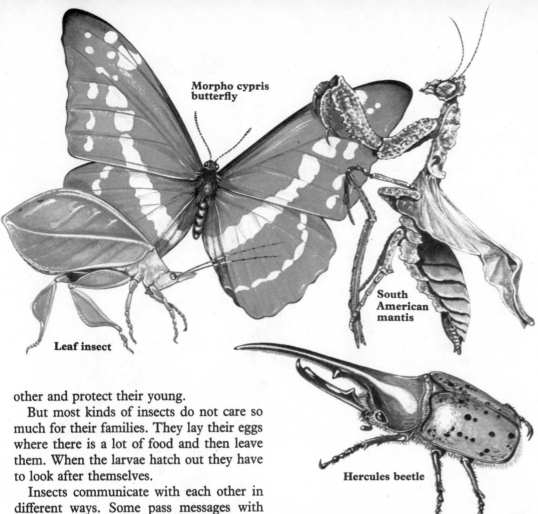

Morpho cypris
butterfly

South
American
mantis

Leaf insect

Hercules beetle

Left: Insects live, by the million, all over the world. The dazzling morpho butterflies live in the trees of Central and South America. The praying mantis eats insects and even small lizards and frogs. It looks as if it is praying, but is waiting to pounce. Beetles form the largest single group in the animal kingdom. There are 278,000 different kinds already known. They are easily recognized by their shell-like front wings, called elytra. Their mouthparts are well developed for chewing. Leaf insects are a good example of an insect protecting itself by looking like something else.

other and protect their young.

But most kinds of insects do not care so much for their families. They lay their eggs where there is a lot of food and then leave them. When the larvae hatch out they have to look after themselves.

Insects communicate with each other in different ways. Some pass messages with scent or by chirping, some by rubbing their legs on their wings. If you watch a procession of ants marching toward an anthill, you will see that they communicate by touching their feelers.

Eight-legged Animals

Spiders are not insects. They have eight legs, not six, and their bodies are divided into two parts not three. If you look at a spider's eyes you can see that they are not in sections like the large eyes of an insect. Spiders use silken nets and webs to catch insects and other small animals for their food. The spider makes its beautiful web out of thread which it spins from its own body.

There are many different kinds of spiders. Some of them are really tiny, but others, such as bird-eating spiders, are as big as a man's hand. Many spiders have a poisonous bite which they use to kill their victims but only a few large spiders can hurt humans.

Spiders belong to a much larger group of eight-legged animals called arachnids. The spiders' relatives among the arachnids include mites and scorpions. A scorpion has a long tail with a poisonous sting in it. Scorpions live only in warm countries.

Interesting Facts

Bees pass messages to each other by 'dancing'. Different 'dances' tell other bees where they can find food.

In a colony of ants, termites or bees only one insect, the queen, lays eggs.

The dragonfly catches its food in mid-air.

Some insects, such as wasps, are not good to eat, and birds learn to avoid them. Such insects have what is called 'warning coloration', usually yellow and black. A number of other insects that are perfectly edible have developed similar colouring, so birds avoid them, too. This is known as mimicry.

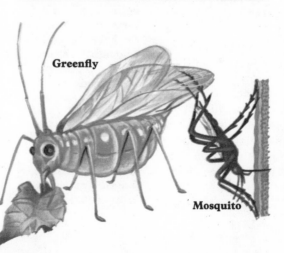

Greenfly

Mosquito

Left: Insects feed on both plants and animals and their mouthparts vary depending on the way they feed. Mosquitoes have a piercing mouth which sucks blood from animals. Aphids, such as greenflies, feed on plants and are a pest to gardeners.

59

Animals as Pets

All sorts of animals share homes with us as pets. Many people keep dogs and cats, but there are many more unusual pets. Pets are often kept as companions but there are other reasons for keeping them. For example, an aquarium full of tropical fish is a very pleasant sight and canaries and budgerigars are both beautiful and tuneful. Some insects and reptiles make fascinating pets.

Some animals are happy living with people, but it would be very cruel to keep wild animals in cages and boxes. Large or fierce animals do not make good pets, although some people keep snakes or even young lions in their homes.

If you go to any dog show you will see that there are hundreds of different kinds of

Below: Budgerigars make ideal pets. They are happy in captivity and are easily looked after. Breeders have cross-bred them to produce many colours for show purposes.

The Golden Hamster

Did you know that the golden hamster, so popular as a pet, was a rare animal at one time? Naturalists first saw a specimen in 1839—and then nobody saw another for nearly a hundred years. In 1930 a zoologist in Syria found a female with 12 young. Nearly all the golden hamsters kept as pets today are descended from this one family. The name 'hamster' comes from a German word meaning 'hoarder', because hamsters hoard any food they cannot eat. They are clean animals that hibernate in the winter.

dog. Big dogs such as German shepherds (alsatians) need a lot of food and exercise. Many people prefer to keep medium-sized dogs, such as terriers, because they do not need so much room and some people like very small dogs such as the chihuahua. Dogs are very intelligent animals and can be easily trained.

Cats are also common pets. There are many different types of cats, but all are part of the same family as lions and tigers. They do not need as much attention as dogs because they are very independent animals. They are also very curious and often go out exploring on their own.

If you live in a small house or an apart-

Right: The hamster is a rodent which is often kept as a pet. It has short legs, a bobbed tail and large cheek pouches for holding food. The name comes from a German word meaning 'hoarder'. Any food a hamster does not eat he will hoard. All pet golden hamsters are descended from one female and her litter of 12 babies.

Homes for Pets

Wild animals usually make their own homes if they need one, but pets often need some sort of house to live in. An outdoor kennel is a good home for a large dog and pet birds are best kept in a cage large enough for them to move around freely. Small pets such as mice, rats and hamsters can be kept in small cages but larger animals such as rabbits and guinea pigs should have a bigger cage or a hutch.

Many people have fish as pets. If they are coldwater fish, they can live in an aquarium or a fish pond in the garden. Tropical fish need a lot more looking after and will die unless they are in a warm tank with an air pump. Stick insects can be kept in a jar with fine net tied over the top. Ants can also be kept in a glass container where you can see them working in their tunnels.

Most pets also like something to do. It would be a very boring life for a budgerigar in its cage without a ladder and a bell or a mirror. Hamsters and mice love exercising on a treadwheel. Another thing that is essential in a cage or hutch is a supply of fresh food and water that is changed daily. Fish, too, need more than just a home. A fish tank should have a floor of gravel and a few stones. It is also a good idea to have some plants growing in the water, to help the fish breathe properly.

ment without a garden, it makes more sense to keep a small pet. Mice, rats and hamsters make good pets. They can be kept in cages and are cheap to keep. Small lizards and salamanders can also be kept at home, but only if you can provide the special environments they require.

There are several types of bird that make good pets. Canaries, budgerigars, parrots and finches are all very pretty and some of them sing sweetly. Mynah birds are not so colourful but they can learn to talk.

Rabbits and guinea pigs often live in hutches in the garden. Tortoises can be kept in the garden as long as they are safely fenced in. Many people keep goldfish and keeping tropical fish in a heated aquarium can soon become a fascinating hobby.

Above: Cats do not need a great deal of attention apart from food and drink. There are more than 30 pure breeds of cats divided into two main groups: short-haired (including orientals and tabbies) and long-haired (Persian and Angora).

Left: A cocker spaniel. Dogs have been 'man's best friend' for many thousands of years. They were first used in the role of hunting companion and for guarding homes and families. They can now be trained to act as guide dogs for blind people.

HISTORY OF MAN

BC

10,000–2500	Middle and New Stone Ages (use of stone tools).
8000	The first farmers.
3200	Bronze Age (use of bronze tools by Sumerians).
1500	Iron Age (use of iron tools by Hittites).

Timechart

	EUROPE		AFRICA AND THE MIDDLE EAST
BC			
		About 4000	Civilization of Sumer.
		1184	End of Trojan War.
753	Traditional founding of Rome.	814	Carthage founded by the Phoenicians.
510	Rome becomes a republic.		
356	Birth of Alexander the Great.	30	Egypt becomes part of the Roman Empire.
58–51	Julius Caesar conquers Gaul (France).		
44	Julius Caesar murdered in Rome.		
27	Augustus becomes first Roman Emperor.		
AD			
43	Roman invasion of Britain.	293	Roman Empire divided into 'Western' (European) and 'Eastern' (Byzantine).
313	Roman Empire becomes Christian.		
476	End of the Roman Empire in Europe.		
711	Muslims invade Spain.	630–660	Muslims conquer the Middle East.
1095	Pope Urban II calls for a Crusade.		
1096	Start of the First Crusade.		
1099	Crusaders capture Jerusalem.		
1215	King John signs Magna Carta.	1230	Sondiata becomes King of Mali.
1303	Last Crusaders defeated in the Holy Land.		
1347–51	The Black Death (bubonic plague) in Europe.		
1439	Johann Gutenberg develops printing press.	1453	Ottoman Turks capture Constantinople. End of Byzantine Empire.
1450 (approx.)	Start of the Renaissance.		
1517	Martin Luther begins Reformation.		
1517	Ferdinand Magellan starts first voyage round the world (completed 1522).		
1649	King Charles I of England executed. England becomes a republic.		
1660	Restoration of the monarchy in England. Charles II becomes king.		
1700–25	Peter the Great modernizes Russia.		
1733	Start of the Industrial Revolution.		
1769	Birth of Napoleon Bonaparte.		
1789	Start of the French Revolution.		
1804	Napoleon becomes Emperor of France.	1869	Opening of the Suez Canal.
1815	Napoleon defeated at Waterloo.	1899–1902	Boer War between South African Boers and Britain.
1830	First public railway (British).		
1848	Revolutions in Europe.		
1861	Unification of Italy.		
1870	German states come under the rule of Prussia.		
1914–18	First World War.	1957	Ghana gains independence. First African British colony to do so.
1933	Adolf Hitler and Nazis come to power in Germany.		
1939–45	Second World War.		
1945	Start of the 'Cold War'.		

The history behind the development of Man and civilization is both dramatic and fascinating. In this chapter we describe life from the time of the cavemen through all the great advances made in the fields of science, technology, the arts, philosophy, religion and revolutions to the age in which we live.

THE AMERICAS

1300	Olmec civilization founded in Mexico.
900	Toltec civilization founded in Mexico.
1000	Incas founded Cuzco, in Peru.
1325	Aztecs founded Tenochtitlan in Valley of Mexico.
1438	Inca Empire founded.
1492	Christopher Columbus arrives in America.
1519-40	Spanish conquest of Mexico and Peru.
1607	English colony founded in Virginia.
1776	American Declaration of Independence.
1783	End of American War of Independence.
1809-25	Wars of Independence in South America and Mexico.
1860-65	American Civil War.
1903	Wright Brothers fly first aircraft.
1945	United Nations set up.
1969	First men on the Moon.

ASIA

1500	Advanced civilization in China.
1000	First Hindu states established in India.
207	Great Wall of China completed.
1206	Genghis Khan becomes Mongol leader.
1211	Mongols invade China.
1250	Mongol Empire at its greatest extent.
1497-98	Vasco da Gama sails to India.
1526	Moghul Empire established in northern India.
1857-58	Indian Mutiny. British Government rule India.
1947	India and Pakistan gain independence.
1949	China taken over by Communists.

AUSTRALASIA/PACIFIC

1642	Abel Tasman discovers New Zealand.
1770	Captain James Cook discovers eastern Australia.
1911	South Pole reached for the first time by Roald Amundsen.

Early Man and the First Civilizations

The first human beings on Earth were hunters. They followed herds of animals and killed them. The flesh provided food and the skins gave clothing. The hunters had no homes. At night, they slept in shelters made from brushwood, or in caves.

In some places, though, the hunting was so good that families could live in caves for long periods of time. While the men went hunting, the women, children and older people scraped skins, gathered firewood, or made tools from pieces of flint (stone) and animal bone. The age in which these people lived has been called the Stone Age.

Growing their Food

In about 7000 BC, people discovered how to grow grain. They became farmers. They also kept small herds of goats and sheep.

The best place to live was near a large river, where the land was fertile and could be easily irrigated. Because farmers could grow plenty of food, large numbers of people could live there. So, the first towns and the first civilizations began to grow up. One of the first was at Sumer, between the Rivers Tigris and Euphrates in Mesopotamia. Some 5,500 years ago, the Sumerians were constructing canals, using ploughs in their fields and building beautiful palaces

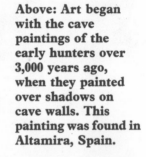

Above: Art began with the cave paintings of the early hunters over 3,000 years ago, when they painted over shadows on cave walls. This painting was found in Altamira, Spain.

Above left: The map shows the importance of the Tigris and Euphrates rivers to the existence of Sumer. The Sumerians had the first civilization based on trade.

and, some time later, temple towers called ziggurats. Some Sumerians became very rich. They wore splendid embroidered robes and jewels. They even used perfumes. The Sumerians wrote in cuneiform (wedge-shaped) letters. They scratched their writing onto baked clay tablets with hard reeds.

Civilizations along the Hwang Ho River in China began about 4,000 years ago. The Chinese grew millet, barley and rice along the Hwang Ho. They kept herds of

Cave Paintings at Lascaux

One day in 1940, a boy wandered into a cave at Lascaux in south-western France and made a tremendous discovery. There, on the walls of the cave, were some very ancient pictures of animals.

Archaeologists and scientists became very excited when they learned of these pictures. It was not surprising, because the pictures were about 20,000 years old. They were painted on the walls of the cave by the people called Cro-Magnon who lived in Europe during the Stone Age. The Cro-Magnon artists painted their pictures with charcoal and coloured earth mixed with oil. This was their paint. Their paintbrushes were sticks, feathers—or their fingers!

Some scientists believe the Lascaux cave pictures were meant to give hunters good luck when they went after the animals shown in the paintings. After 1940, more pictures were found on cave walls in France, and also in Spain.

Left: An early Chinese bronze vessel belonging to the Shang period (14th-12th century BC). The vessel shows a tiger protecting a man.

Above: Indus Valley sculpture from the 3rd century BC.

Above: Sumerian ziggurats were thought to be the dwelling places of the gods.

Left: The all-powerful pharaohs supervised the building of their pyramids.

cattle. They learned how to make silk from the cocoon (cover) of silkworms.

The civilization in the Indus Valley of India arose 4,500 years ago. Its centres were Mohenjo-Daro and Harappa. The Indus Valley peoples grew wheat and barley, and lived in houses made from bricks. Like the Sumerians, they wrote in the form of pictures.

The Ancient Egyptians, too, used picture-writing. Their hieroglyphics (pictures) have been found by archaeologists on the great tombs which were built for the pharaohs of Egypt. Civilization began in Egypt over 4,000 years ago. Here, as in Sumer, rich people lived in great luxury. Poorer people in Ancient Egypt had to work very hard. Egyptian farmers used to irrigate, or water, their fields with water from the River Nile. They used machines like the 'shaduf', which was a bucket on a pole. You can still see Egyptians lifting water from the Nile with a 'shaduf', and pouring it on the land to water it, just as their ancestors did.

65

Ancient Greece

About 4,000 years ago, wandering tribes from central Europe made their homes in the country we now call Greece. These first Greeks were farmers. They lived in villages with wooden houses. They used horses and carts for transport and grew wheat in their fields.

Later, about 2,600 years ago, the Greeks produced brilliant poets, artists, scientists, builders, craftsmen and philosophers. They also developed the idea of democracy, a form of government in which all citizens have the right to choose their rulers. This idea began in Athens. Athens was one of the city states formed in Greece after about 850 BC. There were other city states in Thebes, Argos, Corinth and Sparta.

Sparta was the chief rival of Athens. It was a military state, which meant that its most important activity was war. The Spartans thought only weak people liked comfort, good food, art, music, poetry or philosophy as the Athenians did. Spartan boys and girls were trained in special schools to make them tough and strong.

Life in Athens was quite different. There, houses had comfortable furniture, and floors made of beautiful mosaics. Craftsmen

Below right: The philosopher Socrates (469–399 BC). He believed that there should be discussion about all aspects of life because wisdom came from knowledge and badness came from ignorance.

Right: A map of Ancient Greece.

Below: The temple of Athena at Delphi, built about AD 300.

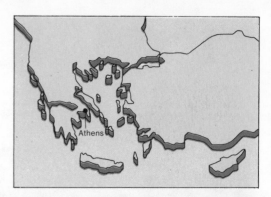

The Greek Gods

The Greeks believed their gods lived in a palace above the clouds on Mount Olympus. Zeus and Hera, father and mother of the gods, sat on beautiful thrones in the palace. Zeus' throne was made of black marble and gold. Its seven steps were in the seven colours of the rainbow. Hera's throne was made of shining crystal, decorated with golden cuckoos. In front of Zeus and Hera sat five gods and five goddesses. One of these gods was Poseidon, god of the sea, rivers and horses. Demeter was the corn goddess. The Romans called her 'Ceres'. From this name, we get our word 'cereal'. Although the gods lived on Mount Olympus, they often disguised themselves as humans and visited the Earth.

Left: The gown which was worn by most Greek men and women was called the *chiton*. It was worn at either knee- or ankle-length and was usually made of wool.

Right: Throwing the discus was one of the most popular sports in Ancient Greece. It was always included in the Olympic Games, which were held in Greece for over 1,000 years.

made mosaics by forming a sort of patterned 'carpet' from small coloured stones. The Athenians loved to play music on lyres or flutes, and they admired beauty in sculpture and architecture. They also liked to see plays performed in theatres and discussed the ideas of great philosophers.

Like other Greeks, Athenians were fond of sport. The Olympic Games were begun in Greece in 776 BC.

If the Spartans, or anyone else, thought Athenians were weak because they lived comfortable lives, they were wrong. The Athenians were brave, skilful fighters. They won many wars against their enemies, including Sparta and Persia. The Athenian navy also won great victories. In 480 BC Athenian ships helped to defeat the Persian fleet at the battle of Salamis. This was a splendid triumph, because the Greek fleet was much smaller than the Persian fleet.

Greek merchants were also brave, adventurous people. They sailed to places all round the Mediterranean Sea and often set up colonies there.

Unfortunately, there were many quarrels among the Greek city states and later, this made it possible for powerful enemies to conquer them. First, King Philip of Macedonia made himself ruler of all Greece in 338 BC. Then, in 130 BC, the Romans overcame the Greeks and Greece became part of the Roman Empire.

The ideas of the Greeks survived, though. Today, many countries have democratic governments, just like the Athenians. Also, many of our ideas about science, philosophy, art, architecture, music and theatre come from those of the Greeks.

Right: A Hoplite, a heavily-armed Greek soldier who, with his comrades, fought in close formation. Hoplites replaced the role of chariots and cavalry.

67

The Roman Empire

In the 8th century BC, two small villages stood on the Palatine Hill above the River Tiber in Italy. The villagers were farmers. They lived in thatch-roofed huts made of wood and wickerwork and covered in clay.

It seems amazing that these villages could grow into one of the mightiest powers Europe has ever known. But that is what happened. From these villages there grew the city of Rome. From the city of Rome, there grew the Roman Empire.

Rome Becomes a Republic

At first, the Romans were ruled, not by emperors, but by kings. The trouble was, some of these kings were cruel tyrants. The Romans decided to get rid of them. In 510 BC, they threw out the Etruscan king, Tarquinius, and made Rome into a republic. The republic was governed by two consuls and a powerful senate, made up of aristocrats or patricians. The poorer people, called plebeians, were represented by elected tribunes. The Romans, both patrician and plebeian, hated kings. The famous dictator and general Julius Caesar was murdered in 44 BC because some people thought he wanted to make himself king in Rome.

Right: A map of the Roman Empire.

Above: Augustus became the first emperor of Rome in 29 BC.

Right: Two consuls were elected every year to govern the Roman Empire.

Below: The remains of the Forum in Rome. Meetings were held there.

Caesar was the greatest and most powerful of all the Roman generals who led the Roman Army. Rome's army was by far the best organized and most disciplined of its time. Their victories built up an empire which finally stretched from the north of England east to the deserts of Arabia.

A Fine Existence

Life inside the empire could be very comfortable. Rich Romans lived in splendid mansions warmed by hypocausts. This was an early central heating system whereby heat from fires in the basement was spread through pipes into the hollow walls of the rooms. At great banquets held in these mansions, people lay on couches and ate enormous meals of meat, fish, cheese, vegetables and fruit. While they ate and drank, they were entertained by dancers, musicians and poets. There were also many

people in Rome whose lives were very hard. The poor lived in blocks of flats called *insulae* (islands). Insulae were usually badly built and often fell down, killing many people. Others died in fires which burned down the insulae or from the diseases caused by dirt and lack of hygiene in their homes.

The life led by slaves was even harder. Some became gladiators and fought in the arena to entertain huge crowds. When a gladiator fell or was injured, the crowd could decide whether or not his opponent should kill him. People also watched wild animals fighting in the arena, and enjoyed the very dangerous chariot races held in the Circus. The charioteers were usually slaves, like the gladiators.

The Empire Crumbles

Far away from Rome, out on the borders of the empire, the Roman Army stood guard against wild barbarian invaders. As long as the Army was strong, the inhabitants of the empire could lead their lives in peace and travel the magnificent Roman roads in safety. However, in the 5th century AD, the Roman Army was finding it more and more difficult to keep back the barbarians. Rome itself was attacked, by the Visigoths (AD 410) and the Vandals (AD 455). Later, more and more barbarians flooded into the empire. At last, in AD 476 a barbarian called Odoacer made himself king of Italy. So, after 750 years, the Roman Empire came to an end in Europe.

Romulus and Remus

The Romans believed that their city was founded, in 753 BC, by the twins Romulus and Remus. According to Roman legend, the twins were thrown into the River Tiber by a great-uncle who was jealous of them. They floated down the river and came ashore near the place where Rome now stands. There, they were fed by a she-wolf and eventually rescued by a shepherd.

When they were building the city of Rome, Remus made fun of the city wall which Romulus was building. For this, Romulus killed him. Later, Romulus became the first king of Rome. When he died, Romulus was believed to have become a war god called Quirinus.

Top: Gladiators were usually slaves who fought with weapons to entertain the Roman crowds. The most famous gladiator was Spartacus, who led the other slaves into revolt. He, however, was killed, as were about 6,000 of his followers.

Above: Roman shopkeepers selling their goods in the market place.

Civilizations of Asia and Africa

About 1,200 years ago, the civilization of China was the richest and most advanced in the world. Its capital, Chang-an, was the world's largest city—more than one million people lived there. There was a rich trade in furs, jade, skins, carpets, jewels, spices and other luxuries. Very good roads were built, and in the harbours of Chinese sea ports, there were hundreds of sailing ships. These ships carried Chinese porcelain, silk and tea to other countries. Long before printing was known in Europe, the Chinese were printing books from wood blocks. They also invented gunpowder, which was used for firework displays. Like the Japanese, who copied their civilization, the Chinese loved to make ornamental gardens, with bushes, trees and pools that looked like living paintings. Chinese herbal medicine, surgery, astronomy and mathematics were also the most highly developed in the world.

Life in India

The Indians were Hindus, and they were very interested in philosophy, science, medicine and art. By about the 5th century AD, Indian mathematicians had worked out a system of numbers, and the sciences of algebra and trigonometry. Indian writers produced many wonderful books. At this time, too, the Indians developed yoga. This

The Mongols

In the year 1212, Temujin, later known as Ghenghis Khan, came to believe that he was meant to conquer the world. At the time, this sounded ridiculous. For Ghenghis was the leader of the poor, wandering Mongol tribes. However, the Mongols were splendid warriors and great fighters. The empire they conquered became the largest land empire ever known. By about 1250, it extended from eastern Europe, down into India and right across China.

Later Ghenghis' grandson, Kublai Khan, became Emperor of China. Babur, one of Ghengis' descendants, founded the Moghul (Mongol) Empire in northern India in 1526.

Above: Buddhist temples were often highly decorative.

Right: A silk-screen painting of Chinese ladies about AD 800.

70

was a form of meditation (thinking) and it is still practised today.

The influence of Hindu India spread to other parts of Asia, such as Malaysia, Indonesia, Kampuchea and Sri Lanka. Hindu ideas also spread throughout India and remained strong there even after India was invaded by the Muslims in about AD 700.

Above left: An earthenware statue, splashed with coloured glazes, of a tomb guardian. This dates from the Chinese T'ang Dynasty which lasted from AD 618-906.

Above: Genghis Khan (1162-1227) was the military leader of a group of people called the Mongols. His ambition was to rule the world and in 1212 his armies began to sweep through China, Asia and Persia.

Left: The kingdom of Benin produced some beautiful examples of bronze sculpture. This bronze head represents a peak in African art.

The Muslims originally came from Arabia. There, in AD 622, the prophet Muhammad founded the new religion of Islam. In less than 100 years, the Muslims, followers of Islam, had spread their religion from Spain in the west to India in the east. Islam also spread into Africa. There, the Muslim kings of the central African empire of Mali were so rich and learned that their fame was known in Europe.

One of the richest was Mansa Musa who became king of Mali in 1307. Mansa used to sit on a throne of ebony decorated with elephant tusks. All his weapons of war were made of solid gold. Timbuktu, capital of Mali, was known as a great centre of Muslim learning and trade.

There were other great trading civilizations in Africa. The Kingdom of Ghana (not the Ghana of today), founded in about AD 300, was known as the Land of Gold because of its rich trade in that metal. Axum, on the east coast of Africa, had a very valuable trade in ivory. On the east African coast, too, Muslim cities like Malindi had ships in their harbours which were loaded with silk, ivory and gold.

Later, in west Africa, there arose the kingdom of Benin. This was a great centre of art and culture, deep inside the forests. The bronze sculptures produced by Benin artists after the 15th century AD were such that Europeans thought they were as beautiful and inspiring as the work of Renaissance artists.

Civilizations of America

The first inhabitants of the Americas came from Asia. About 20,000 years ago, they began crossing a land bridge now covered by the Bering Strait. Gradually, they spread all over North and South America. These were the people Christopher Columbus called 'Indians' when he arrived in America in 1492 because he thought that he had reached India. Most of them lived by hunting wild animals, fishing or gathering plants for food. Some had become farmers. Others had set up villages and towns after 1500 BC and had powerful chieftains as their rulers.

At about the same time, Indian civilizations began to grow up in Central and South America. The earliest was founded in about 1300 BC by the Olmecs who lived around the Gulf of Mexico.

The three Indian civilizations about which we know most arose much later. The first was the civilization of the very learned, very skilful Mayas, who lived in southern Mexico and Guatemala. By about AD 300, they were writing hieroglyphics (picture signs) and setting down their history on large stone slabs. Mayan astronomers studied the stars and knew how to calculate the length of a year. Mayan sculptors made beautiful statues and carvings, and architects built splendid pyramid temples. Then, in the 9th century AD, the Mayan civilization collapsed. The reason may have been some disease, or a war. No one yet knows for sure.

Five hundred years later, the Aztec civilization was developing in the Valley of Mexico. The Aztecs' capital city, Tenochtitlan, was an amazing place. The Spaniards who went there in 1519 found it was larger than any European city of the time. Begun in 1325, Tenochtitlan was built on Lake Texcoco. It had 60,000 houses, 350,000

Rooms of Gold and Silver

In 1532, when Pizarro arrived in Tahuantinsuyu, he made the Sapa Inca Atahualpa his prisoner. Knowing the Spaniards were greedy for gold, Atahualpa offered a magnificent ransom for his freedom: a room full of gold and two rooms of silver. The Inca people brought gold and silver statues, ornaments and other subjects from all over Tahuantinsuyu. They even took gold and silver from the walls of temples. The rooms were filled, as Atahualpa promised. But the Spaniards feared he would lead his people against them, and they put him to death.

Top left: The map shows the empire of the Incas, which, over a period of 2,500 years, extended 4,000 km north to south over what is today Ecuador, Peru, Bolivia, Chile and north-west Argentina.

Above: Between AD 300 and 850 the Mayas built many beautiful cities, palaces and shrines. This temple is a typical example of their buildings. It is pyramid-shaped with steep staircases leading to the top.

inhabitants and was joined to the shores of the lake by three huge causeways. Each causeway was wide enough to allow ten horsemen to ride along it side by side. The Aztec ruler, Montezuma, lived in a palace which had 300 rooms and 20 entrances. The economy was based on agriculture. Aztec farmers planted chinampas, or 'floating gardens' on the lake. They also grew maize, fruit and other crops.

Above: The historic meeting in 1519 between Hernando Cortes, the Spanish explorer, and Montezuma the emperor of the Aztecs.

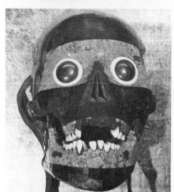

Left: This turquoise and mosaic skull mask, found in Mexico, represents the art of the Aztecs.

Below: The lost city of the Incas, Machu Picchu, was discovered high in the Andes in 1911.

Meanwhile, in the Andes Mountains of South America, a great empire called Tahuantinsuyu (Peru) had been conquered by rulers called Sapa Incas (Supreme Lords). The empire stretched 4,000 km (2,500 miles) through the Andes mountains and encompassed almost six million people. The Incas built a system of roads to link all parts of the empire with the capital at Cuzco. Swift runners carried messages from one end of the empire to another. Like the Aztecs, the Incas worshipped the Sun, but they did not make human sacrifices as the Aztecs did. They treated conquered tribes well, and the Inca state was a 'welfare state'. Everyone had enough food, clothing and a home to live in, and everyone knew exactly his duties to society which he was obliged to carry out.

Both the Incas and the Aztecs were conquered by the same people, the Spaniards, and it happened in the same way. Both peoples believed that a white-skinned god would come across the Great Water (the Atlantic Ocean) to reclaim their lands. When the white-skinned Spaniards arrived in Mexico (1519), their leader Hernando Cortes, was mistaken for this god. In 1532, the Incas made the same mistake about the Spanish leader Francisco Pizarro. These mistakes helped the Spaniards conquer both Mexico and Peru which they afterwards ruled for 300 years.

The Middle Ages

Some historians have looked on the 1,000 years from the end of the Roman Empire to the Renaissance (see pages 76-7) as a sort of 'in between' time. This is why these thousand years have been called the Middle Ages, or medieval times.

The Romans had given Europe an organized government. When this was gone, barbarians ran wild all over western Europe. Visigoths, Vandals and other tribal nations created havoc in France and Spain. In England, the inhabitants were attacked by the Anglo-Saxons from Germany, and after the 8th century AD, by the Vikings from Scandinavia. These attackers burned villages and farms, robbed and killed the inhabitants or carried them off as slaves. They raided

Christian monasteries and murdered the monks.

People lived in village communities under the protection of a lord of the manor. This became known as the feudal system. Peasants became subjects or vassals of great noblemen. The peasants worked on the estates of their lords, who were their military commanders when fighting broke out. The nobles, in their turn, were vassals of kings or dukes. In return for the king's protection and his gifts of land, the noblemen provided him with troops in time of war.

Of course, all vassals had to be absolutely loyal and obedient to their 'liege lords'. If a vassal broke his oath or fealty (fidelity), or betrayed his lord or harmed him in any way, this was a terrible crime. Anyone who did

The Crusades

In the year 1095, Pope Urban II called on all Christian knights in Europe to go to the Holy Land of Palestine and fight against Christ's enemies, the Muslims. These wars were called the Crusades.

The First Crusade was a great success. The Crusaders took Jerusalem (1099) and set up the Kingdom of Jerusalem. People in Europe danced in joy when they heard the news. Soon, 'taking the Cross' (going on crusade) became the finest thing Christians could do.

During the next 200 years, thousands of Crusaders went to the Holy Land on a total of eight Crusades. But not all went to fight for the sake of Christ. Some went because they loved war, others because they wanted to win riches and lands.

Top: In 1348, the Black Death reached Europe from China. It was caused by a virus carried by fleas which lived on rats. It killed up to a third of the population of Europe.

Above: Part of the Bayeux tapestry, which represents the Norman conquest of England in 1066. It is one of the best records we have of feudal life.

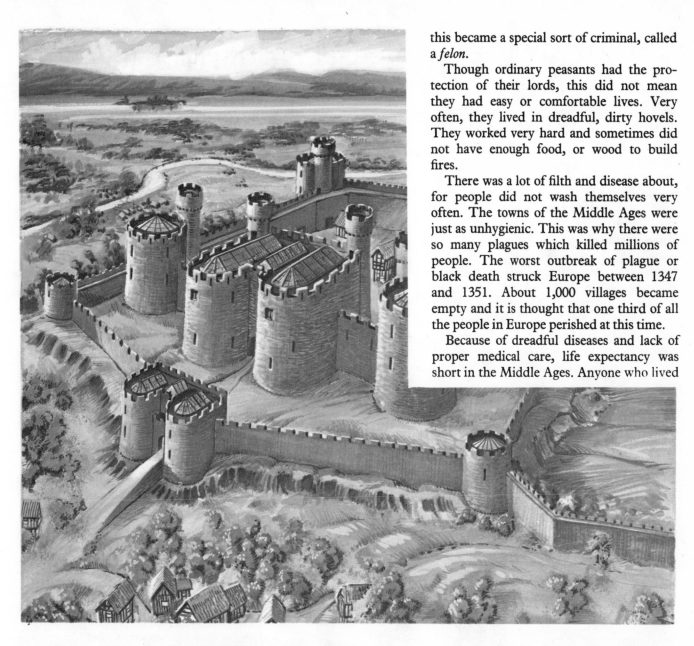

this became a special sort of criminal, called a *felon*.

Though ordinary peasants had the protection of their lords, this did not mean they had easy or comfortable lives. Very often, they lived in dreadful, dirty hovels. They worked very hard and sometimes did not have enough food, or wood to build fires.

There was a lot of filth and disease about, for people did not wash themselves very often. The towns of the Middle Ages were just as unhygienic. This was why there were so many plagues which killed millions of people. The worst outbreak of plague or black death struck Europe between 1347 and 1351. About 1,000 villages became empty and it is thought that one third of all the people in Europe perished at this time.

Because of dreadful diseases and lack of proper medical care, life expectancy was short in the Middle Ages. Anyone who lived

Above: Each medieval town or city had a castle which served as a means of defence.

Left: King John signed the Magna Carta in 1215. It considerably lessened his power over the English barons.

to the age of 40 was thought to be old. In the face of invasion, war and disease, the Roman Catholic Church served as a guardian of intellectual life in Europe. In the monasteries and later, in a few universities, the study of philosophy, history and Latin survived. Art was preserved in richly illustrated scripts called illuminated manuscripts, in church decoration, and in the building of the great cathedrals. The Church became a strong unifying force in a period when society was torn in many directions.

The Renaissance and Reformation

Because life was so dangerous and uncertain in the Middle Ages (pages 74-5), most people had no time for learning, art or poetry. Few people could even read or write. All they thought about was how to survive and avoid death or slavery at the hands of their enemies. However, learning, education and the arts did not die out altogether. People became interested in these subjects again after about 1450, when Europe was a much more peaceful place. About that time, there began, in Italy, a 'Renaissance' or rebirth of interest in the civilizations of Ancient Greece and Rome. The Renaissance did not end there, however. There were new facts to be learned about science, astronomy, art and also about the world.

Discovering the World

Previously, European ships had only sailed around the coasts of Europe and in the Mediterranean Sea. Now, great voyages of exploration were made across the oceans. In 1492, Columbus reached America. Between 1519 and 1522, Ferdinand Magellan's ship made the first voyage round the world. This proved that the world was round. Before, most people thought it was flat.

Above: Johann Gutenberg (1397-1468) invented printing with movable type.

Left: Leonardo da Vinci (1452-1519) left behind many notebooks full of his thoughts and anatomical drawings.

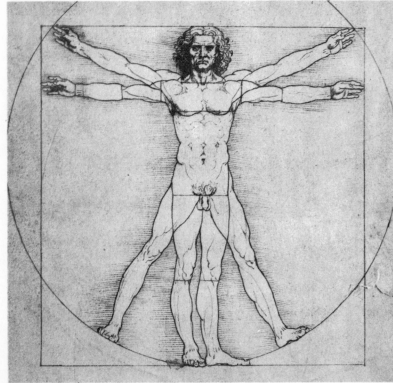

In the Middle Ages, people thought the Earth was the centre of the Universe and that the Sun and other planets revolved around it. Renaissance astronomers proved this was not true. Instead, the Polish astronomer, Copernicus, found the Earth and the planets went round the Sun, and others used improved instruments to back up his findings.

Renaissance artists painted pictures that were quite different from those painted before. Until then, paintings had looked rather unreal. The people shown in them seemed rather 'flat'. In Renaissance paintings, people looked more as they did in real life. The artists and also sculptors who made statues were following Greek and Roman ideas of how people should look.

Painting the Sistine Chapel

Michelangelo, the great sculptor, produced many beautiful works of art. One of his greatest works was the painting on the ceiling of the Sistine Chapel in Rome. This consisted of 145 separate pictures. They showed scenes from the Bible and took Michelangelo four years to complete (1508-1512). Two of the most famous scenes are the Creation of Adam and the Fall of Man, when Adam and Eve were forced out of the Garden of Eden.

Michelangelo worked while standing or lying on scaffolding (a tower made of wooden poles and planks). For hours on end, he painted his pictures looking upwards at the ceiling to see what he was doing. His arms and neck ached terribly, and paint dripped into his eyes and beard. Today, this painting can still be seen in the Sistine Chapel.

Above: Galileo Galilei (1564-1642) was an Italian astronomer and scientist who conducted many experiments.

Left: Martin Luther (1483-1546) pinned up his protests against the authority of the Church in 1517.

Below: A map showing the extent of the Reformation in Europe. John Calvin (1509-1564) founded the Calvinist Churches.

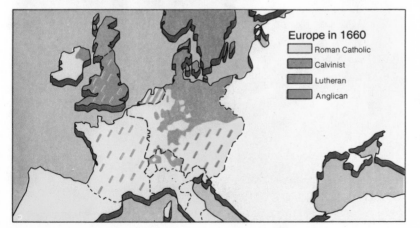

Europe in 1660
- Roman Catholic
- Calvinist
- Lutheran
- Anglican

The Spread of Ideas

The printing press developed in about 1439 by the German, Johann Gutenberg, helped to spread these new ideas. Ideas spread by means of printed books made people question and criticize everything about them. In particular, they began to question religion and how it was taught by the Church.

This led to the serious split in the Christian Church known as the Reformation. In 1517, a monk called Martin Luther protested about some of the practices of the Church. The people who agreed with Luther became known as 'Protestants'. There were now two Churches instead of one: the Catholic Church, which remained loyal to the Pope in Rome, and the Protestant Church, made up of people who did not want the Pope to rule over them. Luther's ideas and his new Church soon spread to Sweden and to Denmark.

The Reformation came to England under King Henry VIII. When Henry asked the Pope for permission to divorce his wife, Catherine of Aragon, the Pope refused him. The King was angry and declared that the Pope did not have supreme power. Henry replaced the Pope as head of the Church of England and divorced Catherine. In 1534, Henry dissolved all the monasteries in England and seized Church lands.

At about the same time, John Calvin was leading the Reformation in Switzerland. His teachings were taken up in Scotland and, in 1560, the Church of Scotland was established under Calvinist principles.

The Industrial Revolution

The word 'revolution' means a turning round, or a complete change in the way things are done. A very important change of this kind took place between 1733 and about 1840. It was called the Industrial Revolution. During this time, machines began to do much of the work which people formerly did by hand. A large number of people had no alternative but to work on these machines in factories, instead of working as craftsmen and craftswomen in their own homes.

This first happened in northern England, with the spinning and weaving of cloth. For centuries, they had been done by hand. Then, in 1733, John Kay invented a machine which could throw a weaving shuttle from side to side on a loom ten times more quickly than weavers could do it by hand. This machine was called the Flying Shuttle and it put many weavers out of work.

James Hargreaves' Spinning Jenny (1764–69) could do the work of eight hand spinners. Richard Arkwright's Water Frame (1769) was a machine driven by water which twisted thread to make a harder, stronger

Above: In 1812, riots broke out by unemployed workers against the use of machines.

Below: The Water Frame was invented in 1769 by Richard Arkwright.

Canals and Railways

By greatly increasing production, the Industrial Revolution created a need for improved methods of moving goods. At the same time, the new technology also provided methods of solving problems of transport.

Manufacturers found that it was both cheaper and safer to ship goods on water than on land. They began to build canals across the countryside. The first canal in Britain was finished in 1776 and carried coal from collieries in Bridgewater to Manchester, where it fuelled the growing cotton industry.

The first railways were developed when engineers discovered that Watt's steam engine could be used to make a self-propelled engine that would pull a carriage on a rail. A Cornishman, Robert Trevithick, built the first steam-powered locomotive in 1804.

Some other famous early locomotives were William Hedley's *Puffing Billy*, built in 1813, and George and Robert Stephenson's *Rocket*, built for a competition sponsored by the Liverpool and Manchester Railway in 1829. The *Rocket* made history when it ran at 30 miles per hour, winning its designers a prize of £500.

Left: Lord Shaftesbury (1801-1885) promoted new laws which benefited workers in factories and mines.
Below: Iron foundries and coal mines provided machines and power for the new factories.
Bottom: Young children worked long hours in factories and mines under harsh conditions.

yarn than could be made by hand. The Water Frame could be operated by children and manufacturers began to hire even very young children to run the machines.

Most important of all was the steam engine developed by James Watt in 1764-5. At first, most large machines of the Industrial Revolution were driven by water power. But machines powered by steam engines could work better, longer and more reliably. They created a large demand for coal as a fuel. This led to an increase in deep coal mining rather than open-cast mines. It also led to an increase in the iron industry as machines made of wood were no longer strong enough to withstand the power of the steam engines.

The new factories also required large quantities of raw material and, for a time, the demand for raw cotton helped to perpetuate the slave trade. Traders from Liverpool would take black slaves from Africa to America where their labour was used to produce cotton. In exchange, the traders would receive raw cotton for English cotton mills.

Before long, machinery was being used in other industries, like pottery making and machines were introduced into factories in other European countries.

Appalling Conditions

Conditions of work in the factories were terrible. At first, machinery was not fenced in, and many workers were killed or badly injured when they fell against them. Children were made to work so long and hard that they often fell sleeping into the machines. The air was stifling and thick with dust and in some rooms the workers were soaked to the skin with steam, which led to rheumatism and consumption.

Men, women and children worked 13 or 14 hours a day for very low wages. They had to live in dirty and overcrowded hovels because they could not afford anything else. They were often ill because they worked so hard in such unhealthy conditions and because they never had enough to eat. If they could not work they had to find someone to take their place, or pay a fine.

It was a long time before laws were passed in Britain to improve this dreadful situation. After 1842, there were laws which prohibited women and children from working such long hours, but bad conditions in factories and mines persisted well into the 20th century.

Great Revolutions

One night in 1773, a group of Americans crept on board three ships in Boston harbour. They grappled the ship's cargo of tea and threw it into the water. This was later called 'The Boston Tea Party'. Their protest against a tax on tea was one of the first defiant acts of American colonists against their British rulers.

Following the Boston Tea Party, the Parliament in London passed other laws that the colonists found intolerable. Many colonists felt that their rights as free people were not being respected by the King and Parliament. They wanted to have a say in decisions about the taxes they paid, the way they carried on trade, and how they would be governed. In July 1776, the colonists voted to declare their independence from Britain.

The ideas set forth in this Declaration of Independence were democratic ideas, similar to those of the ancient Athenians. Naturally, the British and other governments did not like these ideas because they had a lot to lose. At that time, European countries were rather like the personal possessions of the king or the 'ruling class' of nobles. They owned all the land and most

Above: In protest against the British attempt to control their taxes, Bostonians boarded an East India Company ship and threw the cargo of tea into the harbour.

Left: On 14th July 1789, the French people stormed the Bastille prison in Paris, releasing prisoners, killing the governor and burning the building. This marked the beginning of the French Revolution.

The Long March

Between October 1934 and October 1935, the Chinese communist leader Mao Tse-tung made an amazing escape from his great enemy and rival, Chiang Kai-shek, the general of the government forces. Mao set out with 100,000 men on a journey of 9,656 kilometres (6,000 miles) right across the vast land of China. The journey took 368 days. During that time, Mao and his army crossed 18 ranges of mountains and 24 rivers. Mao and his army fought 15 big battles with their enemies. Only 5,000 of Mao's men survived to reach safety in a town near the Great Wall of China. This meant that 19 out of every 20 communists who set out with Mao had died on the way. Those who survived the Long March are very highly regarded in China today.

of the wealth, and governed exactly as they wished.

The governing class did not want to share their power with the people. The people, however, took their power from them, by force in revolutions. In America, the colonists fought a long war against the British. In 1781, they gained their independence and formed the country known today as the United States of America.

In France, ordinary people paid very heavy taxes while nobles, churchmen and the king lived in luxury. The French thought this was unjust. Revolution broke out in 1789. The king, Louis XVI, was overthrown and executed. So was his queen, Marie Antoinette, and thousands of nobles.

After this, there were many revolutions in which people rose up against bad rulers or foreign masters. In 1804, the slaves in the Caribbean colony of Haiti threw out their French masters. By 1830, the Spanish colonies in South America had driven out the Spaniards. The French again rebelled against their kings in 1830 and 1848. The year 1848, in fact, saw revolutions all over Europe, in Italy, Austria, Hungary and Germany.

These European revolutions were defeated, sometimes very cruelly. However, the rulers who did this could not kill the wish of ordinary people to be governed in a democratic way. What is more, even greater and more violent revolutions were about to happen. These were the 'Communist' revolutions inspired by the ideas of Karl Marx (1818-83). Karl Marx believed that countries belonged to the people who lived

in them, and that the rightful rulers were not kings or nobles, but ordinary workers.

The first successful Communist revolution took place in Russia in 1917. The Tsar (king) Nicholas II believed he had been chosen by God to rule Russia. However, ordinary peasants and workers lived in dreadful poverty. Led by the Communists, the Russians overthrew Nicholas. Later, he and his family were murdered. Russia has had a Communist government ever since.

In China, too, people were desperately poor and very harshly governed. Here, in 1949, the Communists led by Mao Tse-tung achieved a Communist revolution.

Above: The last Tsar of Russia, Nicholas II and his wife Alexandra. His rule was overthrown by the Bolsheviks and he and his family were executed.

Below: Mao Tse-tung (1893-1976). His influence left its mark on many aspects of Chinese political, social and cultural life.

The World Wars

Stretcher bearers, carrying wounded soldiers to safety, often had to struggle knee-high through the mud of the battlefield. The opposing armies on the Western Front sheltered in trenches—deep ditches—dug in the muddy ground.

The two worst wars in history were both fought in the 1900s. World War I lasted from 1914 to 1918, and World War II from 1939 to 1945. In each, tens of millions of people were killed, and millions more were injured or left homeless.

WORLD WAR I

World War I was caused by rivalry between certain large countries. The *Central Powers*, on one side, included Germany, Austria-Hungary and Turkey. The *Allies*, on the other side, included Britain and France. The Allies won.

Russia was one of the Allies until the Russian Revolution of 1917. In 1917, too, the USA joined the Allies.

Terrible battles were fought on the Western Front in France and Belgium. Often, thousands of men died just to gain a few metres of ground.

High above the battlefield, pilots from the warring countries fought each other in their flimsy airplanes. Those who shot down several enemy planes became famous as 'aces'.

Events of World War I

Aug. 1914   Germany won the Battle of Tannenberg against the Russians.
Apr. 1915   Poison gas first used in war.
May 1916   Battle of Jutland. British and German High Seas fleets clash.
Dec. 1916   Allies won the Battle of Verdun, in France.
Sep. 1916   British used first tanks.
Feb. 1917   German submarines started to attack all ships friendly to Allies.
Aug. 1917   Germans halted Russian attack.
Nov. 1917   Allied tank attack at Cambrai.
Mar. 1918   Last German offensive.
Aug. 1918   Allies attacked on Western Front.
Nov. 3, 1918   Austria made peace.
Nov. 11, 1918   Germany made peace.

WORLD WAR II

In World War I, great armies fought each other for months at a time without moving more than a few kilometres. But World War II was a war of movement. Powerful forces of fast-moving tanks and guns fought their way deep into enemy territory. Parachute troops dropped from the air behind enemy lines. And huge fleets of airplanes bombed enemy cities.

More than 50 countries took part in the war. Most were among the *Allies*, who included Britain, the Commonwealth countries, France, Russia and the USA. Opposing them were the *Axis* countries, including Germany, Italy and Japan.

At the beginning of the war, German armies quickly seized much of Europe. In 1941, they invaded Russia. In the same year, Japan attacked the USA without warning. The Japanese, too, had success at first, and took over many colonial countries of Asia.

Later in the war, the Russians began to push the Germans back. Allied armies invaded western Europe, and defeated the

Winston Churchill was British prime minister for most of the war. Even when the allies were losing every battle, he believed in victory.

Dictators in conference. Adolf Hitler (left) led Germany into a war of conquest that ended in defeat. Benito Mussolini (centre) gave him Italy's help. With the dictators is the skilful German General von Kluge.

Axis forces there. In May 1945, Germany surrendered. And the war with Japan ended shortly afterwards when the Americans dropped atomic bombs on two Japanese cities.

Above: A British bomber. Fleets of bombers attacked enemy cities, factories, and railways.

Below: A German tank hunter. The Germans led the way in armoured warfare.

Events of World War II

Sep. 1, 1939 Germany invaded Poland.
Sep. 3, 1939 France and Britain declared war on Germany.
June 22, 1940 France surrendered.
June 22, 1941 Axis invaded Russia.
Dec. 7, 1941 Japan attacked American naval base at Pearl Harbor.
Oct. 1942 British offensive against Axis troops at El Alamein.
Feb. 1943 Germans at Stalingrad surrendered to Russians.
Sep. 3, 1943 Allies landed in Italy.
Mar. 1944 Japanese reached the Indian border.
June 6, 1944 D-day. Allies invaded Normandy, and began their drive towards Germany.
Oct. 1944 American naval victory over Japanese in Battle for Leyte Gulf.
Jan. 1945 Russians captured Warsaw.
May 7, 1945 Germany surrendered.
Aug. 1945 Americans dropped atomic bombs.
Sep. 1945 Japan surrendered.

The World Today

For much of history, the lives people led were almost the same as those led by their parents and grandparents. This situation is not the same for people who live in the world today. This is because scientific progress has been very fast in the last two or three decades.

More Gadgets

Twenty years ago, for example, most people did not have central heating, television, transistor radios, tape recorders, washing machines, dishwashers and refrigerators. Today many homes have some or all of these objects. Not so very long ago, most people in Europe did not find it easy to travel to other continents. It is now possible to fly to the other side of the world in a day.

Jet aircraft and machines in the home are only some of the machines which have changed people's lives in the last few years. In offices, for example, there are now electric typewriters, photocopying machines and electronic calculators.

Above: Nuclear power plants are being built all over the world to replace coal and oil as a source of power. The first of these plants was built in Britain in 1936.

Left: A United Nations Observer team. These people help to keep the peace between countries who are in dispute with each other.

Living in the Future

Today, some planners think that in the future, people will live in cities built on the sea. These cities, they believe, might solve the problem of overcrowding in cities today.

The Sea City which these planners have designed is built inside a heated lagoon. Around the city, there is a high wall to keep out the cold winds from the sea and to stop storms from disturbing the calm waters of the lagoon. The inhabitants of Sea City will live in large floating blocks of flats. Covered moving pathways run from the flats to the shops. People can travel around the lagoon in electrically-powered boats.

Left: The work of the medical profession has been greatly helped by the development of more life-saving machines.

Below: Jumbo jets are a fine example of the high degree of technology which has been developed by the aircraft industry within the last few decades.

Bottom: *Telstar* was the first active communications satellite to be launched by the United States in 1962.

Today we think it is quite normal for astronauts to travel to the Moon, or to see television programmes that come from the other side of the world. Thirty years ago, these things seemed practically impossible. It was also impossible to think that rockets could be sent from Earth to carry spacecraft to other planets like Venus, Mars, Jupiter and Saturn. Today, men have lived for over six months in space stations, thousands of kilometres above the Earth's surface. And there are other artificial satellites far out in Space which circle the Earth and send back information about the weather and military installations.

Medical Progress

Medicine, too, has made great advances in the last few years. It was only after 1945 that doctors were able to make regular use of antibiotics to cure infections. There are also new drugs and medicines to help reduce pain, and doctors can now cure many diseases which once killed or crippled thousands of people. New surgical techniques allow doctors to replace joints in the

body with artificial ones and to transplant organs such as the kidneys and even the human heart.

Of course, these advances have not benefited everyone. In parts of South America, Asia and Africa, life is still poor and backward. Fortunately, though, international organizations like the United Nations can send doctors, scientists, teachers and engineers to help poorer countries. With this help, poorer countries can improve the health, farming methods, industry and education of their citizens.

Flags of the World

43 Canada

42 USA

41 Mexico

40 Venezuela

39 Peru

38 Brazil

37 Bolivia

36 Chile

35 Argentina

34 Angola

NORTH AMERICA

43

42

41

40

39

38

SOUTH AMERICA

37

36

35

ATLANTIC OCEAN

PACIFIC OCEAN

1

2

3

8

10

12

30

29

31

AFRI

NI

32

33 Zaire   32 Nigeria   31 Mauritania   30 Morocco   29 Algeria

28 Libya

1 Iceland 2 UK 3 Norway 4 Sweden 5 Finland 6 Poland

7 East Germany 8 West Germany 9 Belgium 10 France 11 Switzerland 12 Spain

13 Italy

14 USSR

15 Turkey

16 Iran

17 Saudi Arabia

18 India

19 China

20 Japan

21 Australia

22 New Zealand

23 S. Africa

24 Tanzania

25 Ethiopia

26 Sudan

27 Egypt

ASIA

PACIFIC OCEAN

INDIAN OCEAN

AUSTRALIA

6 CONTINENTS AND COUNTRIES

As transport and communications are bringing continents and countries nearer to each other, our interest and fascination in other lands and the traditions and customs of the people of those lands steadily increases.

Asia

Asia is the world's largest continent. It also has more people than any other continent. Its area equals almost one-third of the Earth's total land area, and nearly 60 per cent of the total world population live there. In Asia's huge expanse lie some of the world's driest deserts and some of its wettest regions. The world's highest mountains contrast majestically with some of the deepest depressions.

The Land

Asia's shores are washed by the Arctic Ocean in the north and the Indian Ocean in the south. The Ural Mountains separate the continent from Europe in the west, and the Pacific Ocean lies between Asia and North America in the east. In the south-west it borders Europe along the Caspian Sea, the Black Sea, and the Mediterranean. Only the Suez Canal separates Asia from Africa. And in the north-east, the gap between Asia and North America narrows to 72 kilometres (45 miles) across the Bering Strait.

Northern Asia is a vast, cold, often featureless region that includes Russian Siberia. Several huge rivers drain these lowlands. In the middle of the continent the Himalayan mountain range forms a towering triangular mass that is sometimes called 'the roof of the world'. It includes Mount Everest, the world's highest peak, which soars up to 8,848 metres (29,028 feet). Mongolia, parts of western China, and Tibet meet in this central region.

To the south of the Himalayas the land forms a series of ancient plateaux. The teeming nations of Bangladesh, India, Pakistan, Bhutan, and Afghanistan are found

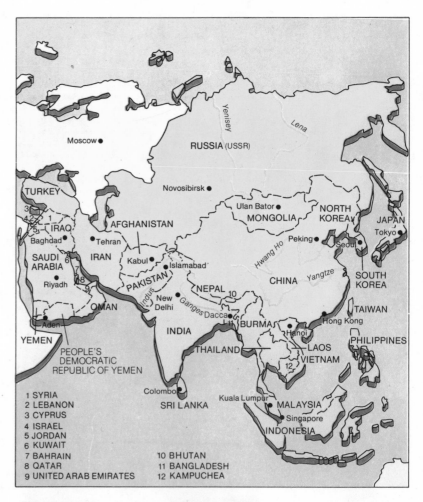

1 SYRIA
2 LEBANON
3 CYPRUS
4 ISRAEL
5 JORDAN
6 KUWAIT
7 BAHRAIN
8 QATAR
9 UNITED ARAB EMIRATES
10 BHUTAN
11 BANGLADESH
12 KAMPUCHEA

Left: The Dead Sea lies on the borders of Jordan and Israel. It is 395 m (1,296 ft) below sea-level and is so salty that swimmers can float easily on its surface without sinking.

there. To the south-west the land dries out into a region known as the Middle East, where Asia nudges Europe. Turkey, Iran, and the Arabian Peninsula form part of the area.

South East Asia is that part of the continent located to the east of India and south of China. It is a region largely made up of forested islands and peninsulas, and includes Malaysia, Vietnam, Indonesia, Thailand, and the Philippines.

In the extreme east, a region known as the Far East, is a mountainous area, parts of which are regularly disturbed by earthquakes. Korea, China, and Japan are found there, and their combined populations add up to more than half the people of Asia.

Rivers, Lakes and Deserts

Some of the world's greatest rivers water the huge plains of Asia. In India the Ganges and Brahmaputra flow into the Bay of Bengal, and the Indus empties into the Arabian Sea. The Hwang Ho and the Yangtse rise in Tibet and flow through China. The Ob, Lena, and Yenisei, which wind across northern Russia, are frozen over parts of their courses during six months of the year. In the warmer parts of Asia, river valleys and deltas (flat areas at the mouths of rivers) are the chief population centres.

Most of the Middle East is hot desert and is thinly-populated except near the few rivers and around oases (waterholes). There are also bleak, cold deserts in the interior of Asia, notably the vast Gobi desert of China and Mongolia.

Top: Mount Everest, 8,848 m (29,028 ft) high, soars above the Khumbu glacier in Nepal.

Above: Tropical rain forest in Indonesia. Indonesia consists of about 3,000 mostly mountainous islands.

Left: The River Ganges at Varanasi, in India. Many Hindus gather here to bathe in the waters of this holy river.

Asia (2)

Asia has more people than all the other continents put together and nearly 60 out of every 100 people in the world live there. Its population increases by about 100,000 every day.

Asia has people from all the chief racial groups—Mongoloid, Caucasoid and Negroid. They speak hundreds of different languages and belong to many different religions of which Buddhism and Hinduism have the most followers. Some live in remote

Tibet

This Chinese province is the highest country in the world. The plateau of Tibet is more than 4,876·8 metres (16,000 feet) above sea-level and many summits are 6,096 metres (20,000 feet) in height. Few people can live there as it is so high and so cold and most of those who do live in the south of the country and can earn a living from their livestock which produce leather, skins, wool, butter, milk, eggs, meat and cheese. Many men studied there to become Buddhist monks or *lamas* before the Chinese took over in 1958.

desert areas. Others live in the most crowded cities of the world. One of the main problems in Asia is how to grow enough food for the population. Millions of Asians live at subsistence level—they have barely enough food to eat. Not all Asian countries are poor. Japan, for example, is one of the richest countries in the world.

The Taj Mahal at Agra in India is often called 'the world's most beautiful building'. It was built in the 1600s by the Emperor Shah Jahan as a tomb for his wife.

Chinese children enjoy a meal at school. Rice and wheat are the most important foods for hundreds of millions of Asians.

Far left: Asians in many countries find work in the rice paddies—small fields surrounded by low mud walls. Many Asians, however, are now receiving a good education and are leaving the land for work in the cities.

Left: Tokyo, the capital of Japan, is one of the world's largest and most crowded cities. Most of the streets have no names, but each block of buildings is numbered.

Important Dates in the History of Asia

3000s BC The Sumerians developed the first city civilization in Mesopotamia in south-western Asia.

2500s BC Cities were built in the Indus Valley in the Indian Peninsula.

1500s BC Beginning of the Shang dynasty in China, probably the first dynasty.

1500s BC The Aryans from northern Asia settled in the Indus Valley.

1200s BC The Israelites left Egypt.

500s BC The Buddha was born in India, and Confucius was born in China.

336–323 BC Empire of Alexander the Great.

300s BC The building of the Great Wall of China began.

about 6 BC Jesus Christ born in Palestine.

AD 570 Muhammad born in Arabia

618 Beginning of the T'ang dynasty in China.

1206 Genghis Khan led the Mongols in the conquest of China and Central Asia

1264 Kublai Khan began his rule of the Mongol Empire.

1526 Babar created the Mogul Empire in India.

1500s European traders and adventurers began to visit Asia.

1757 The British East India Company began its rule in Bengal.

1774 Warren Hastings was appointed the first British governor-general of India.

1857–58 The Indian Mutiny

1876 Queen Victoria was declared Empress of India

1911 End of the Chinese Empire.

1939–45 World War II. The Japanese invaded many countries, but later suffered defeat.

1940s–1960s Many Asian countries became independent of colonial rule.

Asia (3)

Natural Resources

Much of Asia's soil is useless for growing food. As a result, farming land is precious all over the continent. Rice, which is the main food for most Asians, is often grown in flooded paddy fields that are terraced all the way down steep hillsides, to take advantage of every cultivable scrap of land.

In the drier parts of Asia other field crops are grown. These include cereals, such as maize, wheat, millet, and soybeans; and items for selling abroad, such as tobacco, tea, rubber, dates, jute, olives, and cotton.

Asian forests provide some of the world's most valuable timber. This includes pine and teak.

Animals are used mainly for work and transportation. Among such animals are reindeer (in the north), yaks, horses, donkeys, camels, buffalo, and elephants. Cattle, sheep, and goats are raised mainly for meat.

A Wealth of Minerals

Asia is particularly rich in minerals. Most of the world's oil—its most valuable fuel in the late 1970s—comes from south-western Asia. About three-quarters of the world's tin comes from South East Asia, and China sells large quantities of tungsten and tin overseas. Turkey and the Philippines supply chromite, and manganese and mica come from India and China.

Top: Tea grown in Asia is exported all over the world. These Sri Lankan women are picking the leaves by hand.

Above: Silk is an important Asian product. It is made from the cocoon of a moth which lives on mulberry leaves.

Left: China is becoming a great manufacturing nation. This factory in Shanghai produces optical lenses.

Asia's Industries

Virtually all Asia's heavy industry is located in Asian Russia, Japan, China, and Israel. Most of the other nations rely on such rural industries as handicrafts, fishing, and tourism for their income. The four major nations, especially Japan, which leads the world in many industries, produce automobiles, electric and electronic equipment, weapons, ships, precision tools, textiles, machinery, and iron and steel.

The Outlook

Many Asian nations are making desperate efforts to increase their factories and compete more closely in world markets with Japan and the Western nations. At the end of the 1970s, for example, China largely dropped its policy of self-imposed isolation started by Chairman Mao Tse-tung and openly invited Western experts to help with their industrial know-how. Other parts of Asia, such as Taiwan and Hong Kong, expanded their factories and produced a flood of cheap electronic products and watches. One major problem is that, in many nations, the population is increasing quickly. For example, India's population is rising by 2.1 per cent per year so that, every year, India must provide for an extra 12 million people. This makes it hard to raise the people's living standards.

Above: Rubber trees are native to South America but are now cultivated in South East Asia. The liquid rubber, or latex, oozes from cuts made in the bark of the trees.

Below: Rice fields in the Philippines. The young plants are grown in flooded fields, or paddies. Rice is grown widely in Asia and for many Asians it is their staple diet.

Europe

Europe extends from the North Atlantic Ocean in the west to the Ural Mountains and the Caspian Sea in the Soviet Union. Hence, it is essentially a large peninsula (a piece of land almost totally surrounded by the sea) attached to Asia. There are dozens of smaller peninsulas. Along the Mediterranean coast the Italian Peninsula is one of the largest. Immediately to the east of this is the Balkan Peninsula, made up of Yugoslavia, Romania, Albania, Greece and European Turkey. Farther east, the Crimean Peninsula juts into the Black Sea.

In the south-western corner of the continent, separating the Mediterranean Sea from the Atlantic Ocean lies the Iberian Peninsula, made up of Spain and Portugal. The small peninsula of Denmark, in the north-west of the continent, is separated from the much larger Scandinavian Peninsula to the north by the Skagerrak and Kattegat straits. Norway, Sweden, and part of Finland make up the Scandinavian Peninsula. In the far north, the Kola Peninsula separates the White Sea from the Barents Sea.

With so many peninsulas, as well as hundreds of bays, inlets, harbours, and gulfs, Europe's coastline covers about 80,500 kilometres (50,000 miles). This is more than three times longer than Africa's coastline, although Africa is three times as big as Europe.

Some important islands lie off the mainland. The largest of these are the British Isles. Others include the Balearic Islands, Corsica, Sardinia, Sicily, and Crete.

Left: A view of Prague, the picturesque capital city of Czechoslovakia. It lies on the Moldau river.

Above: Mont Blanc is the highest mountain peak in Europe at 4,810 m (15,781 ft). It is on the French/Italian border.

Rivers and Lakes

Europe is criss-crossed by several large and important rivers. Many of these are linked to other waterways by means of canals and have become busy highways for the transportation of goods and passengers.

The longest river is the Volga, which flows north to south through the Soviet Union and empties into the Caspian Sea. Other major Russian rivers are the Don, the Dnieper, and the Dniester. Europe's second longest river is the Danube, which rises in Germany's Black Forest and flows into the Black Sea. One of the most important rivers, historically and commercially, is the Rhine. It rises in Switzerland and flows through West Germany and the Netherlands before emptying into the North Sea.

Although Europe's lakes are small compared with those of some other continents, they are among the most beautiful in the world. Millions of tourists are attracted to the lakes of Switzerland and Italy. The saltwater Caspian Sea is sometimes regarded as a lake; it is the largest inland body of water in the world.

Mountain Ranges

In the past, Europeans tended to be separated into many groups by the several high mountain ranges that stretch across the continent. But the people were never completely isolated because there were always passes through the mountains, and many of these are still in use today.

The major mountain system in southern Europe is the Alps. These mountains range from south-eastern France, through northern Italy, southern Germany, and Switzerland. Two major arms of the Alps are the Apennines, which form a great barrier down the middle of Italy; and the Carpathians, which ring the Hungarian plain. The Caucasus, which run from the Black Sea to the Caspian Sea, claim the highest peak in Europe—Mount Elbrus at 5,634 metres (18,481 feet).

Above right: Corsica, an island in the Mediterranean Sea which belongs to France. Most of Corsica consists of low mountains and rugged hills reaching down to the sea.

Right: Norway is a country of great splendour with pine-topped mountain ranges and narrow deep-sided fiords like the Sogne Fiord seen here.

95

Europe (2)

The People

Europe holds about 650 million people, which means that it has more people than any other continent except Asia. It is also more crowded than any of the other continents. One reason why Europe has always been so important and why so many people live there is that the continent stands at the crossroads of eastern and western nations, and northern and southern nations. The earliest civilizations grew up along the coasts of the Mediterranean and that sea for centuries was a highway for trade and colonizers, and for the exchange of new ideas.

Another reason is Europe's climate, which is generally mild, with enough rain to water the fertile soil all the year round. The warm waters of the Gulf Stream flow round Europe's western and southern coasts and keep the harbours there ice-free. The winds also help because they usually blow from the west, sweeping warm air across the continent.

Europe has many large and famous cities. London, Paris, Rome, Madrid, Dublin and other historic places attract visitors all the year round to enjoy their sights and sounds. Southern cities, such as Barcelona and Naples, where the climate is generally warm and sunny, encourage customers to sit outdoors on the sidewalk at cafe tables. More northerly centres, such as London and Oslo, are colder and wetter. They have more indoor entertainment.

Above: Artists working in the open air in the Place du Tertre, Montmartre. This quarter of Paris has long been famous as an artistic centre.

Below: Moscow lies in Europe. These visitors to Lenin's tomb are waiting outside the Kremlin, a citadel which houses the government.

The peoples of Europe can be conveniently grouped according to the languages they speak. One major group is made up of so-called Germanic peoples. These include the Germans, English, Dutch, Swedes, Norwegians, Danes, and Icelanders. The Latin peoples originally spoke Latin and are descended from the inhabitants of the Roman Empire. They are made up of Italians, Romanians, French, Portuguese, and Spanish. Russians, Bulgarians, Serbo-Croats, Poles, and Czechs belong to the Slavic group. Many of the people who live in Brittany in France, and in Wales, Scotland, and Ireland are Celts. Another group is made up of Turks, Estonians, Lapps, Finns, and Hungarians. The Albanians, Armenians, Greeks, and Basques each form separate groups of their own. More than one language is spoken in several countries. Language differences may lead to conflict if the people who speak minority languages feel that their local culture is threatened.

Left: Amsterdam, the capital of the Netherlands, was built on a system of canals. Visitors may tour the city in glass-sided motorboats like these.

Below left: The coastline of Norway is deeply indented by fiords. Many Norwegians still make their living by fishing.

Below: Venice, in northern Italy, was built on a group of islands linked by canals and bridges. It has many fine churches and palaces.

Ways of Life

Although they all live on the same continent, Europeans vary widely in their ways of life. There are many reasons for this — politics, religion, history, language and education being the main ones.

Such differences have caused many wars in the past. In the last 30 years, West European peoples have drawn closer together because of such things as increased travel and the setting up of common markets.

Europe (3)

Natural Resources

Some of the world's richest farmland is in Europe and, as a result, more than half the land is used for farming. But methods are extremely varied. In Western Europe and European Russia, farmers use the latest methods and the most up-to-date machinery. But in many southern and eastern regions primitive ploughing and hand labour is common.

Europeans produce most of their own food. This includes wheat, potatoes, barley, rye, oats, sugar beet, beans, corn, fibre flax, tobacco, olives, peas, dates, figs, grapes, and citrus fruits. Denmark, Great Britain and the Netherlands have huge dairy herds of cattle. Pigs, sheep, goats, poultry, and beef cattle are also raised in various parts of Europe for meat.

European fishermen sail the world in search of big catches. Iceland, Great Britain, Norway, the Soviet Union, and Spain are among the world's leading fishing nations.

Industrial Muscle

Industry usually means the making of things, as well as digging for minerals hidden deep in the ground, and the building of anything from offices and houses to ships and cars.

Raw materials in plenty are needed for healthy industry, and these are found in

Right: An oil production platform operating in the North Sea. During the 1970s several companies successfully drilled for oil and natural gas in these waters.

Above right: Cattle grazing on pastureland in Ireland. The mild, rainy climate of Ireland is well-suited to dairy farming.

Right: Europe is well-known for the variety and high quality of its wines. Grapes (the main ingredient of wine) are grown in sunny fields or on slopes. After harvesting, the grapes are pressed to extract their juice which is then fermented.

various parts of Europe. Coal is one of the most important items, and three-fifths of the world's coal comes from Europe. The richest coalfields lie in East and West Germany, Great Britain, Czechoslovakia, Poland, and the Soviet Union. Half the world's iron ore is found in Europe, and a quarter of its *bauxite* (the ore from which aluminium is made). Sweden, France, and the Soviet Union lead in the production of iron ore, while bauxite is found mainly in Hungary, Yugoslavia, the Soviet Union, France, and Greece. Iron ore is used in industry to manufacture steel. The Soviet Union, Sweden, France and Spain are leading producers of iron ore.

Heavy industry is located mainly in East and West Germany, Great Britain, France, Poland, and the Soviet Union. This includes iron and steel production, machinery, and the building of cars and ships. Light industry is found in nations such as Switzerland, the Netherlands, and Belgium, where the people make clothing and process food. Traditional craftsmen, such as watch and clockmakers, are still found in the Black Forest region of Germany and in Switzerland.

In addition to coal, Europe relies on a number of other sources for power. In common with most of the rest of the world, Europeans understand that oil and natural gas reserves will run out before long. As a result, they are turning to nuclear energy, hydroelectricity (electric power obtained from falling water) and solar energy. Hydroelectricity is important in nations such as Norway and Switzerland, which have plenty of rivers flowing down steep slopes.

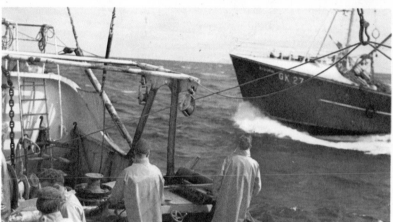

Top: Tourists resting on the steps of the Propylaea, the gateway to the Acropolis in Athens. Athens was an important city of ancient Greece and reached the height of its power in the 5th century BC. Today it is the capital city of Greece.

Above: Fishing is an important European industry. Factory ships are able to freeze or can their catches while still at sea. The north Atlantic has rich fishing grounds but now there are fears that some areas are being overfished.

Below: Harvest-time in Hungary. Like those of other nations with Communist governments, Hungary's farms are organized on a collective system. Individual farmers do not own their own land but work on state-run farms.

Africa

Africa is the second largest continent. It was once called the 'dark continent', because it was largely unexplored and thought to be covered with dense forests. Actually, forests cover less than a fifth of Africa. The rest of the land is more or less equally divided between desert and grassland.

Today, this huge region is going through a period of great change. By 1900, nearly all of Africa was under the rule of European powers. Even in 1950, only four African countries—Egypt, Ethiopia, Liberia and South Africa—were independent. But many Africans were inspired by the conviction that they should govern themselves. The opposition to the colonial powers was mainly political but, in some places, there were long, costly wars. One after another, the colonies won nationhood. Today, Europeans retain control only in southern Africa. Africa's chief problems are now economic, because many Africans are desperately poor.

The Land

The equator crosses the middle of Africa. Much of the northern half is covered by the Sahara Desert, the world's greatest desert. To the north of the Sahara, along the Mediterranean coast, lie the Arab countries of Morocco, Algeria, Tunisia, Libya, and Egypt. To the south of the Sahara are the Negro countries. The Sahara is made up mostly of shifting sand dunes and barren rocks. Oases here and there, and a fertile strip along the River Nile are the only places where farmers can raise crops. Two other, smaller, deserts are the Kalahari Desert and the Namib Desert, both in south-western Africa.

There are mountains in the north-west of the continent (the Atlas Mountains) and high plateaux in the east and south. The Drakensberg Range, with some peaks rising to more than 3,400 metres (11,000 feet), covers a large area of the south-eastern part of the continent. Africa's highest peak is Kilimanjaro, an extinct volcano in Tanzania that is 5,895 metres (19,340 feet) high.

Right: The Sahara, in northern Africa, is the largest desert in the world. It covers an area of 8,600,000 sq km (3,320,000 sq miles).

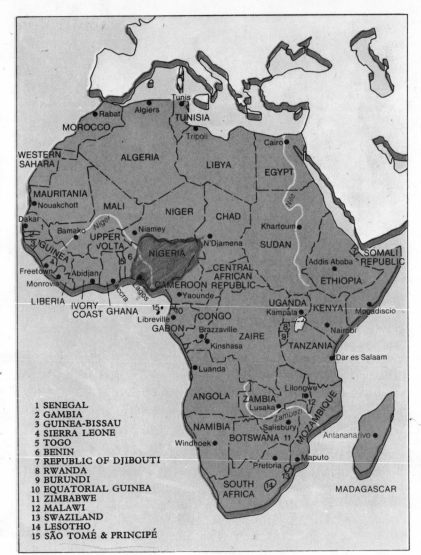

1 SENEGAL
2 GAMBIA
3 GUINEA-BISSAU
4 SIERRA LEONE
5 TOGO
6 BENIN
7 REPUBLIC OF DJIBOUTI
8 RWANDA
9 BURUNDI
10 EQUATORIAL GUINEA
11 ZIMBABWE
12 MALAWI
13 SWAZILAND
14 LESOTHO
15 SÃO TOMÉ & PRINCIPÉ

Left: Victoria Falls, one of the world's greatest waterfalls. It lies on the Zambezi river and divides Zimbabwe from Zambia.

Below: The River Nile is seen here flowing past Cairo, the capital of Egypt. The Nile is the world's longest river. It is regulated by several dams, the most important of which is the Aswan dam, which controls Egypt's irrigation.

Tropical rain forests cover much of the Zaire River basin and the coastal regions of West Africa. There are also forested areas in south-central Africa, the highlands of Ethiopia, in parts of South Africa, and on some of the mountain slopes of north-western Africa. Between the rain forests and the deserts, there are vast regions of savanna, or tropical grassland. In areas where there is abundant rainfall, the savanna is characterized by frequent clumps of trees and tall, luxuriant grass. But, towards the deserts, trees become less and less common and the grass is shorter. Finally, there is a zone of dry scrub between the savanna and the deserts. The savanna, especially in eastern Africa, is the home of some of the world's greatest populations of wild animals. However, hunting and the destruction of many animal habitats have threatened many species with extinction.

One other outstanding feature of the continent is the Great Rift Valley. This is a series of valleys that link up and cut through much of East Africa. The Rift Valley stretches from Syria in Asia to Mozambique in south-eastern Africa. It was formed when blocks of land sank down between roughly parallel sets of faults (cracks) in the Earth's surface. Cracking also occurred on the valley floor. Molten rocks welled up through the cracks. This has widened the Rift Valley by about 10 kilometres (1.6 miles) in the last 20 million years.

The Rivers of Africa

The Nile, the world's longest river, rises in east-central Africa and flows northwards for 6,741 kilometres (4,187 miles) through the deserts of northern Sudan and Egypt before emptying into the Mediterranean Sea. Its source is Lake Victoria, Africa's largest lake and the world's second largest freshwater lake.

Other great rivers are the Niger and Zaire. The Niger rises quite close to the coast of Guinea in West Africa, but it flows northwards and eastwards before turning south into Nigeria, where it empties into the Gulf of Guinea. It is 4,000 kilometres (2,485 miles) long. The Zaire River was formerly called the Congo River, when the country through which it flows was named the Belgian Congo. When the country was renamed Zaire, the river's name was also changed. The Zaire River is 4,370 kilometres (2,715 miles) long.

Two important rivers, the Limpopo and Zambezi, empty into the Indian Ocean in south-eastern Africa. The Zambezi is interrupted by the continent's greatest waterfall, the Victoria Falls.

Africa (2)

The People

Although more than 400 million people live in Africa, their land is so large that in many parts there are no people at all. About 70 out of every 100 Africans are Negroes, who live south of the Sahara. Most of the remainder are Arabs and Europeans, who live on the Mediterranean coasts of North Africa. Some Europeans also live in South Africa and in Zimbabwe (Rhodesia).

Eight out of ten Africans live in the countryside and most of them are farmers. Those who live on the plains of eastern and southern Africa are herdsmen, looking after cattle. But more and more young Africans are moving into the cities, where they work at whatever jobs they can find.

In southern Africa the richer white people can afford to employ black people in business, industry, government, or domestic service. In South Africa, the official policy of *apartheid* (which means 'apartness' in Afrikaans) keeps whites and non-whites apart. In practice it has meant that non-whites have had to make do with inferior housing, schooling, jobs, justice, rights, and recreation. This has led to deeply bitter feelings among the majority of non-whites.

A few Africans are still wanderers and hunters. These include the pygmies, who live in the rain forests of the upper Zaire River basin. They are noted for their small size, few of them growing to more than 1.5 metres (4 feet 10 inches) tall. Other primitive hunters are the Bushmen of the Kalahari Desert. They are yellowish brown in colour and live in small bands, hunting small desert animals and eating roots where they can find them. The Hottentots are related to the Bushmen and live in desert regions of south-western Africa.

Education varies from country to country. In some places six or seven people out of ten can read and write; in others there may be only one out of ten who can do so. Most

Top: Church Square in Pretoria, South Africa. The modern office block contrasts sharply with the older European-style buildings.

Above: African people in ceremonial dress at a tribal gathering.

Left: Supplies are delivered to a remote part of Ethiopia in north-east Africa.

Left: The Tuareg are a nomadic people of northern Africa. They travel across the Sahara with their herds, stopping only to make temporary camps. Their long robes protect them from the fierce heat of the sun and the cold desert nights. Tuareg men also wear long blue veils.

nations try to send all of their children to school, but some are too poor to provide free education for everybody.

Africa has more than 1,000 languages and dialects. In some areas, people must learn a common language so that they can communicate with each other. For example, in East Africa, most people speak Swahili. A European language is also often used as the common and official language. South Africa's official languages are English and Afrikaans, a tongue derived from Dutch. Arabic is the main language in North Africa.

Africans who live outside the cities live mostly in villages with houses made of sun-dried mud bricks. Many have dirt floors and thatched roofs. Some African men have more than one wife, and a household may be made up of brothers all living together with their wives and children, as well as their parents and grandparents.

Herders who live in or near the Sahara and keep camels, cattle, and goats live mainly on milk, butter, and cheese. Many African farming people eat a thick porridge made from grain, fresh or dried root crops, meat when it can be had, all cooked in a variety of sauces, and bananas. Women do most of the heavy farm work, planting, weeding, and harvesting the crops.

Above right: A herd of impala, accompanied by a family of giraffes, visit a waterhole in the African bush. Much of Africa's wildlife is declining in numbers but some countries have set up special safari parks with game wardens to protect the animals.

Right: A group of Moroccan musicians playing traditional instruments in the ancient city of Marrakesh.

103

Africa (3)

The Natural Wealth of Africa

Although many African tribes still use primitive farming methods, more scientific methods are gradually taking over. Much land is useless for farming but other parts have been cleared and turned into profitable industries.

Western Africa supplies about 70 per cent of the world's cacao, from which cocoa and chocolate are made. About three-quarters of the world's palm oil and palm kernels, for use in cosmetics and soap, come from Africa. Other important farm exports include coffee, bananas, olives, cotton fibre and cotton seed, tea, tobacco, rubber, and pyrethrum (used in insecticides). Africa also exports a huge amount of peanuts, and farms in eastern Africa supply about two-thirds of the world's sisal, which is used in making rope.

Manufacturing and Mining

Apart from growing food, the natural wealth of the continent is unevenly divided. Some nations have hardly any natural wealth in the way of minerals or raw materials.

Most of the continent's factories are in South Africa. Other nations that have important and growing manufacturing

The Future of Africa

Some countries, such as Ivory Coast, have made steady progress since independence. Others have benefited from the discovery of valuable minerals. For instance, Nigeria's economy has expanded greatly because of its oil production. The progress of many nations, however, has been marred by instability, with the armed forces seizing power from elected governments. Recently there have been hopeful signs. For example, in 1979, the people of Central African Republic, Equatorial Guinea and Uganda removed their military dictators, while the military leaders of Ghana and Nigeria held elections and restored civilian rule in their nations. Africa's main problem, however, remains. How can living standards be raised in this poor continent?

Top: A copper refinery in Zambia, a land-locked country in south-central Africa. Zambia has rich deposits of copper which it exports to the industrial nations of the world.

Left: Washing gravel to extract diamond deposits at an African diamond mine. Africa is the world's main supplier of these precious gems.

industries are Zaire, Kenya, Algeria, Morocco, Tunisia, Egypt, and Zimbabwe (Rhodesia).

The mining picture is quite different. In some places, Africa is a treasure house of minerals. Nearly all the world's diamonds come from African mines and much gold comes from South Africa.

South Africa is also extremely well-endowed with other minerals apart from gold. It is a leading producer of gem-quality diamonds, copper, chrome ore, asbestos, iron ore, uranium and other metals.

Except for South Africa, the leading producers of diamonds are Zaire (mainly industrial diamonds), Botswana, Ghana, Namibia and Sierra Leone. Africa's other copper producers are Zambia and Zaire. Chrome ore and asbestos are also mined in Zimbabwe, while the other main iron ore producers are Liberia and Mauritania. South Africa and Niger are the two leading producers of uranium. Bauxite (aluminium ore) is mined in quantity in Guinea.

In the late 1970s, the leading oil producers in Africa were Nigeria, Libya, Algeria, Egypt, Gabon, Angola, Tunisia, Congo and Zaire.

Transport

Because of Africa's great size, there are problems of transport. Of Africa's total railways, which amount to about 72,000 kilometres (45,000 miles) of track, nearly four-fifths is in only 11 countries.

Railways are costly to build and roads are the main form of transport in most of Africa, although, even today, many roads have earth surfaces and turn to mud in the rainy season. For non-bulky, high value goods, air transport is ideal and Africa's air services have expanded greatly in recent years.

Above: The mighty Kariba dam spans the Zambezi river on the borders of Zambia and Zimbabwe. The 128 m (420 ft) high dam provides hydroelectric power for both countries. Behind the dam lies Lake Kariba, one of the largest reservoirs in the world.

Top: East African fishermen prepare for the day's catch in their Arab dhows (sailing boats).

Below: Herdsmen driving their camels at an oasis in southern Tunisia.

North America

North America is the world's third largest continent, after Asia and Africa. It includes Canada and the United States, Mexico, the countries of Central America, and the islands of the West Indies.

The Land

The three great landform regions are made up of a huge chain of mountains running down the west of the continent, and known as the *Cordillera;* a smaller, older mountain system covering mainly the eastern region of the United States and part of Canada; and the Great Central Plain, which lies between the two mountain systems.

The Cordillera (a Spanish word meaning 'chain of mountains') is made up of the Rocky Mountains and the Sierra Madre. The Rockies stretch from northern Alaska to the south-western United States. The Sierra Madre is a southern continuation that runs through Mexico.

The Appalachians stretch from the Gulf of St Lawrence in Canada southwards to central Alabama. Quite different from the rugged Rockies, they have been worn smooth over the centuries, and few peaks rise more than 1,800 metres (6,000 feet).

The Great Central Plain stretches from the Arctic to the Gulf of Mexico. In the north the land is frozen or swampy, and

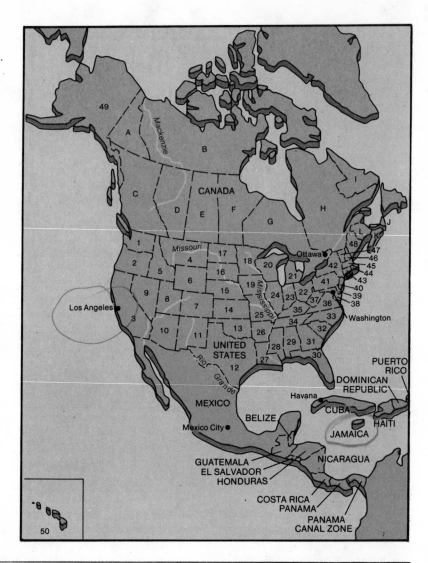

The United States of America

Pacific Coast States
1. Washington
2. Oregon
3. California

Rocky Mountain States
4. Montana
5. Idaho
6. Wyoming
7. Colorado
8. Utah
9. Nevada

South-western States
10. Arizona
11. New Mexico
12. Texas
13. Oklahoma

Mid-western States
14. Kansas
15. Nebraska
16. South Dakota
17. North Dakota
18. Minnesota
19. Iowa
20. Wisconsin
21. Michigan
22. Ohio
23. Indiana
24. Illinois
25. Missouri

Southern States
26. Arkansas
27. Louisiana
28. Mississippi
29. Alabama
30. Florida
31. Georgia
32. South Carolina
33. North Carolina
34. Tennessee
35. Kentucky
36. Virginia
37. West Virginia
38. Maryland
39. Delaware

Mid-Atlantic States
40. New Jersey
41. Pennsylvania
42. New York

New England
43. Connecticut
44. Rhode Island
45. Massachusetts
46. New Hampshire
47. Vermont
48. Maine
49. Alaska
50. Hawaii

The Provinces and Territories of Canada

A. Yukon Territory
B. Northwest Territories
C. British Columbia
D. Alberta
E. Saskatchewan
F. Manitoba
G. Ontario
H. Quebec
I. Newfoundland
J. Prince Edward Island
K. Nova Scotia
L. New Brunswick

quite useless. Farther south it becomes more temperate and is famed for the huge lakes that lie on the borders of Canada and the United States. South of where the Mississippi and Missouri rivers join, the plains are grassy and well watered in the east, drier in the west. On the coasts of the Gulf of Mexico there is a low, flat, hot plain that winds all the way from Texas to Mexico.

Rivers and Lakes

North America is a well-watered continent. Two of its most famous rivers are the Mississippi and the Missouri, which water the Great Central Plain. Other great rivers are the St Lawrence, which flows into the Atlantic; the Colorado, which flows into the Gulf of California; and the Rio Grande, which forms part of the border between the United States and Mexico.

North America is noted for its numerous beautiful lakes. Among these are Lake Superior, the largest of the Great Lakes that straddle the border between Canada and the United States, with an area of nearly 82,900 square kilometres (32,000 square miles); Great Salt Lake, in Utah; and Lake Nicaragua, which is the largest lake in Central America. Other natural wonders include the Niagara Falls, between Lake Erie and Lake Ontario, Florida's Everglades, the active volcanoes of Central America and the spectacular Grand Canyon in north-western Arizona. California's bleak Death Valley contains the lowest place on land in North America. It reaches 86 metres (282 feet) below sea-level.

Top: An airplane flies past the breathtaking scenery of the Grand Canyon in Arizona, USA.

Above: Thousands of people flock to see Niagara Falls on the borders of Canada and the USA.

Right: The coastline of the independent republic of Haiti lying in the Caribbean Sea. The island has a mountainous terrain.

North America (2)

The People

Most of the people who live in North America originally came from Britain, France, Spain, and Africa. The first inhabitants were the American Indians and the Eskimos, both of whom are thought to have travelled from Asia many thousands of years ago.

The British settled mainly in Canada and the northern United States. The French became established in the Quebec and Montreal regions of Canada and in some southern parts of the United States. The Spaniards colonized most of the southern United States, Mexico, Central America and the larger islands of the West Indies. Negroes from Africa were carried in slave ships to the southern United States and the West Indies and later, when they were freed, set up their own communities in these areas. In the late 1800s and early 1900s millions of people (Poles, Greeks, Italians, Dutch, Swedes, and others) fled from Europe to the United States in the hope of starting a new and better life there. Later, they were joined by large numbers of Chinese and Japanese.

Languages

Most of the people of North America speak English. But in and around Quebec, in Canada, most of the people speak French, and many of them would like to be free from the rest of English-speaking Canada. In Mexico, Central America, and some islands of the West Indies such as Cuba, Puerto Rico, and the Dominican Republic, the people speak Spanish. In the other islands of the West Indies language varies according to the nationality of their last conquerors: it may be English, French, or Dutch.

Life of the People

Because North America is so vast, its climate and landscapes vary considerably. The people, too, come from widely separated areas of the world and bring their own customs with them. As a result, there is no single North American way of life. But as in most countries, there is a steady drift of workers from the countryside to the cities, where they hope to make more money for easier work.

Above: A cowboy rides a bull at a rodeo in Cheyenne, Wyoming, in the American West. These popular displays of the cowboy's skill also include bareback bronco-riding and steer wrestling.

Top: The Statue of Liberty overlooks the skyscrapers of Manhattan Island in the heart of New York City. The first Europeans to settle there were the Dutch, in 1625.

Many North Americans, especially in the United States and Canada, travel long distances to work in their cars and, as a result, there is little public transportation compared with, for instance, the cities of Europe.

Food Favourites

Food for most North Americans is plentiful. The continent produces more food than its people can eat. In Canada and the United States, turkey, chicken, steaks, hamburgers, hot dogs, corn on the cob and apple pie are strong favourites. In the Spanish-speaking nations they prefer hot chili dishes and pancakes made of maize-meal, such as *tortillas*, which they eat, instead of bread, with spicy meat and vegetable dishes. *Enchiladas* are tortillas which are stuffed with meat and cheese and baked in a spicy sauce. Many people in the West Indies are poor and live mainly on fish, fruit and beans. But the wealthier people have distinctive dishes which include ingredients and employ methods which originated in far-away Europe, Asia and Africa.

North Americans are lucky in having plenty of wide open spaces for leisure and play, and most people make full use of these. They can swim and sail from thousands of beaches. There are mountains for climbing and skiing down, forests to hunt in, and rivers and lakes for fishing. Farther south the people favour spectator sports of a more gory kind, such as bullfighting and cock-fighting.

Top: A palm-fringed beach on the island of Tobago in the West Indies.

Above: The futuristic architecture of the City Hall at Toronto, Canada. Toronto is the capital of Ontario province.

Right: Chicago, on the shores of Lake Michigan, is the chief city of the American mid-West. It markets farm products and manufactures machinery.

North America (3)

Natural Wealth

The soil provides some of North America's greatest wealth. The United States and Canada have been called the granary of the world. They produce corn, wheat, soybeans, hay, flax, and vegetables in such abundance that not only have they enough for their own peoples but have plenty to export to the rest of the world as well. The main farming regions are located on the vast plains in the interior and in the coastal areas. Some cotton, rice, and fruits are also grown—the latter especially in Florida and California.

The rolling prairies and the foothills of the Rockies support huge herds of cattle both for dairy products and for meat.

Farther south, food production is spread unevenly because much of the land, in the shape of mountains, deserts, and forests, is unusable. Mexico raises livestock such as goats, chickens, and cattle, and also grows enough maize for the needs of the people. The Central American republics have long been noted for their coffee. They also produce bananas by the million, and are rich in sugar-cane, rice, and tobacco.

The West Indian islands rely mainly on sugar-cane, citrus fruits such as grapefruit, lemons, limes, and oranges for export, and tourism for their income. Their sunny weather, uncrowded beaches, and beautiful scenery attract holidaymakers from all parts of the world.

In addition to its wealth of food most of North America is very rich in minerals and sources of power. The United States is a major producer of iron ore, zinc, lead, molybdenum and copper. Iron ore, zinc, and copper are also found in large quantities in Canada which is the world's largest producer of nickel. Mexico has large deposits of nickel, silver and lead.

Power for the Factories

Until the 1970s North America had more or less all the power it needed to carry on its enormous factory output. The energy came from coal, oil, natural gas, and electricity. Great bodies of moving water, such as those found at Niagara and in some fast-flowing rivers, provide power that can be harnessed to make electricity. Water is also important

Top: The vast prairies of Kansas, USA, are a major area for wheat production. Much of the grain is exported.

Above: A steel foundry in Pittsburgh, USA. This important industrial centre also has coal mines and oil refineries.

Left: Golden cobs of maize (Indian corn) are harvested by machine. Maize is native to the American continent.

because it provides a cheap method of transportation. That is why most of North America's heavy industry is centred on the Great Lakes region. Cars, machinery, weapons, tools, clothing, instruments of various kinds, are all made there. But there are also factories of every kind scattered throughout the continent. As a result, everything that can be made by man is made somewhere in North America.

The Rich and the Poor

The United States and Canada are by far the greatest manufacturing nations of the continent. The gross national product (GNP) per person is a way of measuring the wealth of a country. This is worked out by adding up the total value of all goods and services produced in a country in one year, and then dividing it by the population. The GNP per person in the United States in 1976 was US$7,900. Canada was not far behind, with US$7,500. To the south, however, the GNPs of the countries of Central America and the West Indies are much lower. For instance, Mexico's GNP per person was less than one-seventh of that of the United States. However, Mexico is becoming richer as it expands its industries and oil production. Most nations in Central America and the West Indies had GNPs per person in 1976 of less than US$1,000, and some GNPs were less than US$500. Poverty has led to unrest in many places.

American Inventions

1793 Cotton gin	1877 Phonograph
1819 Patent leather	1878 Cash register
1834 Reaping machine	1884 Linotype
1840 Electric telegraph	1889 First fully automatic
1852 Safety elevator	machine gun
1854 First practical sewing	1903 First successful airplane
machine	1911 Motor car electric self-
1857 Steam plough	starter
1868 Typewriter	1947 Polaroid Land camera
1868 Air brake	1947 Transistor
1876 Telephone	

Above: Sugar-cane is harvested by hand in Barbados, a fertile island of the West Indies. Sugar-cane is the world's major source of sugar.

Left: A paper factory in Minnesota, USA. The extensive forests of North America provide wood in abundance for paper-making.

South America

South America is the fourth largest of the world's continents. Although it is twice as large as the United States, it has only about the same number of people. This means that there are huge areas that are completely uninhabited, and some parts that are still unexplored today.

The Land

South America is shaped roughly like an upside down triangle, with its broad base facing the south of North America and the Caribbean, and its point aiming straight at the South Pole. The continent is surrounded by sea, except for a narrow bridge of land in the north-west corner that links it to Panama and Central America.

The equator cuts across South America near the continent's widest point, and more than three-quarters of the land lies in the tropics. The long chain of the Andes Mountains runs down the whole of the western coast and towers above the Pacific Ocean. Lower, and older mountains form the north-eastern highlands. About three-fifths of the land is made up of the central plains. In the north these take the form of dense, hot rain forests, especially around the Amazon River. Further south they give way to scrubland and semi-desert—the *Chaco*—and still further south to the lush grasslands of Argentina and Uruguay called the *pampas*.

Climate varies a good deal with altitude. The higher you go, the colder it gets. In the Amazon basin the weather is generally very hot and muggy. The tops of the Andes, on the other hand, are always covered with snow, even at the equator.

Natural Resources

South America is rich in minerals. Copper is found in Chile, and Bolivia mines large quantities of tin. Venezuela produces nearly all of the continent's oil, and Brazil has very large deposits of diamonds and iron ore. Colombia produces more emeralds than any other country in the world; and Guyana and Surinam are rich in bauxite, an ore from which aluminium is made.

Right: The vast expanse of the Amazon rain forest. Plans are being formed to clear large areas for industrial use.

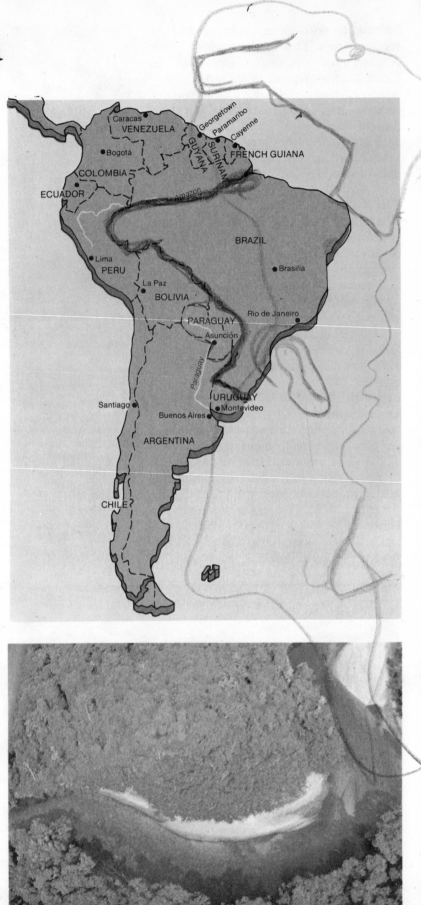

and French in French Guiana. The only countries where non-Romance languages are officially used are Guyana, where English is spoken, and Surinam, where Dutch is used. The people of South America are descended from three main groups: American Indians, Europeans and Africans. People of mixed origin are called *mestizos*. The American Indians were the earliest inhabitants. One group, the Incas, built up a great civilization in the Andes. This civilization was destroyed in the early 1500s by Spanish soldiers. Spain and Portugal colonized most of the continent and, in some areas, they imported African slaves to work on their plantations.

Most South Americans work on the land and are poor. But every year, the cities attract more and more people from the countryside. The cities are growing so fast that new arrivals have nowhere to go except into expanding slum areas around the cities. There is a great contrast between the many poor and the few rich people. However, the people still show their natural gaiety in carnivals, when everybody dresses up and dances and sings in the streets, eating and drinking for days on end.

Most South American governments today are developing new industries, which means more jobs for the people. They are also building more houses and opening up the interior of the continent with new highways. But there is still a long way to go before large-scale starvation and disease are wiped out in many parts of South America.

Huge herds of cattle and sheep graze on the rich pasturelands of the pampas. As a result, the people of Argentina are able to sell wool, hides, and beef to much of the world overseas. Brazil and Colombia are famous for the coffee grown there. The vast forests that cover the northern part of the continent provide valuable timber for many different uses.

But travel and transportation is still difficult in South America and much of it has to be done by air. This means that most of the continent's natural riches still remain to be made use of.

The People
More than 200 million people live in South America. They are mostly Latin Americans —that is, they speak Romance languages derived from Latin, namely, Spanish in most of the continent, Portuguese in Brazil

Top: Rio de Janeiro, at the foot of the Sugar Loaf Mountain. Rio is one of the most highly developed cities in Brazil.

Above: Coffee beans are dried and graded in the sunshine on this plantation in Colombia.

Right: The brightly-dressed citizens of La Paz, capital city of Bolivia, sell their wares on market day.

Australasia

Australia

Australia is both the smallest inhabited continent and the largest island in the world. It is the only continent inhabited by a single nation.

The Land

Australia is geologically older than any other continent. It is made up mostly of broad, rolling plains eroded from ancient mountains and hills. The land can be divided into three vast natural regions that run across Australia from north to south.

The eastern edge is made up of a range of mountains that runs for about 3,200 kilometres (2,000 miles) along the eastern coast. This range is called the Eastern Highlands, or sometimes the Great Dividing Range.

Westwards of the mountains is the dry Central Lowland. This region makes up about a third of the continent and is covered mostly with grasslands and scrub. Thousands of cattle and sheep are grazed there.

In the west are the deserts of the Western Plateau, an enormous region that covers nearly half of Australia.

The Nation and the People

Australia is a commonwealth (a group of states that are linked politically). There are six states. The five mainland states are Queensland, New South Wales, Victoria, South Australia, and Western Australia. The sixth is the island state of Tasmania.

Australians are generally easy-going, sporting, outdoor types of persons. Their wealth once came from wool and meat. Farming remains important, but mining and manufacturing are the most valuable industries. Most Australians live in cities. More than half live in either Sydney, Melbourne, Brisbane or Adelaide.

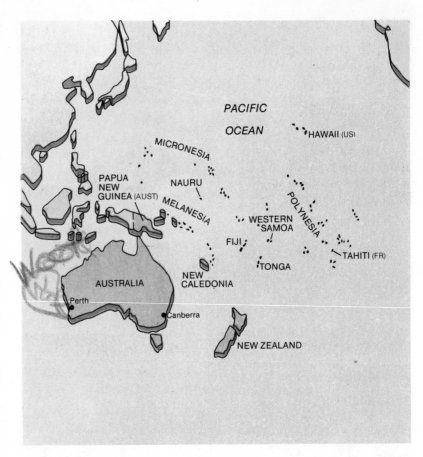

Above: Australasia is a collective name for Australia, New Zealand, New Guinea and the islands of the South Pacific.

Below: A view of Sydney harbour, Australia, with its famous bridge.

Fiji is a group of islands in the Pacific. Once part of the British Empire, it is now independent. The members of this cult (left) are taking part in a fire-walking ceremony.

Centre left: Sheep grazing in South Island, New Zealand. In the background are the peaks of the Southern Alps. Sheep farming is an important part of New Zealand's economy.

New Zealand
New Zealand is an independent nation made up of two main islands located in the Pacific Ocean to the south-east of Australia. The two islands are called North Island and South Island and they are separated by a stretch of water called Cook Strait. Although New Zealand is a little larger than Great Britain in area, only about 3 million people live there.

The Land
North Island has a varied landscape. The sub-tropical climate of the far north gives way to lakes, volcanoes and hot springs further south. Most of the region is dairy country, but citrus orchards and vineyards abound.

The mountainous South Island is dominated by the Southern Alps, a high chain of mountains that runs down the western part of the island. The huge flat region known as the Canterbury Plains is an outstanding feature of New Zealand. There sheep, cattle, and pigs in their millions are raised.

The People
In the 1800s and early 1900s many people from Britain went to seek a new life in New Zealand. There they found a warlike people with light brown skins, called Maoris. After a lot of fighting, white New Zealanders and Maoris today live in peace and cooperation.

Most of New Zealand's wealth comes from farming. The country has about 56 million sheep, 10 million cattle and half a million pigs. Wool, meat and dairy products are sold abroad. Arable farming is less important than pastoral farming.

The island continent of Australia was isolated from the rest of the world for millions of years. Lack of competition from more highly-evolved mammals enabled Australia's marsupials, such as the kangaroo (below), to flourish. Young marsupials are born at an under-developed stage and are then nursed in their mother's pouch.

Polar Regions

The Arctic

The Arctic is not a continent in its own right. It is mainly made up of the Arctic Ocean. Within this region there are thousands of islands, including Greenland. There are also the northern parts of the continents of Europe, Asia, and North America.

Although the Arctic is very cold, most of it is free of snow and ice during the short summer. At that time the days are so long that there is almost no night there. The reverse is true in the long winter when darkness covers the land for most of the time.

Plant life is low-growing, scattered, and short-lived. It is made up mainly of mosses, lichens, sedges, grasses, and low shrubs. The most common animals are reindeer. There are also many fur-bearing animals such as sables, foxes, martens, bears, and ermine, which are often shot or trapped. In the air, ducks, ptarmigan, puffins, petrels, gulls, and terns are common; while in the sea whales and seals abound.

There are probably rich mineral and fuel deposits in the Arctic but because the subsoil is permanently frozen, they are difficult to extract.

People living in the Arctic have adapted to the cold, harsh conditions. They wear thick clothing made from animals' skins, and eat plenty of fat taken from the land animals and fish which they hunt and kill. The best-known and most widespread of these peoples are the Eskimos. They are found in Greenland, through northern Canada and its offshore islands, to Alaska and north-eastern Asia.

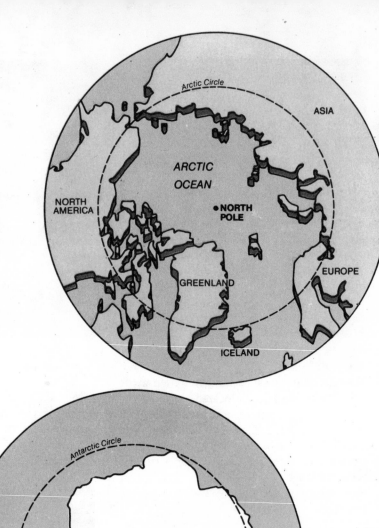

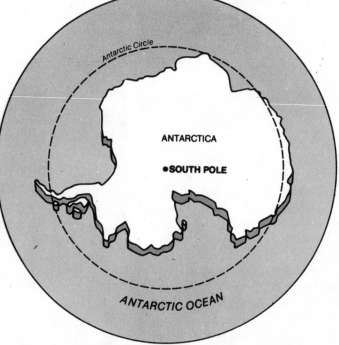

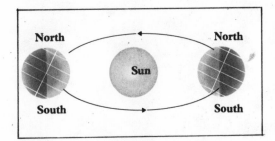

When the Northern Hemisphere is tilted towards the Sun, the Arctic has almost continuous daylight, and the Antarctic has almost continuous night.

Explorers and Exploration

Arctic

1909 Robert Peary Led first expedition to reach the North Pole.

1926 Umberto Nobile With Roald Amundsen he flew over the North Pole in an airship.

1926 Richard Byrd With Floyd Bennett, he flew over the North Pole in an airplane.

Antarctic

1911 Roald Amundsen First man to reach the South Pole.

1929 Richard Byrd Flew over the South Pole.

1957-58 Sir Vivian Fuchs Led the Trans-Antarctic Expedition which made the first overland crossing of Antarctica.

The Antarctic

Unlike the Arctic, the Antarctic consists of a large, uninhabited continent called Antarctica. This region is the coldest and bleakest place on earth. Gale force winds howl over a landscape that is ruggedly mountainous and covered with a mass of ice and snow. Freezing seas surround the land and huge icebergs, many kilometres across, regularly break off and float out into the waters.

Nobody lives there permanently, and parts of Antarctica are still unexplored. The seas around the continent are sometimes called the Antarctic Ocean, but they are really portions of the Indian, Pacific, and Atlantic Ocean that meet at the foot of the world.

Plant life in the Antarctic is almost non-existent, and land animals are confined to a few tiny insects and similar creatures. Penguins are the best known birds in the region, and there are also several flying birds, such as fulmars, skuas, and petrels. Thousands of whales and seals swim in Antarctic waters.

Ever since the Norwegian explorer Roald Amundsen reached the South Pole in 1911, Antarctica has been a centre of interest for scientific exploration. Today there are a number of manned scientific stations located in various parts of the continent. Several countries also claim portions of Antarctica as part of their national territory. Nations with such claims include Great Britain, Argentina, Chile, France, Australia, New Zealand and Norway. Antarctica is thought to contain considerable mineral wealth which might, one day, be exploited.

Above: Reindeer, or caribou, live in herds and feed on lichen in winter.

Left: Seals have layers of fat under their skin to protect them from the intense cold.

Below left: Penguins spend much of their time in the sea but raise their young on land.

Below right: Eskimos traditionally wore clothes of fur and animal skins.

7 EXPLORATION AND DISCOVERY

Men have wanted to explore the world about them since the Stone Age. They had to explore to find food to eat and enjoyed the challenge of going into new territory. The challenge of exploration and the thrill of discovery are just as strong today.

FAMOUS EXPLORERS

The Seas

Eric the Red	(Norse)	Sailed to Greenland in about 980.
Leif Ericson	(Norse)	Probably the first European to sail to America in about 1000.
Bartolomeu Diaz	(Portuguese)	First European to sail round the Cape of Good Hope in 1487.
Christopher Columbus	(Italian)	Made several voyages to the West Indies between 1492 and 1504.
John Cabot	(Italian)	Sailed across the Atlantic to Canada in 1497.
Amerigo Vespucci	(Italian)	Travelled to the West Indies and South America between 1497 and 1503.
Vasco da Gama	(Portuguese)	First European to sail to India in 1498.
Pedro Alvares Cabral	(Portuguese)	Discovered the Brazilian coast in 1500.
Ferdinand Magellan	(Portuguese)	Sailed round the world in 1521.
Sir Martin Frobisher	(English)	Looked for the Northwest Passage in the 1570s.
Sir Francis Drake	(English)	First Englishman to sail round the world in the 1570s.
Abel Tasman	(Dutch)	Discovered Tasmania and New Zealand in 1642.
Vitus Bering	(Danish)	Explored the Bering Straits and the coasts of Asia and Alaska in the 1720s.
James Cook	(English)	Made several journeys especially to the South Pacific in the 1760s and 1770s.

Africa

Mungo Park	(Scottish)	Explored the River Niger in 1796 and 1805.
David Livingstone	(Scottish)	Discovered the Victoria Falls and explored the River Zambezi from 1852 to 1856.
Sir Richard Burton	(English)	Explored Africa and Arabia in the 1850s. Discovered Lake Tanganyika.
John Hanning Speke	(English)	Discovered Lake Victoria in 1858.
Sir Henry Stanley	(Welsh)	Explored the Nile and Congo Rivers in the 1870s and 1880s.

Asia

Marco Polo	(Italian)	Explored China, India, Ceylon and Persia in the late 13th century.
Sven Anders Hedin	(Swedish)	Explored Asia between 1885 and 1933.
Roy Chapman Andrews	(American)	Explored the Gobi Desert and Tibet between 1910 and 1930.

The Americas

Vasco Nunez de Balboa	(Spanish)	Crossed Panama and discovered Pacific Ocean in 1513.
Hernando Cortes	(Spanish)	Conquered Mexico in 1521.
Francisco Pizarro	(Spanish)	Explored Peru in the 1530s.
Francisco de Orellano	(Spanish)	Explored the Amazon in 1541.
Sir Alexander Mackenzie	(Scottish)	Explored Canada and discovered the Mackenzie River.

Polar Explorers

William Baffin	(English)	Discovered Baffin Bay in 1616.
Sir Ernest Shackleton	(Irish)	Explored Antarctica from 1908 to 1916.
Robert Peary	(American)	First man to reach the North Pole in 1909.
Roald Amundsen	(Norwegian)	First man to reach the South Pole in 1911.
Robert Falcon Scott	(English)	Reached the South Pole shortly after Amundsen.
Sir Vivian Fuchs	(English)	First man to cross Antarctica in 1958.

Left: The Norsemen were among the first explorers. Eric the Red discovered Greenland in 982. He gave it an attractive name to encourage other settlers. His son, Leif Ericson, was probably the first European to land in North America. He landed in a place he named Vinland, which may have been Newfoundland. He called it Vinland because he found grapes growing there.

Early Explorers

The first explorer we know of was an Egyptian called Hennu. He lived about 4,000 years ago and sailed from Egypt to a land he called the Land of Punt, which was probably on the Red Sea coast of Somaliland.

The Egyptians were not really a seafaring nation, but the Minoans, who lived on the island of Crete, explored most of the Mediterranean in their tiny boats without any kind of navigation instruments. Crete was captured by Achaean Greeks in about 1400 BC and another nation, the Phoenicians, succeeded the Minoans as the sea traders of the Mediterranean. They made much bigger and better boats which could travel further and faster. They sailed through the Strait of Gibraltar about 600 BC and explored the Atlantic coast of Europe as far north as England. The next great exploring nation was Carthage in North Africa. The Carthaginians explored south of the Mediterranean as far as Cape Verde.

Across the Hellespont

Before about 300 BC the Ancient Greek civilization was at its height and explorers like Alexander the Great and Pytheas made great journeys of discovery. Alexander the Great crossed the Hellespont (now the

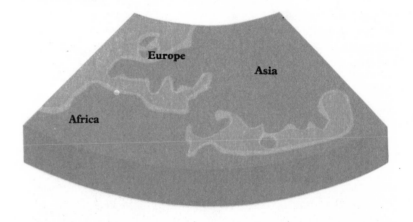

Dardanelles) into Asia and marched through Phrygia and Afghanistan to India. He went as far as the Indian Ocean before returning home. At about the same time, Pytheas was exploring Europe.

In the Middle Ages very little exploration was done until the Vikings made their great voyages from Norway across the northern seas to the Faroe Islands and then to Iceland, Greenland and eventually America. These voyages took place between about AD 800 and 1000.

One explorer of Asia was Marco Polo, who came from Venice. He set out in 1271 and travelled as far as China. Marco Polo was received in the court of the Chinese Emperor, Kublai Khan, and remained in China for 20 years. When he returned to Venice, he wrote an account of his experiences. It was his discovery of the size and riches of Asia that led to people wanting to find new routes to Asia.

Above: Europeans of ancient times had very little knowledge of the world as we know it now. Their experience was limited to the lands around the Mediterranean. A Greek named Ptolemy summarized this knowledge in his book *Geography* written in the second century AD. Ptolemy underestimated the size of the Earth, but his book remained a standard work for 1,400 years.

The Great Age of Exploration

During the Middle Ages, very few voyages of exploration were made from the more advanced European countries. Then, during the 1450s, the Great Age of Exploration began.

There are several reasons why this Great Age started when it did. In 1453 the Turks closed the main route to the East, which meant that European traders had to find a new way to get the silks and spices they wanted. Another reason was that Christian countries wanted to convert other countries to their religion. But the main reason may have been that people felt the urge to explore just as they had done years before.

Henry the Navigator

Perhaps the most important man at the beginning of the Great Age was not an explorer at all. The King of Portugal's brother, Prince Henry, opened a school of navigation in 1416. He also studied ship designs and helped to develop a new ship called the caravel, which was good for long ocean voyages.

Because of Henry the Navigator, Portugal became a nation of explorers. Many Portuguese had explored Africa looking for a sea-route to the East and Bartolomeu Diaz went round the Cape of Good Hope into the Indian Ocean. An Italian called Christopher Columbus went to Portugal and announced that he wanted to sail west to India, the other way round the world. The Portuguese would give him no assistance so Columbus persuaded the Spanish rulers to help him. He sailed across the Atlantic in 1492 and reached some islands he thought were off the coast of Asia. They were in fact the Bahama Islands off America, but Columbus called them the Indies. They are now called the West Indies.

Trade with Asia

One of the reasons that Marco Polo made his journey to China was to see if it was possible to trade directly with Asian countries. Before he went there, Europeans bought all their silk and spices from the Arab merchants who had bought them from China and India. Marco Polo discovered that it was easier and cheaper to deal with Asia direct.

The caravel was an ocean-going ship developed for use in exploration by the Portuguese and the Spaniards. The ships were small but they had room for good supplies of water and food. They had two main types of sail. A square sail was used for moving fast when there was a strong wind behind the ship. Triangular sails, called lateens, were used when the wind was very light, or from the side.

Exploration East and West

The Portuguese still believed the best way to the East was round Africa. In 1497 Vasco da Gama succeeded in reaching India round the Cape of Good Hope. The route to the East was open.

Columbus's discovery had led other nations to travel west from Europe. John Cabot set out from England in 1497 to explore the coast of the country we now call Canada. Many people still thought that this land was Asia, but a few realized that it could be a new continent.

Other explorers followed Columbus from Spain, also. The explorations of Balboa, Cortes and Pizarro firmly established Spain's claim in the land people were beginning to call the New World. There the Spaniards found gold to rival the riches of Asia. Yet the desire to find a western route to the East remained strong.

The Portuguese were not particularly interested in exploring the new continent. They still wanted to reach the spice islands. A Portuguese explorer called Ferdinand Magellan asked Spain to support him in his latest venture. He planned to sail round the new continent of America and on to Asia. He set out with five ships in 1519 and by the end of 1520 he had reached the southern-most tip of South America. Beyond that he discovered a huge sea which he called the Pacific Ocean. After a terrible voyage across this ocean, his expedition reached the spice islands, but Magellan had been killed on the journey. Only one of the five ships returned by the route around Africa. It was the first ship to sail completely round the world.

Now that a south-west passage had been found to Asia, explorers began to search for a north-west passage. Although nobody found this until 1906, the search brought great discoveries in the huge continent of North America. All the European countries joined in the exploration and eventually wars were fought about who owned different parts of North America. The Spanish, French and English all claimed part of the land, and it was not until after the Declaration of Independence in 1776 that their fighting stopped.

The Southern Continent

By this time, navigators had fairly accurate maps of most of the world but there were still a few gaps. For thousands of years, people had thought that there was another continent in the south. In 1776 James Cook

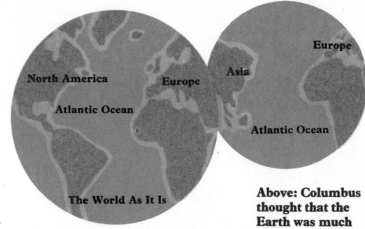

North America

Europe

Atlantic Ocean

Asia

Europe

Atlantic Ocean

The World As It Is

set out to explore the Pacific Ocean. He found many small islands and sailed around New Zealand, and also discovered that there was a southern island continent, now called Australia.

In the 19th century explorers turned to the unknown continent of Africa. The most famous of them was David Livingstone, who spent nearly 25 years as a missionary crossing unknown parts of the continent.

By 1900, nearly all the continents of the world had been explored, but there were still some areas about which men knew very little. These included the polar regions.

Above: Columbus thought that the Earth was much smaller than it is. When he reached the other side of the Atlantic Ocean he thought he had reached Asia.

Below: Sailors in the 1400s feared long sea journeys. They thought that they might be attacked by vast sea serpents, or might fall off the edge of the Earth.

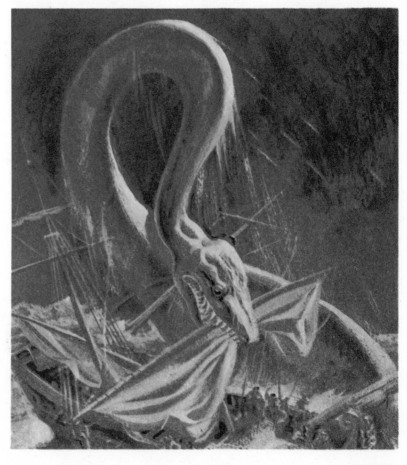

Polar Exploration

The Arctic region is a very cold area and many men died trying to sail through the Arctic Ocean to find the Northwest Passage. The mistake they made was to try to cross the Arctic during the summer, when the sun never sets there. In the summer the Arctic ice melts a little and breaks up into huge ice floes or islands. It is extremely difficult to navigate ships safely between these ice floes, and only a few explorers, such as Roald Amundsen, succeeded in sailing through these dangerous waters.

Explorers finally decided it would be easier to explore this region during winter when the Arctic ocean is completely frozen and can be crossed on foot with dog sleds. The weather is very much worse at this time of the year and the Arctic is in continual night. In 1909, however, Robert E. Peary braved these conditions and reached the North Pole.

A Race to the South

The South Pole did not have the same problems as the North Pole as it is, in fact, land. It is still a difficult place to reach, however, because it is so terribly cold. Robert Falcon Scott explored part of the continent in 1902 with the British Navy and was later to reach the South Pole itself. In 1908 Sir Ernest Shackleton crossed far inland to within 200 kilometres of the Pole, but it was first reached by Roald Amundsen in 1911 (see picture, left). His team beat a team of Englishmen, led by Scott, to the Pole by a month. After suffering from scurvy, frostbite and other hardships in blizzards and in the intense cold, Scott and his companions died on the return journey. His diary was found later and tells us of his disappointment at being beaten so narrowly by Amundsen. The first complete crossing of Antartica took place in 1957-8.

The conditions and weather of the polar regions are now studied by scientists in research stations there.

Right: Polar exploration has been made very much easier by the invention of vehicles that can cross snow and ice. Sno-cats have caterpillar tracks. They are very much better than teams of dogs and sleds.

Exploration Today

Now that even the polar regions have been discovered and explored, you may think that there is very little left to explore. This is certainly not true. There are still many parts of the world where no man has set foot, and we still know very little about the huge areas that are under the oceans. Exploration has also begun of the vast unknown space of our universe.

New inventions have changed the way

that explorers work, and people can discover much more about lands and seas than before. Explorers in the 19th century sometimes travelled by balloon on their voyages of discovery, and the invention of the airplane meant that explorers could visit even more places quickly and observe them from above. One of the first explorers to make use of the airplane was Amundsen, and he was followed by Commander Richard Byrd. Byrd flew over the North Pole in 1926 and then in 1929 over the South Pole. Nowadays, airplanes are used on many explorations and the aerial photographs that can be taken are very useful to map-makers.

Other means of transport have helped men to explore new regions of the world. Hovercraft have now been used to explore parts of the River Amazon, because they can travel equally well over open water, marsh, and flat country. Cars are also being adapted for this type of exploration.

Oceanic Exploration

More than two-thirds of the Earth's surface is covered by sea, and it is now being explored very thoroughly. The early submarines were not very good for exploring the oceans as they could not go very deep and had to surface frequently for air. But today there are nuclear-powered submarines that can make long journeys deep under the ocean's surface. As early as 1958, a nuclear submarine went under the Arctic ice-cap to the North Pole and surfaced on the other side. Scientists also use small submarines connected to ships on the surface. These often use bathyscaphes, to study the bottom of the oceans and the animals that live there. Scientists have developed new techniques in underwater photography and they can use drills to take samples of the ocean floor. They are particularly interested in finding oil and other valuable minerals under the oceans.

Exploration is now continuing outside our world. Space explorers are travelling out of the Earth's atmosphere and have already explored parts of the Moon's surface. Mars, Venus, Mercury and Jupiter and its moons are also being observed. This space exploration helps scientists to explore the Earth. Satellites out in space can send back pictures of the Earth's surface which give new information about unknown lands, and enable map-makers to make even more accurate maps. Satellite pictures also provide information about the weather.

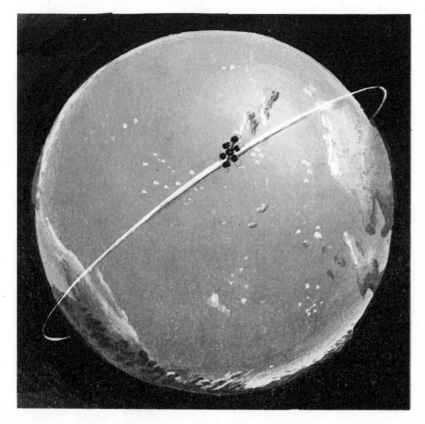

SPACE TRAVEL

Man has dreamed for hundreds of years of travelling in space. That dream has recently come true. The challenge of unexplored places has led us to make the first space flights. Scientists have learned much about the universe, and will discover much more.

Getting into Space

The first problem that has to be overcome before we can send anything into space is the pull of gravity. Gravity is the force that pulls objects towards the Earth (or any other body in space). Everything that is dropped near the Earth's surface falls to the ground and accelerates or gets faster on its way down. To beat this force of gravity, objects must travel away from the Earth very fast. When you throw a stone into the air this defeats gravity for a short time before the stone starts to fall back to the ground. But rockets can now travel fast enough to escape the pull of the Earth's gravity.

To do this, they have to travel at more than 40,000 kilometres (25,000 miles) per hour. This is an enormous speed which even our fastest jet planes cannot reach. Scientists had to invent new kinds of engines to propel rockets into space. The most powerful rocket engines are powered with liquid fuels, such as hydrogen and a substance similar to kerosene, but there are some that work on solid fuels. Ordinary jet engines would be useless in space because they need air to work properly. So rockets carry a supply of oxygen as well as fuel to propel the rocket. The propellants, as the oxygen and fuel are called, are burnt in a combustion chamber at the base of the rocket. A jet of hot gases shoots out from this chamber and pushes the rocket forward. Liquid fuel engines have several advantages over solid fuel ones. They are easier to control and can be restarted.

Because space rockets have to carry so much fuel to push them out of the Earth's gravity, they are very big. The smallest are about 40 metres (130 feet) high and some are more than 100 metres (330 feet) high.

Rockets as Weapons

The rocket was first invented in China over a thousand years ago. It was just like the firework rocket of today but was used as a weapon. These rockets were powered with the solid fuel, gunpowder, and it was not until 1926 that a liquid-fuelled rocket was made. These rockets were not powerful enough to travel very far, and certainly not to get into space.

The Space Age really began in 1957 when the Russians launched the first artificial satellite into space. The rocket that took it into space was developed from the V2 rockets used by the Germans in the 1940s. Very soon after the first satellite, another was launched with a dog on board. The success of the early space flights with animals showed that it was possible to put a man into space without harming him.

Man in Space

On 12 April 1961 the first man was launched into space. His name was Yuri Gagarin. This was the first of many manned space flights and the beginning of an exciting period of exploration.

The largest rocket yet built was the massive Saturn V that successfully launched the Apollo spacecraft on their voyages to the Moon. It was 111 metres (365 feet) tall and it was the most powerful rocket ever launched.

Space is a very difficult place for human beings to survive in. Outside the protection of the rocket they would die immediately because there is no air, and because of the extreme heat and cold. But astronauts do have to leave their spacecraft now and again to do repairs on the exterior, to check cameras or even to walk on the Moon. So when they do this they have to wear protective spacesuits. Spacesuits have several layers which protect astronauts from radiation and temperature. They are also pressurized and supplied with oxygen, to give astronauts the same atmospheric conditions they have on Earth.

An astronaut's spacesuit keeps him at an even temperature and supplies him with oxygen. The thick oversuit and helmet protect him from space particles and radiation.

A First Dictionary of Space Travel

aerial (antenna) A metal wire or rod used to send or receive radio signals.

booster The first stage of a rocket, which usually falls away after launching.

capsule The cabin which the early astronauts travelled in.

cosmonaut The name given to Russian astronauts.

docking When two spacecraft meet and join together in space.

escape velocity The speed needed to escape the Earth's gravity.

heat shield A covering on a spacecraft which will protect it from heat during re-entry.

launch pad The area from which a rocket is launched.

lift-off The end of a countdown when the rocket leaves the launch pad.

module A section of a spacecraft.

orbit The path a satellite takes around the Earth, or any object takes around any other in space.

probe An unmanned spacecraft sent into space to obtain information.

re-entry The time when a spacecraft is coming back into the Earth's atmosphere.

satellite Any small body that circles a planet.

splashdown When a returning spacecraft lands in the sea.

Satellites and Spacecraft

A satellite resembles a man-made moon that orbits around the Earth. Satellites can stay in orbit and overcome the Earth's gravity by travelling very fast, at more than 28,000 kilometres (17,500 miles) per hour. If a satellite were to slow down to below this speed it would be pulled back to Earth.

To launch a satellite into space, rockets are used. A multistage or step rocket is the best way to do this. Step rockets are made in sections which are arranged one on top of the other. When the bottom stage has used up its fuel, it drops away and the next stage takes over. In this way the spacecraft gets faster and lighter as it travels into space.

Use of Satellites

Artificial satellites are of many different shapes and sizes and are sent into orbit for several different reasons. They usually have solar cells to use the energy from the Sun for their instruments and to keep them on the correct course. The first artificial satellite was the Russian *Sputnik 1* which was launched in 1957. Twenty years later, more than 4,000 satellites had been sent into space and were still orbiting the Earth. All satellites orbit at different heights above the Earth. The closer ones eventually fall back into the Earth's atmosphere.

A common use for satellites is to improve international communications. Communications satellites can pick up signals from a point on the Earth and relay them to the other side of the world by amplifying them and then beaming them down to a ground station. This means that radio, telephone and television signals can now be sent round the world.

Some satellites carry cameras which take pictures of the Earth's surface to help meteorologists forecast the weather and map-makers to make accurate maps. Other satellites carry cameras and telescopes which are pointed out into space so that astronomers can get more information about distant stars and planets. These satellites can see into space more clearly than we can from Earth because they are outside the Earth's atmosphere, which distorts images of the stars. Satellites are also used for military reconnaissance.

Satellites do not have to be streamlined to travel through space because there is no air in space. They can be any shape that suits the job for which they are designed. But they all have the same basic units performing different functions. There is an instrument unit, a power unit, and communication and control units.

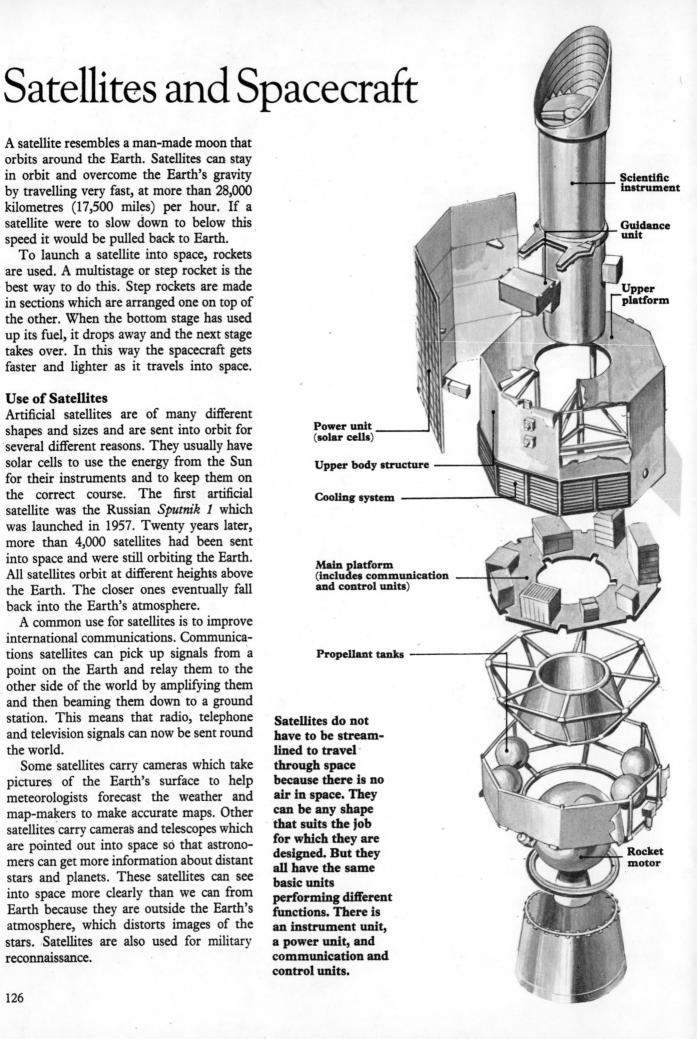

Scientific instrument

Guidance unit

Upper platform

Power unit (solar cells)

Upper body structure

Cooling system

Main platform (includes communication and control units)

Propellant tanks

Rocket motor

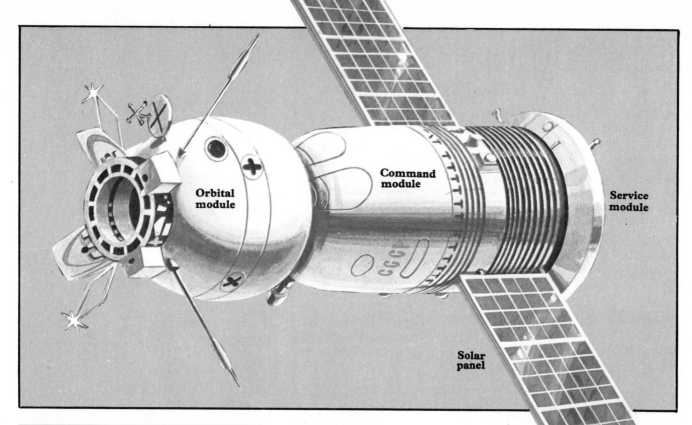

Orbital module

Command module

Service module

Solar panel

Satellites

Ariel A series of satellites designed in Britain for scientific research. They were launched from the United States of America.

Cosmos Scientific satellites launched from Russia.

ERTS Earth Resources Technology Satellite (see Landsat).

Explorer American scientific satellites. The first American satellite was an Explorer.

Intelsat Communications satellites. They relay telephone and television signals over the oceans.

Landsat Satellites that observe the Earth from above. They used to be called ERTS (see above).

Meteor Russian weather satellites.

Molniya Russian communications satellites.

Nimbus American weather satellites.

Sputnik 1 The world's first artificial satellite. Sputnik 2 contained the first live space traveller—Laika, a dog.

Telstar The first communications satellite to carry a live transatlantic television broadcast.

Manned Satellites

Manned satellites are built like unmanned satellites in modules or sections. One of these modules contains the crew, and it is this module that returns to Earth. There are also large satellites which stay out in space to be used as space stations. The US Skylab and the Russian Salyut are examples of these.

Manned satellites do not stay in orbit for long as there is not enough room for the crew to live comfortably. Space stations, however, contain a living area with continually circulated air, toilet facilities and places for the men to sleep and work. They also provide means for the astronauts to exercise to keep fit. Man can stay in space for several months.

Above: Soyuz is Russia's chief manned spacecraft. It is used to take cosmonauts to and from their space station, Salyut. The orbital module is used for working in space. The cosmonauts sit in the command module for take-off.

Left: Communications satellites operate by picking up a radio beam from a ground station, amplifying it, and beaming it back to another station. Many are in orbit 35,900 km (22,300 miles) from Earth. At this height they orbit at the same rate as the Earth turns and so appear to be stationary.

127

The Future

In the future, space travel will change just as rapidly as it already has done. Multi-stage rockets may soon become old-fashioned and be replaced by new types of rocket. Scientists will spend long periods of time orbiting the Earth in space stations and astronauts will travel much farther into space than they can today, to discover new facts about the universe.

Scientists have already developed new kinds of spacecraft which will be used in the 1980s. The space shuttle will replace the multistage rocket. The main advantage of the shuttle is that it can be used many times, but a multistage rocket can only be used once. The shuttle is in three sections. The orbiter looks like a modern jet plane and is

Right: It is hard to imagine how big space is. If you imagine that you are in a rocket you will get some idea of the size from this diagram. It would take 2½ days to reach the Moon, 3 weeks to reach the Sun and thousands of years to reach Proxima Centauri, our nearest star after the Sun. It would take the rocket thousands of millions of years to reach the next nearest galaxy to our solar system.

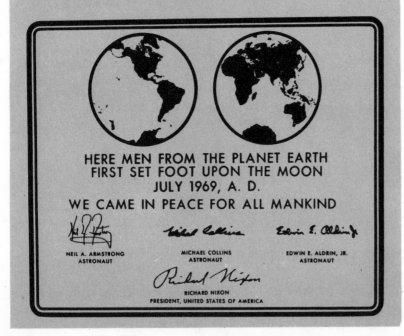

Nearest galaxy
20,000 million years

Nearest star
500,000 years

The Sun
3 weeks

The Moon
2½ days

Earth

Man on the Moon

On 21 July 1969 at 2.56 a.m. GMT Neil Armstrong became the first man to step on to the Moon. He was joined by Edwin Aldrin.

The spacecraft used to get the astronauts to the Moon was the Apollo spacecraft, which was perched high on top of the huge Saturn V rocket. This rocket launched the spacecraft into space where it orbited the Earth before blasting off towards the Moon. The spacecraft then moved into an orbit around the Moon and one of the three modules, the lunar module, separated and descended to the Moon's surface.

After a rest, the astronauts left the lunar module for the first walk on the Moon. In their protective spacesuits, they explored the Moon's surface for nearly three hours and collected samples of the rocks and dust. They left automatic instruments to send back information. After the Moon-walk, the lunar module docked with the main spacecraft and returned to Earth, leaving behind the plaque below.

HERE MEN FROM THE PLANET EARTH
FIRST SET FOOT UPON THE MOON
JULY 1969, A. D.
WE CAME IN PEACE FOR ALL MANKIND

NEIL A. ARMSTRONG
ASTRONAUT

MICHAEL COLLINS
ASTRONAUT

EDWIN E. ALDRIN, JR.
ASTRONAUT

RICHARD NIXON
PRESIDENT, UNITED STATES OF AMERICA

the section which carries the crew and equipment. This is attached to the main fuel tank which contains the propellants that power the spacecraft. There are also two booster rockets which are used for launching.

When a shuttle is launched, the booster rockets fall away and parachute back to Earth, and the orbiter continues out into orbit until the fuel tank is empty. This then drops away and the orbiter continues its mission. Once it has completed the mission, the orbiter returns to Earth and is flown like a glider after re-entry into the Earth's atmosphere.

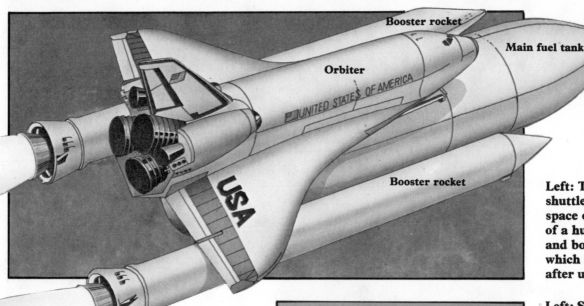

Booster rocket

Main fuel tank

Orbiter

UNITED STATES OF AMERICA

USA

Booster rocket

Left: The space shuttle blasts into space on the back of a huge fuel tank and booster rockets which fall away after use.

Left: Space stations of the future will be constructed on Earth and ferried into orbit by space shuttles one section at a time. In orbit the sections will be joined together by teams of skilled space engineers.

The orbiter can do many things in space. One of its advantages is that it can bring back satellites that need repair and then take them back to their orbit. It will also be used for placing new satellites in orbit.

Spacelab

Its most important cargo will be a space laboratory called Spacelab which is being designed by the European Space Agency. The laboratory, which will have room for four scientists, will be launched in the shuttle's payload bay. When the shuttle is in orbit, the doors of the bay will be opened and Spacelab will have a direct view of the sky for astronomical and Earth observations. It will orbit in the shuttle's bay for up to a month and then be brought down to Earth. It will be re-used about 50 times. The shuttle will also take out parts of new space stations. This means that space stations can be much bigger than before when the whole station had to be launched at the same time.

Now that men have been in space and landed on the Moon, they want to travel even farther into space, to new planets and stars. But there are great problems with travelling so far away from Earth. One of the main problems is the hostile conditions on most other planets' surfaces. There is no air for men to breathe, and the other planets in our solar system are either too hot or too cold, depending on their distance from the Sun, for people to survive.

Another problem which is even more difficult to overcome is the vast distances between Earth and even its nearest neighbours. It took the Viking probes to Mars ten months to get there, and using rockets travelling at the speeds they do today it would take many years to reach even the nearest star. Scientists are working on new ideas for powering rockets with intense beams of light, but even if they could travel at thousands of kilometres per second it would take a very long time to reach the solar system's nearest neighbours in space.

In spite of the problems of space travel, highly reputable physicists and space scientists foresee great advances before the end of this century. Their predictions include a permanent base on the Moon, manned, orbiting space stations supplied by rockets taking off from airports on Earth, the colonization of space, and use of space technology in developing solar energy as a source of heat and electricity.

9 WORLD RELIGIONS

All the earliest-known peoples worshipped gods or spirits and (except in recent times) no tribe or nation has ever existed without religion. Many once-great religions have died out, including those of the ancient Egyptians, Greeks, Romans and Vikings.

Religions from the Middle East

Judaism, the religion of the Jews, began in the Middle East before 1200 BC. The Jews were probably the first people to believe in one, all-powerful God to whom they could speak but not see. Traditionally, Abraham founded Judaism, and the Jews awaited the coming of a *Messiah* (anointed of the Lord) who would lead them through difficult times. Their great leader, Moses, led them out of slavery in Egypt to the 'promised land' of Palestine.

Christianity developed from the teachings of Jesus, a Jew born in Palestine nearly 2,000 years ago. Many people thought Jesus was the promised Messiah and called him *Christos*—a Greek word meaning 'anointed one'. This became *Christ*, and his followers became known as *Christians*. Christians believed that God 'redeemed' their sins because Jesus had taken the punishment upon himself when he was crucified before ascending to heaven as the Son of God. Christianity later became the religion of almost all Europeans.

Islam began in AD 622 when an Arabian merchant, Muhammad, fled from the city of Mecca to Medina. Many Muslim (Is-

lamic) beliefs are similar to those of Jews or Christians. Muslims believe in one God (Allah). The 'revelations' of Allah to Muhammad are recorded in Islam's holiest book, the *Koran*. Muslims pray direct to Allah, facing towards Mecca, at least five times a day wherever they are, but preferably in mosques. They have no priests.

Religions from India

Hinduism is the religion of most Indians. It has hundreds of gods and goddesses, many of whom can be seen as idols in Hindu

Above: A Roman Catholic priest celebrating Mass. Since the Vatican II Council meeting called by Pope John XXIII in 1962, changes have taken place in many aspects of Roman Catholic religious practice and belief.

EIGHT GREAT RELIGIONS

RELIGION	MAIN AREAS	WHEN IT BEGAN	FOUNDER
HINDUISM	India	Before 2000 BC	Unknown
JUDAISM	USA, Israel, USSR	Before 1200 BC	Abraham
SHINTO	Japan	By 600 BC	Unknown
TAOISM	China	By 500 BC	Lao-tzu
BUDDHISM	Far East and South East Asia	About 500 BC	Siddhartha Gautama
CHRISTIANITY	Europe, North and South America	After AD 4	Jesus Christ
ISLAM	From West Africa to Indonesia	AD 622	Muhammad
SIKHISM	Punjab (India)	About AD 1500	Guru Nanak

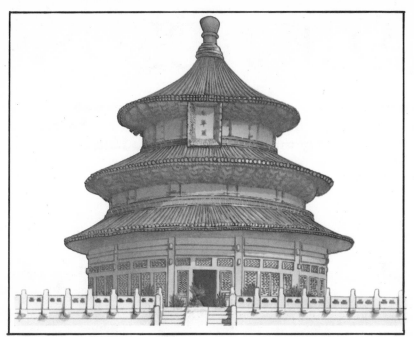

Above: The Hall of Annual Prayer, situated in the compound of the Temple of Heaven in Peking. Built in 1420 and later reconstructed, it was here that the emperor of China offered sacrifices to the god of heaven.

Above right: An Orthodox Jewish family celebrates the festival of *Pesach* (Passover) which commemorates the exodus of the Jews from Egypt in Biblical times. The festival lasts for eight days. The first two evenings are called *Seders*.

Right: When in AD 630 Muhammad led the Medinan army and captured Mecca, he chose this city to be the centre of Islam and the Ka'abah to be the holy shrine. Thousands of Muslims flock here every day to pray at this symbolic site.

temples. But many Hindus say that all these deities are only aspects of one Supreme Being.

Buddhism began in around 500 BC when Siddhartha Gautama, an Indian prince, later called the Buddha, sought a 'middle way' that rejected both the harsh life and poverty of Hindu holy men and the luxury of the wealthy. True Buddhism has no gods, but Buddhists worship images of the Buddha.

Sikhism, begun by Guru Nanak in Punjab, India, over 500 years ago, incorporated aspects of Islam and Hinduism in an attempt to end hatred between followers of the two rival religions. Sikhs believe in one God.

Religions from the Far East
Taoism, said to have been taught in China by Lao-tzu, encouraged men to work in harmony with nature, rather than to strive to change things. Another important Chinese religion was Confucianism, founded in the 6th century BC by the philosopher Confucius (K'ung Fu-tzu).

Shinto, a religion of Japan, is a form of spirit worship. Like Chinese religions it places great importance upon the honouring of ancestors.

10 SCIENCE

When we learn about science, we find out about nature, about the Universe, our world and living things. A good scientist understands how things happen and may make discoveries that help people, or our environment.

What is Science?

Science is a search for knowledge. Scientists watch things, take measurements and work out explanations for the answers. If the explanations are correct a scientist will be able to say how something is going to work. In this way, scientists make discoveries. For example, Sir Isaac Newton watched how the planets move around the Sun, and wondered why they move in this way. He worked out that a force called gravity keeps them moving in their paths around the Sun. With this knowledge, astronomers later searched for and discovered two additional planets, Neptune and Pluto.

Scientific Method
Many scientists carry out experiments to see if their explanations are correct. First, they make observations of something that interests them. Then they form a theory to explain their observations. They test the theory with experiments. If the experiments support the theory, the theory then becomes a law of science. However, new evidence may later cause a law to be modified. A new law will then be formulated.

Kinds of Science
There are several different kinds of science. Biology is the principal life science. Biologists study all forms of life: microbes, plants, animals and human beings. The study of plants is called botany, and the study of animals, zoology.

Physical sciences involve the study of non-living things. Chemists study gases, fuels, new plastics and drugs. Physicists study atoms and states of matter. They also study energy and electronics. Discoveries in the physical sciences are important in engineering, which puts the knowledge to use.

Above: Scientists are always trying to solve problems and setting themselves more and more difficult tasks. Research on any topic often takes many years of careful experimentation and analysis before any practical application can be found for new products. New drugs, in particular, have to be tested and approved before they are marketed to ascertain that they will cause no harmful side-effects.

Other sciences include geology, which is the study of rocks and minerals and how the land is formed. Geologists also study the history of the Earth from fossils and other evidence in the rocks. The atmosphere and weather are studied in meteorology. Oceanography is the scientific study of the oceans. In astronomy, everything in space is studied —the Sun, Moon, comets, meteors, planets, stars and galaxies.

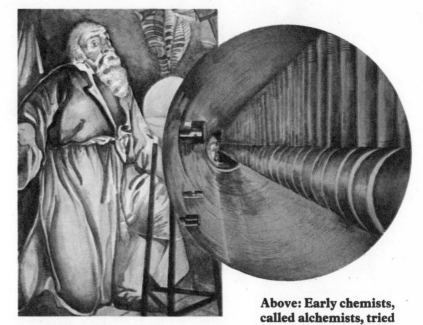

First Dictionary of Science

friction The retarding force that tries to stop one object from sliding over another.

gas A liquid turns into a gas when it boils. A gas always expands until it fills its container.

gravity The force of attraction exerted by any object. The force exerted by a small object is weak, but the force exerted by large bodies, such as the Earth, Moon or Sun, is very powerful.

liquid A solid melts to form a liquid, such as water.

magnetism The result of electrical forces between moving, electrically charged particles.

mass The amount of matter in a body. Mass differs from weight because the mass of a body is the same wherever it may be, while the weight depends on the pull of gravity.

matter Everything having any mass consists of matter.

molecule A group of atoms linked together.

solid A liquid becomes a solid when it freezes. For example, water becomes a solid when it freezes into ice.

theory An attempt to explain an observed result. If a theory is supported by experiments, it will become a law of science.

vacuum Space that is completely empty of matter.

weight The force exerted by gravity on a body. For example, on the Moon an astronaut weighs only one-sixth of his weight on Earth. This is because the force of gravity on the Moon is only one-sixth of that on Earth. But the mass of the astronaut remains exactly the same.

Above: Early chemists, called alchemists, tried unsuccessfully to turn base metals into gold. Radioactive elements such as uranium can now be changed into other elements. Huge machines called linear accelerators are used to split elements. Using this method, gold can be made from mercury.

Left: Sir Isaac Newton studied the movement of the planets. In 1687 he published his theory on the law of gravity, stating that gravitational force kept the planets moving in their paths around the Sun. He made many discoveries and invented the reflecting telescope.

Below: A laser beam is reflected off the Moon to accurately measure the distance from Earth. It is also used in surgery and holography.

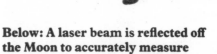

Mathematics and Measurement

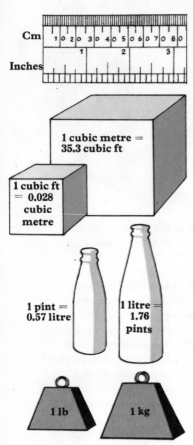

We all need to have some knowledge of mathematics and measurement. When we buy anything, we need to use simple mathematics to work out how much to pay. When we make something, we need to use measurements to make it the right size or shape.

Scientists of all kinds find mathematics essential. When a scientist discovers a new law, he often presents it as a mathematical formula. He also has to be able to make accurate measurements.

The SI System

To measure correctly, we need systems of units. Scientists and engineers use the SI system of units. They use metres to measure length and kilograms to measure weight. There are smaller and larger multiples of these. For example, there are 100 centimetres in a metre and 1,000 metres in a kilometre. SI stands for *Système International d'Unités* (International System of Units). It is based on the metric system of measurement which dates from the 1790s.

Below left: The ancient Egyptians based their units of measurement on the length of various parts of the body.
Below: The metre is based on a wavelength of light given off by the gas krypton. Length can be measured by using an instrument called a krypton interferometer.

The imperial system of measurement is still used in Britain and some other English-speaking countries. Some imperial units are shown on the left. Another unit used in these countries is the degree Fahrenheit (°F) for measuring temperature.

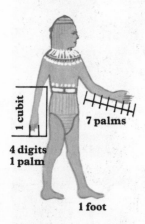

Length

millimetre (mm)
10 mm = 1 centimetre (cm)
100 cm = 1 metre (m)
1000 m = 1 kilometre (km)

Area

square millimetre (mm²)
100 mm² = 1 square centimetre (cm²)
10,000 cm² = 1 square metre (m²)
10,000 m² = 1 hectare (ha)
100 ha = 1 square kilometre (km²)

Volume

cubic millimetre (mm³)
1000 mm³ = 1 cubic centimetre (cm³ or cc)
1000 cm³ = 1 cubic decimetre (dm³)
1000 dm³ = 1 cubic metre (m³)

Capacity

millilitre (ml)
1000 ml = 1 litre (l)
(1 ml is approximately equal to 1 cm³; and 1 litre is approximately equal to 1 dm³)

Weight

milligram (mg)
1000 mg = 1 gram (g)
1000 g = 1 kilogram (kg)
1000 kg = 1 tonne or metric ton

Time

second (s)
60 s = 1 minute (min)
60 min = 1 hour (h)
24 h = 1 day (d)
(7 days equal 1 week; and 365 days are approximately equal to 1 year)

Angle

second (")
60" = 1 minute (')
60' = 1 degree (°)
90° = 1 right angle or quadrant
4 quadrants = 1 circle = 360°

Useful Formulae

It is easy to calculate the area or volume of a simple shape with the aid of a formula for the area or volume. In these formulae, the letters stand for the lengths of the various dimensions of the shapes. For example, if the sides of a square are 6 centimetres (cm) long, then its area will be 36 cm² (6² or 6 x 6). π (pi) is equal to 3.14159 or approximately 22/7.

Circumference

Circle of radius r	$2\pi r$

Area

Circle of radius r	πr^2
Surface of sphere of radius r	$4\pi r^2$
Triangle of base b and height h	$\frac{1}{2}bh$
Square of side a	a^2
Rectangle of sides a and b	ab

Volume

Sphere of radius r	$4/3\pi r^3$
Cylinder of radius r and height h	$h\pi r^2$
Cone of radius r and height h	$\frac{1}{3}h\pi r^2$
Cube of side a	a^3

Decimal Multiples

Units smaller and larger than the SI units have prefixes that indicate their size. For example, kilo means 1,000 times bigger, so 1 kilometre is equal to 1000 metres.

Prefix	Symbol	Multiplication Factor
mega	M	1,000,000
kilo	k	1,000
hecto	h	100
deca	da	10
deci	d	0.1
centi	c	0.01
milli	m	0.001
micro	μ	0.000001

SI Units

Basic Units

Length	metre (m)
Mass or weight	kilogram (kg)
Time	second (s)
Electric current	ampere (A)
Temperature	kelvin (K)
Amount of substance	mole (mol)
Luminous intensity of light	candela (cd)

Derived Units

All the units below can also be expressed by combinations of some of the basic units. However, for simplicity, they are given their own special names.

Frequency	hertz (Hz)
Force	newton (N)
Pressure, stress	pascal (Pa)
Energy, work, quantity of heat	joule (J)
Power	watt (W)
Electric charge, quantity of electricity	coulomb (C)
Electric potential, potential difference, emf	volt (V)
Electrical resistance	ohm (Ω)
Electrical conductance	siemens (S)

Right: Whether you are making a scientific experiment or baking a cake, it is important to understand weights and measures. The ingredients for a cake must be weighted accurately and the cake must be baked at the right temperature.

Below: Modern inventions such as electronic calculators can be a great help in mathematics.

Speedometer

Barometer

Left: Many everyday instruments give us measurements automatically. The speedometer measures speed (the distance travelled in a given time). The barometer measures pressure (the weight of air acting on a given area of the Earth's surface).

Elements

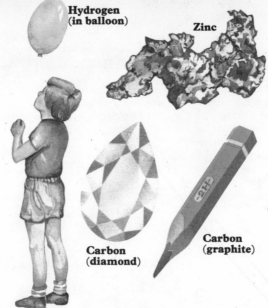

Hydrogen (in balloon)

Zinc

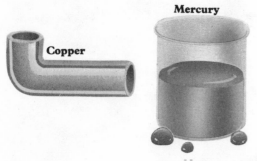

Copper

Mercury

Carbon (diamond)

Carbon (graphite)

Left: Most elements are metals. Metals include copper and zinc (solids), and mercury, a liquid element. Hydrogen is a gas, and carbon is a solid with more than one crystalline form.

The Elements

Elements are the simplest substances, from which everything is made. They are themselves made up of atoms. An atom of one element has different chemical *properties*, or characteristics, from an atom of another element. There are 92 elements which occur naturally on the Earth. A few have been created by scientists. Two elements, bromine and mercury, exist normally as liquids. Eleven, including hydrogen and helium, are normally gases. The rest are solids, mostly metals, such as aluminium and copper. They have widely differing properties. Some are hard, some soft, some are strong, others brittle.

Studying the Elements

It was not until the 1800s that scientists really began to understand the nature of chemical substances. But several of the chemical elements, such as iron and

sulphur, were known in prehistoric times. The ancient peoples did not know these were elements, though. In the Middle Ages, scientists called alchemists tried to make gold from other substances—without success.

The 'father' of modern chemistry was an English scientist, Robert Boyle, who lived in the 1600s. He was the first to say what an element was. More and more elements were discovered in the 1700s and 1800s.

Below: Most metals look glossy and are good conductors of heat and electricity. They can be mixed to form alloys. Brass, for example, is an alloy of copper and zinc.

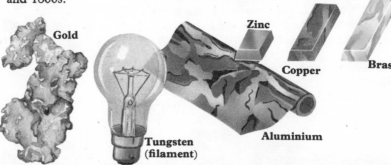

Gold

Zinc

Copper

Brass

Tungsten (filament)

Aluminium

136

The Periodic Table of elements arranges them in groups according to their properties. For example, the 'light metals' are in yellow on the left, the 'heavy metals' in light brown in the centre, the non-metals in light red to the right, and the rare gases in red on the far right.

1	2	3	4	5	6	7	8	9	10	11	12	13	14	15	16	17	18
Hydrogen H 1																	Helium He 2
Lithium Li 3	Beryllium Be 4											Boron B 5	Carbon C 6	Nitrogen N 7	Oxygen O 8	Fluorine F 9	Neon Ne 10
Sodium Na 11	Magnesium Mg 12											Aluminium Al 13	Silicon Si 14	Phosphorus P 15	Sulphur S 16	Chlorine Cl 17	Argon Ar 18
Potassium K 19	Calcium Ca 20	Scandium Sc 21	Titanium Ti 22	Vanadium V 23	Chromium Cr 24	Manganese Mn 25	Iron Fe 26	Cobalt Co 27	Nickel Ni 28	Copper Cu 29	Zinc Zn 30	Gallium Ga 31	Germanium Ge 32	Arsenic As 33	Selenium Se 34	Bromine Br 35	Krypton Kr 36
Rubidium Rb 37	Strontium Sr 38	Yttrium Y 39	Zirconium Zr 40	Niobium Nb 41	Molybdenum Mo 42	Technetium Tc 43	Ruthenium Ru 44	Rhodium Rh 45	Palladium Pd 46	Silver Ag 47	Cadmium Cd 48	Indium In 49	Tin Sn 50	Antimony Sb 51	Tellurium Te 52	Iodine I 53	Xenon Xe 54
Caesium Cs 55	Barium Ba 56	Lanthanum La 57	Hafnium Hf 72	Tantalum Ta 73	Tungsten W 74	Rhenium Re 75	Osmium Os 76	Iridium Ir 77	Platinum Pt 78	Gold Au 79	Mercury Hg 80	Thallium Tl 81	Lead Pb 82	Bismuth Bi 83	Polonium Po 84	Astatine At 85	Radon Rn 86
Francium Fr 87	Radium Ra 88	Actinium Ac 89															

Rare earth group

Cerium Ce 58	Praseodymium Pr 59	Neodymium Nd 60	Promethium Pm 61	Samarium Sm 62	Europium Eu 63	Gadolinium Gd 64	Terbium Tb 65	Dysprosium Dy 66	Holmium Ho 67	Erbium Er 68	Thulium Tm 69	Ytterbium Yb 70	Lutetium Lu 71

Actinide group

Thorium Th 90	Protactinium Pa 91	Uranium U 92	Neptunium Np 93	Plutonium Pu 94	Americium Am 95	Curium Cm 96	Berkelium Bk 97	Californium Cf 98	Einsteinium Es 99	Fermium Fm 100	Mendelevium Md 101	Nobelium No 102	Lawrencium Lr 103

In the mid-1850s, scientists noticed a connection between the relative weights of the elements and their chemical properties. The atomic weights (now called 'relative atomic masses') could at that time be calculated in relation to each other. The Russian chemist Dmitri Mendeleyev built up a Periodic Table of elements. The modern Table groups the elements in order of their atomic number and according to their properties (see the section *Inside the Atom*).

Chemical Symbols

Each element is represented by a symbol consisting of a capital letter by itself or of a capital letter and a small letter. For example, H stands for hydrogen and He for helium. Some of the symbols come from the Latin names of elements. The symbol Pb for lead, for example, comes from the Latin *plumbum*.

Chemical symbols are used in writing chemical equations. An example of an equation is:

$$H_2 + Cl_2 \rightarrow 2HCl$$

This represents the simple reaction between the gases hydrogen (H) and chlorine (Cl), which combine to form hydrochloric acid (HCl), a liquid.

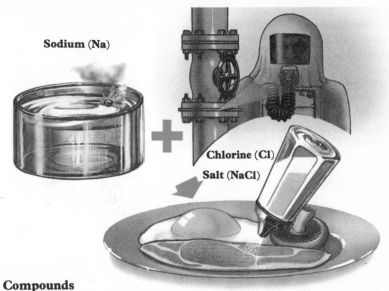

Sodium (Na)

Chlorine (Cl)

Salt (NaCl)

Compounds formed when elements combine are very different from those elements. Sodium (Na) and chlorine (Cl), for example, are unpleasant and highly active alone. Yet they combine to form common salt (NaCl), a harmless substance.

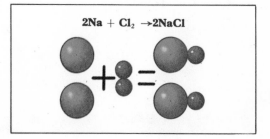

$$2Na + Cl_2 \rightarrow 2NaCl$$

Solids, Liquids and Gases

Solid   Liquid   Gas

Above: Matter exists in three states—solid, liquid or gas. It consists of small particles, called atoms, which are held together by 'cohesive forces'. In the solid state the particles are tightly bound like bricks in a wall. A solid has a definite shape. As the temperature rises, the atoms begin to vibrate and the cohesive forces weaken. The particles are loosely attached and can slide over each other. A liquid does not have a shape but adopts the shape of its container. At higher temperatures the energy within the atoms is much greater than the force binding the atoms. The particles are not attached and fly about at random. A gas has no shape but is limited by its container.

Solids, liquids and gases are the three common states of matter. Most substances are in one of these three states. If it is made cold enough, every substance will become solid. Many substances, such as rocks, are solid at the normal temperature at which we live. Substances that are liquid at normal temperature have to be cooled to make them freeze. Water must be cooled to 0°C (32°F) to change into ice, which is solid water. However, most substances that are gases at normal temperature have to be cooled to a much lower temperature than this to make

them condense into a liquid. Then they have to be cooled even more to make them freeze into a solid. Oxygen, which we breathe in the air, becomes a liquid at —183°C (—297°F) and a solid at —219°C (—362°F).

Everything will become a gas if made hot enough. Water boils at 100°C (212°F) and becomes steam. Some metals, such as solder, melt at temperatures not much higher than this, but iron does not melt until it reaches 1539°C (2802°F); it boils at 2800°C (5072°F).

Pressure also influences the change of

Below: Although a submarine is made of metal which is heavier than water, the air in the ballast tanks allows it to surface. The tanks are filled with water to make the sub sink and when the water is blown out it resurfaces.

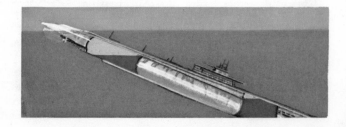

their state. A liquid under high pressure has to be heated more than a liquid at low pressure to make it boil. But if the pressure is reduced, the molecules can escape more readily; at 3,000 metres (10,000 feet), water boils at only 90°C (194°F), so it is difficult to cook a boiled egg! Pressure also affects melting and freezing. No matter how much helium is cooled, it will not solidify unless it is compressed as well.

Atoms and Molecules

Why are some substances normally solid, some liquid and others gaseous? It depends on the forces exerted between the atoms and molecules in the substance. In most substances the atoms are held together in groups called molecules. Even the largest molecules are so small they can only just be seen in the most powerful microscopes. This page is about half a million atoms thick.

In a solid, the atoms and molecules all

Above: Many digital watches use liquid crystal in the display panel. Liquid crystal has characteristics of a crystal and a liquid and many others that are unique.

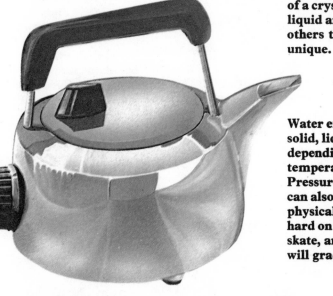

Water exists as a solid, liquid or gas depending on the temperature. Pressure, however, can also alter its physical state. Press hard on ice, as with a skate, and the ice will gradually melt.

Left: Hydraulics deals with the use of a liquid, because of its ability to be compressed and to flow, to perform mechanical work. If a fluid in a pipe is pushed by a piston, the force exerted on the fluid can be made to do work. Aircraft undercarriages use this system.

Piston

occupy fixed positions. This makes the material retain the same shape unless we apply forces which are usually large in order to make the atoms or molecules move past each other.

In a liquid, the atoms or molecules are free to move about, so that the liquid can easily change its shape. It always flows to the bottom of any container. The atoms and molecules stay close together but can slide past each other. Thus, when a ship is pushed through the sea, the molecules of seawater slide out of the way and, after being churned about in the ship's wake, they will return gradually to rest. In doing so they become warmed, as the energy is being supplied by the motion of the ship.

As in a liquid, atoms or molecules in a gas can move in all directions. Unlike a liquid, they can move away from each other wherever they can. Because they are free to move, gases tend to expand indefinitely. Hence, in practice, a small amount of gas will completely fill any container.

Density and Floating

The density of a substance is the relation between its mass, or weight, and its volume. For example, expanded polystyrene foam has an extremely low density and even large pieces seem to weigh hardly anything. But if you hold a comparatively small piece of the metal lead in your hand, it will feel very heavy. This is because lead has a high density, like most metals and rocks. In fact, lead is over 11 times as heavy as an equal volume of water.

Any solid placed in a liquid of higher density will float. Ships made of metal float because they contain empty spaces, which make the boat as a whole less dense than the water.

Forces and Motion

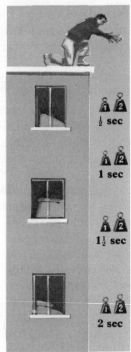

A force is basically a push, a pull or a twist. A force is needed to start a mass moving, to change its speed, to make it change direction, or to bring it to rest.

We use our muscles to produce force. We move ourselves and objects by exerting force with our arms and legs. We also produce force with engines to drive our machines. However, force is not needed to keep objects moving unless there is some resistance. When you throw a ball into the air, you use the muscles in your arm to move your hand and push the ball into the air. The ball is then slowed down by the resistance of the air, and pulled downwards by the Earth's gravitational attraction. If there were no atmosphere and no gravity, the ball would go on at the same speed and in the same direction for ever.

Friction

Almost everything that moves on Earth is resisted by some form of friction, because no surface is absolutely smooth. Hence, friction is the force that slows down a book as it slides across a table. And if you place a brick on a plank, you will soon find how far you will have to tilt the plank before the brick will slide down it.

When a bicycle or car is moving at a constant speed, the force pushing it forward is equal to the friction acting to slow it. Some of the friction is inside the engine (or inside our bodies as we pedal along). Some is in the moving parts of the vehicle. Some is due to the rolling resistance of the tyres, and some to our resistance.

Away from the Earth, out in space, there is no air to cause friction and to slow down a spacecraft. A satellite moving around the Earth, therefore, continues to move in its orbit without stopping. Similarly the Moon always moves around the Earth and the Earth moves around the Sun.

Above left: Racing cyclists use muscle power to move their cycles at high speeds. In doing this they overcome air resistance. Even fast riders try to follow in the 'slipstream' created by the leaders. This reserves power for the final dash to the finish.

Above: Until Galileo proved otherwise, people believed that heavier objects fell faster. Earth's gravity pulls at a constant 9.8m (32 ft) per second per second, but air resistance slows the speed of some falling objects.

Left: Newton's third law of motion states that for every action there is a reaction. When a car hits another the first stops, throwing the driver forwards, and the other accelerates, throwing the driver backwards. Snooker uses this law.

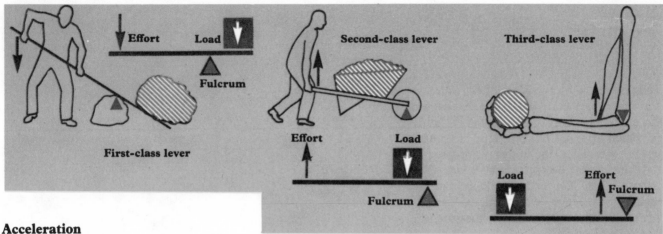

Effort **Load** **Fulcrum** **First-class lever**

Second-class lever **Effort** **Load** **Fulcrum**

Third-class lever **Load** **Effort** **Fulcrum**

Acceleration

If the force pushing a moving object is greater than the total retarding force, the speed increases. If you pedal harder on your bicycle, it accelerates until the increasing friction and air resistance once more balances the force with which you are pedalling. Then the acceleration stops and the bicycle travels at a steady, higher speed.

When you stop pedalling, the forces are again unbalanced and you slow down. If you put on the brakes, you increase the friction. You therefore slow down much more rapidly.

Gravity

Scientists do not fully understand gravity. It is a force that makes objects attract each other. It is quite separate from magnetism, because it is possessed by everything, and depends on mass (the weight of an object). Two people attract each other, but we do not notice this because the force is so small.

What we do notice is the very powerful attraction of the Earth. This is why things fall to the ground. Gravity extends out into space. It is gravity that keeps a satellite circling around the Earth, and the Earth in orbit around the Sun.

Inertia

Imagine a very heavy weight hung from a strong wire. Even though there is little friction, we would have to push hard to start it swinging. Once it was swinging, it would need a large force to stop it. This is because of inertia, which makes every mass resist a change in its motion. The heavier the object, the greater the force you will need to accelerate it to a particular speed, or to make it stop. A force is required to overcome inertia. This explains why, in a moving car which stops suddenly, a passenger will continue to move forward unless stopped by a safety belt.

On the Moon, where there is no air resistance, everything falls at the same rate. On Earth, gravity accelerates everything at a rate of 9.8 metres (32 feet) per second per second. People once thought that heavy objects fell faster than light ones. This was disproved by the scientist Galileo (1564-1642), who is supposed to have dropped two weights of different sizes off the top of the Leaning Tower of Pisa. The weights hit the ground at the same time. Light feathers and pieces of paper fall more slowly only because of air resistance.

Above: A machine is a device which enables energy to be used more efficiently. A lever allows effort applied at one place to create movement at another. The three types of lever shown differ according to the position of the effort applied, load and fulcrum (or point on which the lever turns).

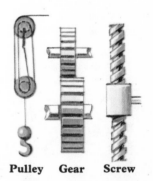

Pulley **Gear** **Screw**

Above: There are several other devices which simplify work. A pulley enables a heavy weight to be lifted with a small amount of effort. A gear is used to transmit motion or to change speed or direction. A screw can be used to raise and support heavy weights.

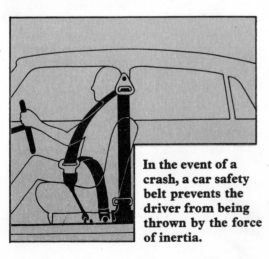

In the event of a crash, a car safety belt prevents the driver from being thrown by the force of inertia.

Above: Cranes are powerful lifting machines which combine the principles of the lever and pulley. Cranes are versatile because they can pivot to move loads horizontally as well as vertically. Many cranes can be moved to different sites.

Heat

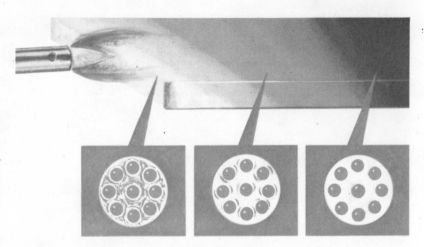

Heat makes us warm. We get heat from the Sun, from fires and radiators. The food we eat produces energy inside our bodies, some of which appears as heat. The more heat anything receives, the hotter it becomes. If anything loses heat, it gets colder. We measure how hot or cold things are by taking their temperature with a thermometer. Temperature is usually measured in degrees Celsius (°C).

A cold substance, for example ice, still has heat, but much less than a hot object. Heat is a form of energy. It makes the atoms or molecules in an object vibrate. The more heat there is in an object, the faster its atoms and molecules vibrate. As an object cools, its atoms and molecules slow down. At a temperature called absolute zero, the atoms and molecules stop moving. This temperature is —273°C (—459°F). It can never quite be reached because nothing can lose all its heat.

Heat travels from a hotter object to a colder object in three ways. Heat spreads through solids by conduction. Very bad conductors insulate heat, one example is glass-wool put on a hotwater tank. In liquids or gases, the heated matter rises causing convection currents. For example, the Sun may heat the ground intensely so that the warm air near the ground rises in a strong current. This air finally cools, spreads out and then sinks again. Heat also travels through empty space by radiation in the form of infra-red rays.

First Dictionary of Heat

boiling point   The temperature at which a liquid changes into vapour. The boiling point of water is 100°C.

Celsius   The standard scale of temperature. It was named after a Swedish astronomer, Anders Celsius (1701-1744).

Centigrade   An old name for Celsius.

degree   Units of the temperature scale. Temperature is usually measured in degrees Celsius (°C).

Fahrenheit   A scale of temperature in which the freezing point of water is 32°F, and the boiling point is 212°F. To convert Celsius to Fahrenheit, multiply by 9/5 and add 32. The scale was invented by a German physicist, Daniel Fahrenheit (1686-1736).

freezing point   The temperature at which a liquid freezes to a solid. The freezing point of water is 0°C.

heat insulator   A substance that does not conduct heat well. Good insulators include a vacuum, air, glass, wool and asbestos.

melting point   The temperature at which a solid melts to a liquid.

temperature   The temperature of an object shows how hot or cold it is. Temperature is measured in degrees.

thermometer   An instrument that measures temperature. In a mercury or alcohol thermometer, the liquid in a small container expands and contracts up and down a thin, graduated tube.

thermostat   A device that keeps a heater or heating unit, such as a central heating system, at a steady temperature.

Above: Heat has an influence on the movement of atoms. The atoms and molecules in a hot flame vibrate quickly, whereas, farther away where it is cooler, they vibrate at a much slower rate. At a temperature of 0° Kelvin (—273°C/—459°F), atomic and molecular movement would stop, but this is an impossible temperature, so atoms and molecules are always moving.

Left: A solar house has insulated roof panels with glass covers. Inside are copper tubes filled with water. These are heated by the Sun, even on cloudy days. The hot water from these panels goes into the heating system of the house to warm the rooms. The Sun's heat is free, and solar houses save fuels such as coal, gas or oil, that are becoming scarce.

Sound

We hear sounds because our Earth has an atmosphere (it is silent on the Moon!). Any disturbance to the air causes waves to expand out from that point, like ripples from a stone dropped in a pond. As the waves pass our ears we hear the sounds.

Sound waves consist of air molecules vibrating to and fro. We cannot feel most sound waves because the pressures are not strong enough. But they make our eardrums vibrate, and this causes us to hear the sound.

Sound waves move through air, at a speed of about 330 metres (1,082 feet) per second (a little faster on a hot day, slower in winter). This is much slower than light. We would see an explosion 1 kilometre (0.62 miles) away in 1/300,000 second, but we would not hear it until more than three seconds had elapsed.

Sound also travels through liquids such as water, and solids such as glass and stone. This happens because these materials, like air, can transmit vibrations. This is why you can hear sounds coming through walls and windows. But sound does not travel through empty space. The astronauts on the Moon had to speak to one another by radio because there is no air on the Moon to carry sound waves.

When a sound wave hits a hard surface, it bounces off it. If you are far enough away from a wall or cliff, you can hear your voice return to you as an echo. The echo is caused by your sound waves bouncing off the wall or cliff. In a large building, a church for example, you may be able to hear many echoes as sound bounces to and fro off the walls. Concert halls are designed to avoid echoes.

The speed at which a sound wave vibrates makes it sound higher or lower. A deep

sound, such as a drum, vibrates slower than a shrill sound, such as a flute. Some sounds vibrate so fast that they are too high for us to hear. These sounds are called ultrasonic, and they have many uses in today's world. This is because ultrasonic waves can be focused, much like a beam of light from a searchlight. Ultrasonic devices are used to locate and measure objects underwater, to separate different signals on the same lines in telephone systems, and so on.

Below: An echo is caused by physical conditions, where sound waves from a noise reverberate off surrounding surfaces, and bounce back to make an echo. Echoes are common in hilly areas.

Above: By sending down sound vibrations from special equipment and calculating the length of time it takes for the echo to bounce back, the warship can accurately gauge how far the submarine has submerged.

Below: Crossing the sound barrier (from left to right). As a plane travels, pressure waves that travel at the speed of sound are created. As it accelerates, the plane catches up with the waves and a shock wave builds up. As the plane crosses the sound barrier a sonic boom can be heard on the ground.

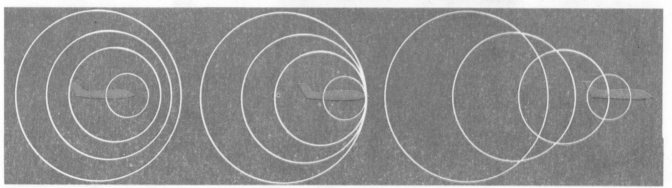

Light

We see objects because light rays coming from them enter our eyes. Most objects do not generate their own light. Only bright objects, such as the Sun or a lamp, are sources of light. They illuminate other objects by sending out light rays which are reflected by the surfaces of the objects into our eyes.

Light is like a succession of waves and also like a stream of particles. Light rays travel in straight lines and move at the tremendous speed of 300,000 kilometres a second. Nothing, in fact, can move faster than light.

Objects produce light if they are made very hot. The Sun shines because it is very hot. The filament of a light bulb glows when

First Dictionary of Light

focus The place near a lens or curved mirror where a sharp image of a distant object forms.

image A picture of a real object produced by a lens or mirror.

lens Pieces of transparent material, notably glass, shaped to bend light rays to form an image. Convex lenses bend outwards and concave lenses bend inwards.

mirror A shiny surface that reflects light rays to give an image. Flat mirrors give images the same size as the object they reflect. Convex mirrors bend outwards and make things look smaller. Concave mirrors bend inwards and can make things look larger. A parabolic concave mirror can send out light from a point source at its focus into a parallel beam, as in car headlights.

prism A triangular block of glass that splits up white light to form a spectrum.

retina The part of the back of the eye that is sensitive to light.

spectrum Each wavelength of visible light corresponds to a colour. The longest waves look red and the shortest violet. The spectrum is all the colour spread out according to wavelength. Sunlight passed through a prism can throw a spectrum on white paper. Sunlight refracted through raindrops makes the rainbow.

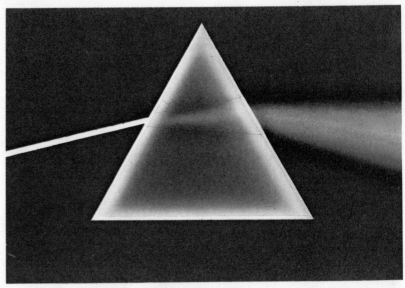

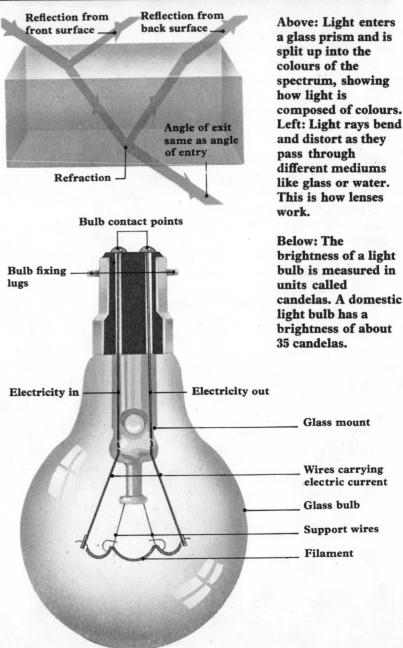

Reflection from front surface

Reflection from back surface

Angle of exit same as angle of entry

Refraction

Above: Light enters a glass prism and is split up into the colours of the spectrum, showing how light is composed of colours. **Left:** Light rays bend and distort as they pass through different mediums like glass or water. This is how lenses work.

Below: The brightness of a light bulb is measured in units called candelas. A domestic light bulb has a brightness of about 35 candelas.

Bulb contact points

Bulb fixing lugs

Electricity in

Electricity out

Glass mount

Wires carrying electric current

Glass bulb

Support wires

Filament

it is heated by electricity. Some substances emit light without getting hot. Strip lights and television sets contain luminous substances that light up when fed with electricity.

The surfaces of most objects are not smooth, and so they scatter light in all directions. If the surface is flat and smooth, each ray of light is reflected in one direction. We call such surfaces mirrors. When you stand in front of a mirror, light rays from your face strike the mirror and are reflected back into your eyes.

Light travels through empty space, and also through transparent substances such as air, water and glass. Whenever it enters a new substance, its speed changes slightly. This makes the light rays bend if they enter the surface of the new substance at an angle. This bending is called *refraction* of light.

Refraction causes strange images to form. A stick when plunged into water appears bent where it enters the water, and things seen underwater look nearer than they are. Lenses like those in a magnifying glass or spectacles refract light rays to form images. A magnifying glass concentrates all the rays at one point, called the focus. If the light from the Sun is focused into a small bright point on dry paper, the paper will soon char and burst into flames. Other lenses can project a beam through a film or slide on to a screen.

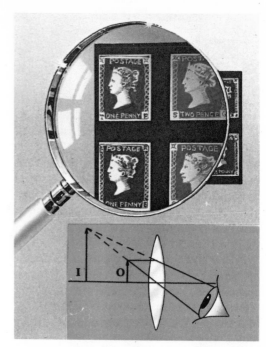

Right: A magnifying glass is a lens with convex surfaces. The lens is fatter in the centre than at the edges. Light rays take longer to pass through the thick part, and this bends them more, so that when they focus the objects being magnified appear larger than they really are. The diagram shows how the object (O) appears as an enlarged image (I).

Light rays are sometimes bent, or refracted, near the Earth's surface so that they create kinds of optical illusions. For example, on a hot day, the shimmer over a road looks like a pool of water. Even more striking are mirages of cool pools of water seen by thirsty travellers in hot, sandy deserts. Sometimes the effect of a mirage is to make distant objects appear to be nearby. Sometimes objects appear to be upside down. For example, at sea, the dense layers of air near the water focus rays from a distant object, such as a ship, into an upside-down image in the sky. Because mirages are caused by light rays passing through layers of air of differing density, they can be photographed as well as seen.

Below left and below: A magnifying glass can be used to concentrate the Sun's rays (see diagram). If the hot rays are focused on to a piece of paper the paper will smoulder and burn. Do not try to do this yourself because you may easily start a fire.

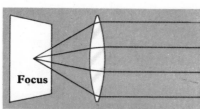

Focus

Above: Light travels very fast—at a speed of about 300,000 km (186,000 miles) per second. It takes 8½ minutes for light to travel from the Sun to the Earth. Special instruments measure very accurately the speed of light. They use lasers and microwave aerials (shown here).

Colour

A transparent prism splits up white light into a spectrum of colours. Raindrops act in a similar way, breaking up sunlight into a rainbow. This happens because sunlight and white light consist of a mixture of colours. As light passes through the prism or raindrops, it is bent or refracted. However, the different wavelengths are bent by different amounts, so the colours in the light are spread out.

White and almost all colours can be made by mixing light of other colours. Black is seen when no light is reflected. A colour television set makes colours by mixing light of three colours: blue, green and red. If you

look closely at the screen, you will see that the whole picture is made up of dots or lines of these three colours. They merge to form a colour picture. Green and red light make yellow light, and all three colours, green, red and blue, make white light. Lights over the stage in a theatre are used to make colours in much the same way.

Most of the colours we see do not come

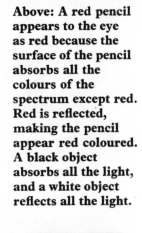

Above: A red pencil appears to the eye as red because the surface of the pencil absorbs all the colours of the spectrum except red. Red is reflected, making the pencil appear red coloured. A black object absorbs all the light, and a white object reflects all the light.

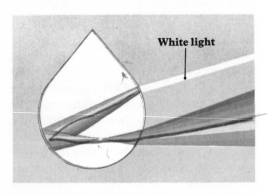

White light

Left and centre left: A rainbow is formed when light is refracted and reflected. The light enters the raindrops which act as thousands of tiny prisms reflecting the light back in the colours.

from original sources of light, but from surfaces that reflect or scatter the light falling on them. Hence a colour television picture is quite different from a colour illustration in a book or a colour photograph, because the light entering the eyes from a colour television is produced by the picture itself. On the other hand, a coloured illustration does not produce light. It is illuminated by the Sun or by artificial light. The light that enters our eyes is, therefore, light that has been reflected from the surface of the illustration or some other object. Each surface absorbs some colours and reflects others. For instance, a blue surface absorbs most colour except blue. The blue light is reflected into our eyes and we see the surface as blue. White cinema screens reflect all colours.

Below left and above: The primary colours in light are red, blue and green. The primary colours in paint pigments are special shades of red, blue and yellow. From these primary colours all shades can be made. In the case of light, a combination of the primary colours produces white.

Energy

Energy is the capacity to do work. It is found inside atoms. Some of this is turned into another form of energy, heat, when the atoms combine chemically in what we call burning. Far more heat is generated in nuclear fission.

Heat, light and radio waves can transmit energy through space. Potential energy is found in a compressed spring, or a rock that could fall from a high cliff. If it fell it would gather speed, gaining kinetic energy. When it hit the ground the energy would be transformed into noise and heat.

We are always using energy. As we digest food, we use its chemical energy to produce body heat and power our muscles. The Sun's light makes daylight and its heat rays give enough warmth for life to exist on Earth. We use the chemical energy in petrol to drive cars, and we use electrical energy to power machines and light our houses. Light rays and radio waves bring us information as we read or look at television. We use the kinetic energy of a hammer to drive in a nail.

Most energy is produced by changing one kind into another. In a power station, we burn coal to raise steam, to drive a generator and make electricity. Burning the coal changes chemical energy in the coal

into heat. This heat is turned into kinetic energy as the steam turns the generator, and the generator turns the kinetic energy into electricity.

Some kinds of energy can be created. Energy is made in a nuclear reactor and inside the Sun and other stars. This is done by using up matter.

Above: An offshore drilling rig. In the search for further sources of fuel, new drilling techniques have been employed to enable valuable gas and oil to be extracted from beneath the sea bed. Special pipes carry the oil or gas inland.

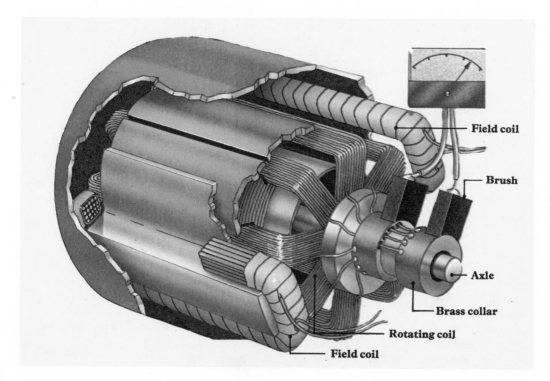

Field coil

Brush

Axle

Brass collar

Rotating coil

Field coil

Left: An electric generator works on the principle of magnetism. A magnetic field is created in a field coil of wire. Several field coils are arranged around moving coils, so that large electric currents are produced. The generator is turned by a water or steam turbine.

147

Magnetism

A magnet will pick up steel pins at close range and hold them. Its force is stronger than the force of gravity. You can feel this force by putting two magnets together. In one position, they cling together and you will have to pull hard to part them. In the other position, they will twist away from each other.

If you hang a bar magnet on a thread it will turn until one end faces north and the other faces south. The end that points north is called the north pole, and the south-seeking end is the south pole.

When two bar magnets are brought together, they pull themselves together if the north pole of one faces the south pole of the other. If the two north poles face each other,

Left: A magnet can separate iron filings from a mixture of iron and other non-metallic mixes. When a magnet picks up a pin, the pin is temporarily turned into a magnet and picks up more pins. The molecules in the unmagnetized pin point in all directions until they are lined up by the magnet. The magnetic field is strongest at the poles (the ends).

Left and far left: The magnetic field surrounding a magnet becomes visible if a sheet of paper is laid over the magnet and iron filings are sprinkled over the paper.

the magnets will repel one another. This is a law of magnetism: like poles repel each other, and unlike poles attract each other.

The force exerted by a magnet falls away as the square of the distance: twice the distance means only one-quarter of the force. Thus, though the effect of a magnet can in theory be felt at any distance, in fact it is felt only within a limited space. We call this space the field of the magnet.

The Earth is a huge magnet, with its poles quite near the Earth's North and South Poles. The Earth's magnetic field extends all over the world, so that every magnet in the world is acted upon by the Earth's magnetic field. Therefore, every magnet that can do so aligns itself with the Earth's field.

A compass needle is a small magnet balanced on a pivot so that it can turn. It responds to the Earth's magnetic field so that it always points to the magnetic poles. These poles do not lie exactly at the North and South geographic poles, so a compass needle does not indicate true north exactly. In fact, the magnetic poles are always

slowly moving. However, their location from one year to the next is well-known, and it is easy to allow for this movement and work out where true north is from a compass. Around the Earth is a magnetic field which may be upset during magnetic storms, when radio communications are interrupted and compass needles swing round. These storms may be caused by a solar wind, which consists of a stream of charged particles emanating from the Sun. The Earth's magnetism is probably caused by movements in the liquid inner core of the Earth.

You can think of the field surrounding every magnet as consisting of many in-

Below: Unlike poles attract and like poles repel one another. The dog's head and the bone both contain magnets and the dog will only accept the bone at one end.

visible lines of magnetic force linking its poles. The lines of force bulge outwards between the poles. You can see where the lines of force extend in a magnet. Place a piece of paper over a bar magnet and sprinkle some iron filings on the paper. Now tap the paper. The filings act as tiny magnets and move to follow the lines of force. They make a pattern of lines between the poles of the magnet. This pattern is an outline of the magnetic field.

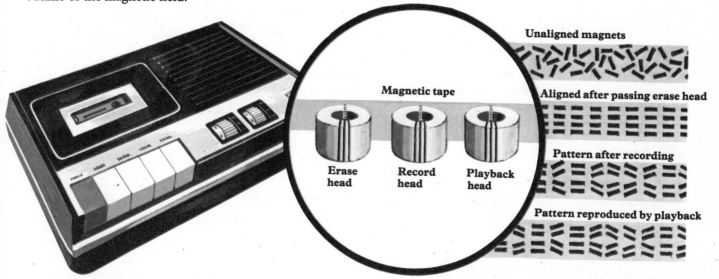

Unaligned magnets

Aligned after passing erase head

Pattern after recording

Pattern reproduced by playback

Magnetic tape

Erase head   Record head   Playback head

It is easy to make iron and steel objects magnetic. When a magnet picks up a pin, its magnetic field turns the pin into a small magnet. However, the pin loses most of its magnetism when it is separated from the magnet. A permanent magnet can be made by continually stroking an iron bar with one pole of a magnet in the same direction. Most magnets are made by placing them in the strong magnetic field inside a coil of wire carrying a current.

Not all materials are magnetic. Iron, nickel and cobalt are among the most magnetic materials. Other metals and materials are only slightly magnetic and cannot be used for magnets. If you cut a bar magnet into pieces, every piece will be found to have its own N and S poles! Thus we can see that a magnet is made of a large number of extremely small magnetic parts. When we magnetize iron we do so by making all the parts rotate to point in the same direction.

Right: The Earth's magnetic lines of force all point along magnetic north and south. These magnetic poles are different from the geographic poles. Magnetic north is 74N 100W and magnetic south is 67S 142W.

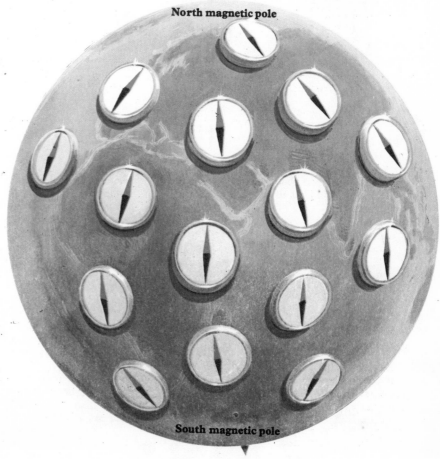

North magnetic pole

South magnetic pole

Electricity

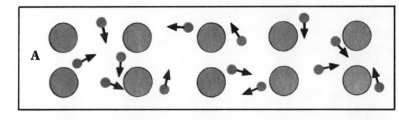

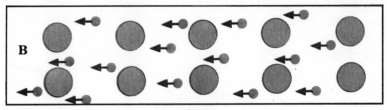

Electricity is a form of invisible energy which is very important to us. In nature, we can see the effect of electricity in a flash of lightning. But electricity can be generated, stored in a battery or carried along a cable. Because it is ready for use whenever we need it, it has been called 'man's most useful servant'. It is also cheap and clean.

There are two kinds of electricity. Current flows along a wire. It consists of a stream of electrons. This is the kind that powers our homes. The other kind is static electricity. Clouds may build up charges of static electricity. When the charge becomes too great, lightning flashes between the cloud and the ground.

You can produce static electricity by rubbing an insulator (something that will not conduct current), such as a plastic comb.

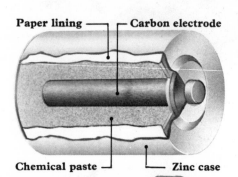

Paper lining — Carbon electrode

Chemical paste — Zinc case

Above: In most materials the electrons (red) move about the nucleus (blue) of atoms in a random motion (A). Electrons have a negative charge while the nucleus is made up of protons (which have a positive charge) and neutrons (no charge). When a current flows (B) through the material, the electrons flow in an orderly manner away from the negative pole towards the positive pole. Some materials, such as copper and aluminium, are good conductors.

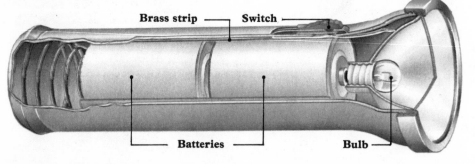

Brass strip — Switch

Batteries — Bulb

Left: A dry cell or battery produces a direct current (DC), i.e. it flows in one direction—from the negatively charged zinc outer case to the positively charged inner carbon rod when a connection is made. Current flows in a torch when the circuit is completed. This is done by moving the switch to join the two brass strips.

First Dictionary of Electricity

accumulator A battery that can store electricity. Unlike a dry battery, it can be recharged.

ampere (amp) The unit of electric current.

conductor Any substance through which electricity can flow. Most metals are good conductors.

dry cell A battery containing dry chemicals.

electrical resistance Every substance resists the flow of electricity to some degree. Conductors have a very low resistance and insulators a very high resistance. Resistance is measured in *ohms*.

fuse A piece of wire that protects electrical machines and wiring from dangerously high currents. The fuse heats up and melts before the machines or wiring are damaged.

insulator Any substance that resists the flow of electric current. Many plastics are good insulators, and are therefore used to cover electric cables and wires.

volt The unit of 'electro-motive force'; we can think of this as being equivalent to pressure in a water pipe. To contain a high voltage we need good insulation.

watt The unit of power (not necessarily electric power). Power is the rate at which something does work. One bar of an electric fire has a power of 1000 watts (1 kilowatt).

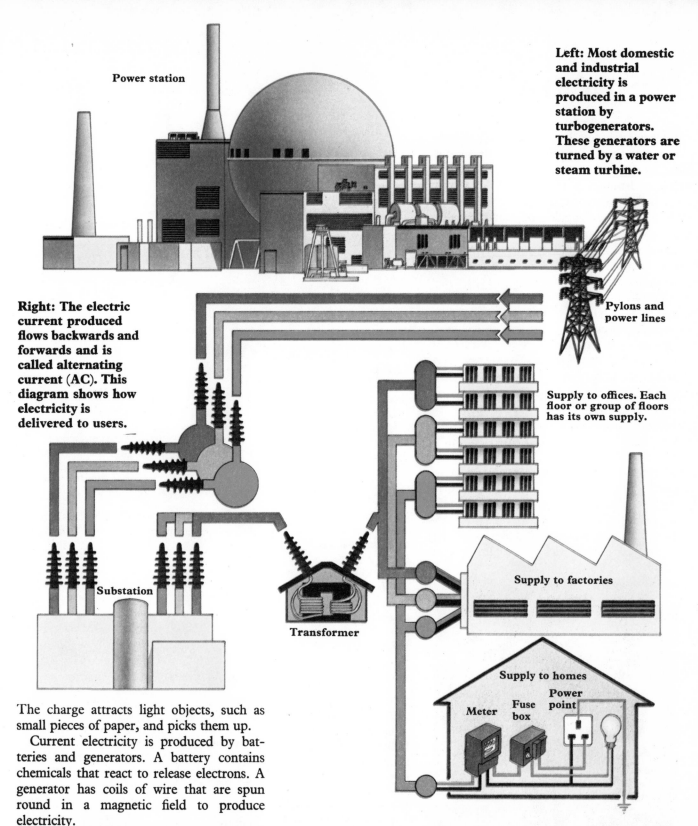

Power station

Left: Most domestic and industrial electricity is produced in a power station by turbogenerators. These generators are turned by a water or steam turbine.

Pylons and power lines

Right: The electric current produced flows backwards and forwards and is called alternating current (AC). This diagram shows how electricity is delivered to users.

Supply to offices. Each floor or group of floors has its own supply.

Substation

Supply to factories

Transformer

Supply to homes

Meter   Fuse box   Power point

The charge attracts light objects, such as small pieces of paper, and picks them up.

Current electricity is produced by batteries and generators. A battery contains chemicals that react to release electrons. A generator has coils of wire that are spun round in a magnetic field to produce electricity.

Many machines run on electricity. Electricity can easily be turned into heat and light. Electric motors use the magnetic effects of an electric current to produce power. Current electricity always flows round a closed circuit, from a battery or other source of current, through the heater, lamp or other device and then back to the source.

Above: Electricity from the power station flows through cables to local substations. There the voltage is regulated and reduced. It is then further transformed for use in homes, offices and factories.
Smaller cables carry electricity into homes. The meter records the amount used and the fuse box controls the current flowing.

Inside the Atom

Except for a very few things, such as light and electricity, everything is made of tiny particles called atoms. An atom is about one hundred-millionth of a centimetre across. Atoms, however, are not the smallest particles. They are made up of even smaller particles. Yet it is these minute particles in the atom that create the power of the Sun, of nuclear power stations and nuclear weapons.

An atom is mostly empty space. At the centre is a group of particles called the nucleus. Around the nucleus move even smaller particles called electrons. We are not even sure if they *are* particles—often they seem to fill a completely hollow shell surrounding the nucleus. Some atoms have several electron shells, which appear to form one inside the other.

Groups of Atoms

There are 92 naturally recurring types of atom. The simplest is that of hydrogen, with a nucleus containing one positively charged proton surrounded by one negatively charged electron. All other atoms are more complex and each type of atom forms

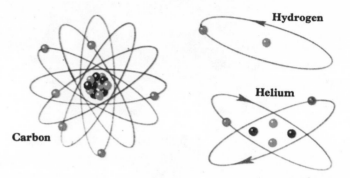

Carbon

Hydrogen

Helium

Above: Atoms consist of protons (red), neutrons (black) and electrons (green). The nucleus of the atom consists of protons and neutrons with electrons circling around it. Atoms have the same number of protons and electrons and it is the number of these that determines the type of element. Hydrogen has one of each, helium two of each and carbon six of each.

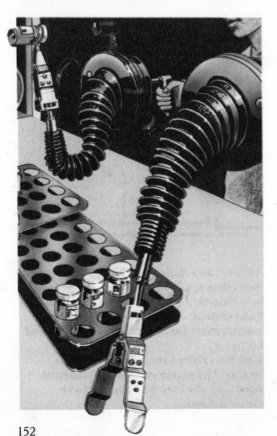

Left: Radioactivity is harmful to human beings. Radioactive isotopes, therefore, have to be handled with mechanical arms like these. The operator is protected by a special glass which prevents rays from passing through and usually protective clothing is also used. Rays are also used by doctors but under controlled conditions.

First Dictionary of the Atom

atom   The smallest particle of an element with the properties of the element. Atoms are made up of electrons and nuclei. Atoms of different elements have different nuclei and different numbers of electrons.

electron   A tiny particle in the atom that moves around the nucleus. It has a negative electric charge.

isotopes   Different forms of the same element, with different numbers of neutrons in the nucleus.

neutron   A particle in the nucleus with no electric charge.

nuclear power   Energy obtained by breaking nuclei apart. The energy is in the form of heat and radiation.

nucleus   A group of particles at the centre of an atom. Nuclei consist of protons and neutrons. The nuclei in the atoms of a particular element always contain the same number of protons, but the number of neutrons varies.

proton   A particle in the nucleus with a positive electric charge.

radiation   Some radiation, such as heat and light, is harmless. The rays sent out by radioactive substances can be dangerous.

radioactivity   Anything that produces nuclear radiation is radioactive. Some elements found in nature, such as uranium, are radioactive.

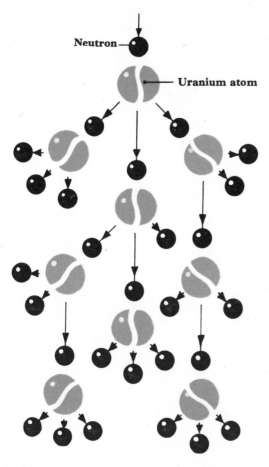

Neutron

Uranium atom

Above: Rutherford's theory said that electrons orbited a solid nucleus.

a substance called an element. Some elements are gases, such as oxygen and hydrogen. Some are solids such as sulphur. Some are metals, like iron. Elements combine to make compounds. Water is a compound of hydrogen and oxygen. Elements may occur in more than one form, because the atoms are arranged differently. For example, carbon occurs as soft graphite and hard diamond.

The number of protons is always equal to the number of electrons. This number is called the atomic number and is different for each element. The nucleus can also contain particles which have no electric charge, called neutrons.

Nuclear Energy
The particles in the nucleus are held together by strong forces. If a nucleus is broken into two smaller nuclei (the plural of nucleus), much energy may be released. This process is called fission. It is used to make energy from the elements uranium and plutonium in nuclear power stations.

Nuclear fusion occurs if small nuclei are joined to make a larger nucleus. This process produces huge amounts of energy in the Sun and in hydrogen bombs.

Above: When uranium atoms are bombarded with neutrons they split and a nuclear chain reaction is set off. The atoms break up, forming other atoms with less concentrated nuclei and release a lot of heat energy and radiation. This is known as fission. The atom bomb is an uncontrolled chain reaction. Fusion is the opposite reaction when atoms combine to form different, heavier elements.

Left: Nuclear power stations are used to produce electricity. In these stations the chain reaction is controlled in a nuclear reactor.

Man the Inventor

We are surrounded by inventions. We take such things as cars, airplanes, computers, fridges and vacuum cleaners for granted. But at one time none of these things existed. They all had to be invented.

The Need for Invention

Man invents to make his life and work easier. Early man invented tools and weapons for such purposes as hunting, skinning and cutting up his prey. When men became farmers, they needed different tools to cultivate the land. They also needed transport to carry their goods. Thus the two most important early inventions were probably the plough and the wheel.

A variety of needs provides the impetus for invention. For example, the need to defeat enemies in war has, over the years, produced a wide range of hand weapons, cannons, guns and bombs, including the atom bomb. The need for communication has stimulated many of our other inventions, such as printing, telegraph and faster means of transport.

Some Important Inventions

DATE	INVENTION	INVENTOR	COUNTRY
4000 BC	Plough	—	Sumeria
3500 BC	Wheel	—	Sumeria
250 BC	Screw water pump	Archimedes	Greece
AD 100	Paper	—	China
AD 800	Gunpowder	—	China
1608	Refracting telescope	Hans Lipershey	Holland
1698	Steam pump	Thomas Savery	Britain
1804	Steam locomotive	Richard Trevithick	Britain
1821	Electric motor	Michael Faraday	Britain
1837	Telegraph	William Cooke	Britain
		Charles Wheatstone	Britain
		Samuel Morse	USA
1867	Dynamite	Alfred Nobel	Sweden
1876	Telephone	Alexander Graham Bell	USA
1877	Electric light	Thomas Alva Edison	USA
1885	Petrol engine	Karl Benz	Germany
		Gottleib Daimler	Germany
1893	Diesel engine	Rudolf Diesel	Germany
1895	Radio	Guglielmo Marconi	Italy
1895	X-ray machine	Wilhelm Roentgen	Germany
1937	Jet engine	Frank Whittle	Britain
1944	Digital computer	Howard Aiken	USA
1946	Electronic computer	J. Presper Eckert	USA
		John Mauchly	USA
1948	Transistor	William Shockley	USA
		John Bardeen	USA
		W. H. Brattain	USA

Top: Many new inventions are patented. A patent gives the inventor the exclusive right to make, use or sell a new product, commodity, process or any kind of improvement.

Above: The Spinning Jenny, the first hand-powered multiple spinning machine, was one of the products of the Industrial Revolution. With this machine it became possible to spin many threads of wool, cotton or flax together rather than singly. It was invented by James Hargreaves in 1767. He named it after his daughter, Jenny.

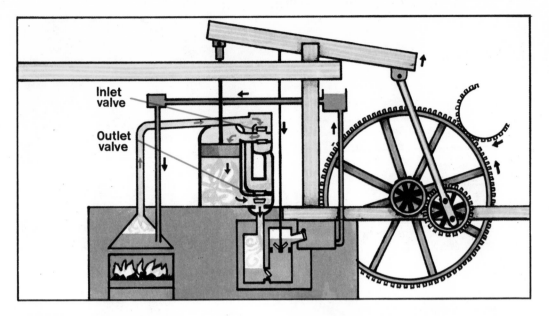

The Effects of Invention

Inventions have had a tremendous effect on the way people live. For example, in the 1700s in England there was an increasing demand for cotton cloth. This led to the invention of several machines that could spin cotton yarn quicker than it could be spun by hand. The owners of the cotton industry built factories to house these machines, and the peasants who had previously spun the cotton in their homes had to go and work in the factories instead. The factories were usually built in towns and so more and more people left the land and went to live in the cities. This process, which was also speeded up by the invention of the steam engine, was called the Industrial Revolution, and it led to very many more inventions. For example, one consequence of the Industrial Revolution was a more rapid increase in population. Inventors therefore sought ways of raising food production. In the 1800s, inventors produced the reaper, the seed drill, better ploughs and combine harvesters driven by steam engines.

Invention is a continuous process. Many inventions lead to others. For example, the invention of the petrol engine gave us the motor car and the airplane. The desire for faster speeds in the air led to the invention of the jet engine. The discovery of electricity led to the electric motor, which in turn has given us many everyday electrical appliances from electric lights to electric toothbrushes. Just as the inventions of the 1700s revolutionized life, so too has the supply of electricity. The modern world would be very different without telephones, television, radio or X-ray machines.

The most important recent inventions have been in the field of electronics and computers. It is now possible to make computers small enough to be used for very many different things. On more and more occasions it will no longer be necessary to have a person working. A computer will do the job instead, and again our way of life will be changed.

Photography

Photography is a method of making a picture using a camera and a plate or film coated with light-sensitive chemicals. The earliest form of camera was called a pinhole camera, or *camera obscura*. Light from an object passes through the pinhole and an image is formed on the screen at the back of the camera. A modern camera works in the same way. However, instead of a pinhole a lens is used. This allows more light to pass through to the film.

Early Photographers

The first known photograph was taken by Joseph Niepce, a Frenchman, in 1826. It was very blurred, but it was the first time anyone had succeeded in preserving the

Right: Joseph Niepce was the first man to succeed in taking a photograph. The results were blurred as the equipment he used was primitive but he was the true 'father' of modern photography.

Words Used in Photography

aperture The opening that controls the amount of light passing through the lens. On some cameras apertures are indicated by symbols for bright sun, hazy sun and cloud. On other cameras apertures are shown by f-numbers, such as f.16, f.8, f.5.6 and f.4 (f.16 is the smallest of these apertures). Generally, small apertures are used in bright light and wider apertures are used in poorer light.

automatic camera A camera in which the aperture and/or shutter speed are controlled by a light meter.

developer A chemical that changes the exposed silver salts in a film into dark grains of metallic silver, producing a negative.

film A length of cellulose acetate wound on to a spool, either with a paper backing or inside a cassette. The surface of the film is coated with a layer of emulsion containing silver salts. When these are exposed to light they change chemically; different amounts of light cause different amounts of change.

shutter speed The length of time for which the shutter opens to allow light to the film. Some cameras have only one or two shutter speeds; others have several, ranging from 1 second or more to 1/1000 second or less. In normal conditions a shutter speed of about 1/60 second is used. However, for fast moving subjects faster speeds may be necessary.

image produced on the screen. In 1835 Louis Daguerre began producing clearer images on metal plates (*daguerreotypes*). In 1841 an Englishman called W. H. Fox-Talbot devised a method of making paper negatives from which several duplicate positives could be produced.

Above: Louis Daguerre was the first to use metal plates in the photographic process. This gave a much clearer image.

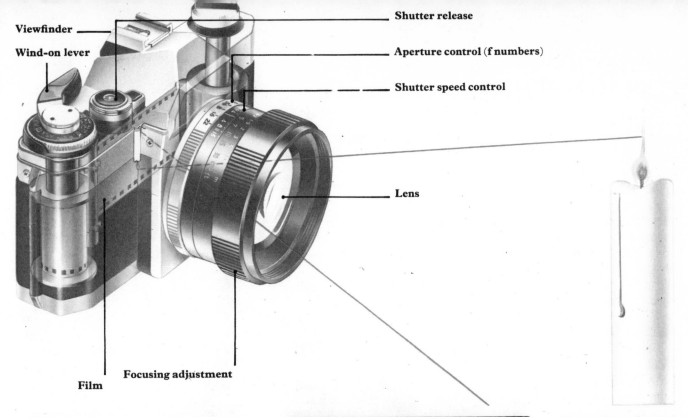

Viewfinder

Wind-on lever

Shutter release

Aperture control (f numbers)

Shutter speed control

Lens

Focusing adjustment

Film

By the 1860s there were many photographers using cumbersome cameras and glass plates. But in 1889 the Eastman Company in the USA produced the first celluloid film, for use in their small, simple Kodak box camera. With this camera anyone could take photographs and photography became the popular hobby it is today.

How to Use Your Camera

Your camera is basically a light-proof box with a lens at the front and a film contained in the back. The lens produces an upside down image on the film.

First, you must decide how much light you can allow to enter the camera to produce an accurate reproduction of the scene you wish to photograph. This is called the exposure, and it requires setting the shutter speed and the aperture if your camera has these controls. For example, to photograph a stationary subject on a bright day you might use a shutter speed of 1/60 second and an aperture of f.16. This combination will change as light conditions change.

Next, you must focus the camera. Just set the focusing adjustment (generally marked in both feet and metres) to the distance between the camera and the subject.

Finally, look through the viewfinder and check that the scene is exactly what you want to photograph. Make sure that you are holding the camera upright and steady and press the shutter.

36 ➡ 36A

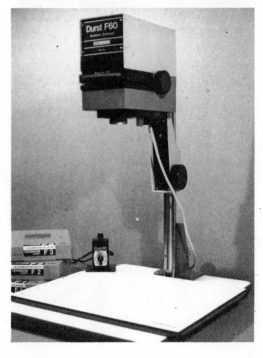

Above: A modern camera. This image of the candle is transmitted by light rays through the lines, which react with the celluloid film to make a negative image.

Above left: A negative photograph. During the developing process the image becomes positive when it is printed on special paper and treated with chemicals.

Left: The image on the film can be increased to many times its size by using a photographic enlarger. The photograph can lose sharpness and clarity if it is enlarged too much.

Radio and Television

Electricity was discovered during the 1700s. As scientists began to learn more about its properties, James Maxwell, a Scottish physicist, predicted that it would one day be used to send messages through the air.

In 1887 he was proved right. Heinrich Hertz, a German physicist, succeeded in sending a signal over a very short distance. By 1901 the Italian Guglielmo Marconi was sending messages from Cornwall to Newfoundland.

What are Radio Waves?

Radio waves belong to a group called electromagnetic waves. They are given this name because of their electrical and magnetic properties. Other types of electromagnetic waves include radar waves, infra-

Radar

In 1904 a German inventor called Christian Hulsmeyer had the idea of using radio waves to detect distant objects.

Guglielmo Marconi suggested the idea again in 1922. By 1932 the Americans, Germans and Japanese were all doing research, but the British led the field. By 1939 Britain was the only country with radar-equipped planes. Radar means *radio* detec-tion *and* ranging.

Radar uses pulses of radio waves. A rotating scanner emits a constant stream of pulses. When these strike an object they are reflected back to the scanner and the inform-ation is transferred electronically to a screen on which the object appears as a bright area or dot.

red rays, light rays, ultraviolet rays and X-rays. The only difference between them is their wavelength. Light rays are a band of waves to which our eyes are sensitive. This band is called the visible spectrum. Ultraviolet rays and X-rays have shorter wavelengths. Infra-red rays and radar have longer wavelengths. Radio waves have the longest wavelengths of all.

Broadcasting

The first radio messages were sent in Morse Code. This system of dots and dashes is sent as bursts of radio waves.

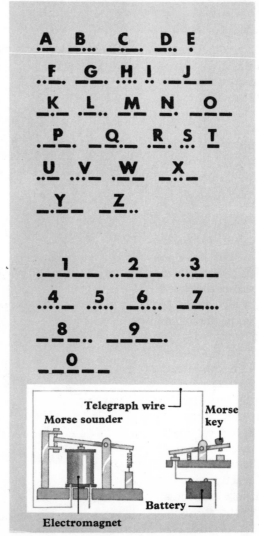

Morse sounder
Telegraph wire
Morse key
Battery
Electromagnet

Above: Guglielmo Marconi (1874-1937) with his radio transmitter and receiver. He produced the first practical wireless telegraph when he was 21 and set about developing this. The Italian government showed no interest in his invention, so he went to Great Britain where, in 1899, he sent the first wireless telegraph across the English Channel. In 1901 he sent the first radio signals across the Atlantic.

Left: Morse Code is a method of telegraphy—a means of sending messages by electricity. It was invented by Samuel Morse (1791-1872).

Below: A colour television receiver. Electron beams pass through a mask to a phosphor dot screen. When the dots are struck by electrons they light up with colour—either red, blue or green.

Above: A television studio during the shooting of a play. Note the quantity of cameras needed to film the action from several angles and the strong lighting for the maximum effect.

By 1918, however, scientists had discovered how to use radio waves to carry speech. Today radio waves are also used to carry television signals.

Sending Pictures

Modern television uses the electronic system devised by the Russian-American Vladimir Zworykin in the 1920s. In a television camera a beam of electrons scans the image of the scene in a series of lines. The information is then converted into a radio signal.

In a television set the signal is used to control another electron beam, which scans the screen. This is coated with a material that glows when it is struck by an electron. In this way the light and dark areas of the original scene are reconstructed on the screen. The process is much the same for colour television. Three basic colours—red, green and blue—are transmitted as one signal, with other signals indicating how they should be mixed.

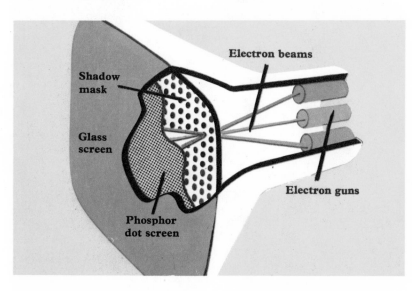

Electron beams

Shadow mask

Glass screen

Phosphor dot screen

Electron guns

Computers

When early man settled down and acquired possessions, he began to develop methods of counting. At first he used his fingers, which is why most civilizations developed systems that involved the numbers one to ten. Numbers have fascinated mathematicians ever since. But in everyday life people needed to be able to do calculations quickly. They therefore developed machines to help them.

Calculating Machines

The first type of calculator was the abacus. This uses beads on wires strung across a wooden frame. Each of the beads on a wire has the same value. The beads on the next wire are all worth ten times as much. The abacus can be used to add, subtract, multiply and divide.

The first calculating machine was invented by the French mathematician Blaise Pascal in 1642. Instead of beads his machine had cogs, each with ten teeth. In 1671 Gottfried Leibniz, a German mathematician, devised an improved mechanical calculator. In the 19th century, Charles Babbage, an English mathematician, invented a small calculator. Then, in 1832, he devised a machine that used most of the

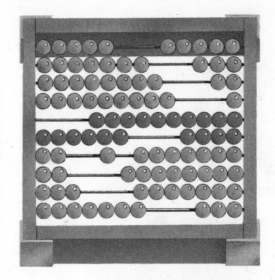

Left: The abacus is the simplest form of calculating machine. It was invented by the Arabs many centuries ago and is still used in many parts of the world today for solving mathematical problems.

Centre left: Today most shops and supermarkets use electric cash registers to add up shoppers' bills and to calculate how much change should be given. Each item is recorded so that at the end of the day, the shopkeeper can quickly see how much money he has taken.

Below: United States space missions are controlled from this room in Houston, Texas. Every modern computer facility is in use to ensure the success and safety of each mission.

160

Numeral Integrator and Calculator. ENIAC used electronic devices called valves. However, in modern computers these have been replaced by much smaller and more reliable devices known as transistors.

The first electronic computers were large. However, modern technology has enabled engineers to miniaturize complicated circuits, including transistors, so that they fit on to tiny slivers of silicon, known as silicon chips. As a result even very complicated computers can be relatively small. At present, pocket calculators are the smallest form of computer.

A computer has to be told what to do. Therefore, information in the form of a program is fed into the input unit. The information is stored in the memory, or core

Left: Charles Babbage was the originator of the modern computer. Between 1813 and 1823 he designed and built a small calculator that could tabulate certain mathematical computations to eight decimal places.

The Language of Computers

Computers use a code language known as the binary code. Any number can be expressed by different combinations of just two digits, 1 and 0. This system can be used to show the presence (1) or absence (0) of certain selected numbers. In practice these numbers are 1, 2, 4, 8, 16, 32, 64, 128 and so on. Some examples are shown below:

128	64	32	16	8	4	2	1		
	1	0	0	0	0	0	0	=	64
1	1	0	0	0	1	0	0	=	196
	1	1	0	0	0	0	1	=	97
			1	0	0	1	1	=	19
				1	1	1	1	=	15

Information in binary code may be fed into a computer in the form of punched cards or tape. A punched hole indicates 1 and no hole indicates 0. Or the presence or absence of electrical impulses on magnetic tape can be used to represent 1 or 0.

Above: Programs are fed into the computer on tapes or cards. Information is translated into 'computer language' by punch-card operators who use a keyboard machine. The information required from the computer is printed on paper or shown on a Visual Display Unit (VDU for short).

features of modern computers. But it was very complicated and he failed to interest people in it. It was not until 1944 that the first successful mechanical computer was developed by the American, Howard Aiken. Aiken's calculator contained counter wheels, electric motors to turn them, electromagnets and other parts. There were 750,000 parts in all.

Electronic Computers
In 1946 Aiken's computer was outdated by a new type of computer. In America J. Presper Eckert and John Mauchly built ENIAC, which stands for Electronic

store. Then the data—the information that is to be used in the calculation—is fed in. The control unit then directs the central processor to carry out the calculation. Because there are no mechanical parts, this process takes only seconds. Finally, the results are produced by the output unit. They may be displayed on a screen or printed out on paper.

The speed of computers has increased and their size has been reduced as smaller and smaller components have been used. The speed of a computer is now set not by the time taken to do calculations, but the speed at which the computer prints out results.

161

11 TRANSPORT

Transport is the means by which people and freight are moved from one place to another. As we will see, the uses to which transport is put have changed throughout history as a result of changes in the methods of transportation.

The Urge to Travel

Prehistoric people were always on the move, in search of food and shelter. The earliest method of moving heavy loads was to drag them on two branches tied together. Sledges and skis gradually replaced the branches. Later, animals were used to drag these, or to carry loads on their backs, the most important being the horse. The invention of the wheel enabled heavier weights to be pulled more easily.

As different groups of people developed special skills and discovered the different things that grew or were found in various parts of the world, they began to trade. One tribe would, for example, exchange woollen

Right: Sir Francis Drake's ship, the *Golden Hind,* made two world voyages.

Below: Stephenson's *Rocket,* built in 1829, was one of the first steam locomotives.

Transport Dates

In ancient times most transport was used for goods, or freight. The dates are not exact, but are estimated from the oldest known examples.

8000 BC   Loads dragged on branches.

5000 BC   Sledges and skis.

4000 BC   Boats with built-up sides and sails.

3500 BC   Invention of the wheel.

3000 BC   Animals used to pull or carry loads. Horses, dogs, oxen, reindeer, elephants, camels and other animals are still used for this purpose.

1500 BC   Road network established in China, probably in the Hsia Dynasty.

Left: Hot-air balloons were invented long before passenger aircraft. The first hot-air balloon was built in the 1780s.

Below: The search for economy in air travel has led to the invention of jumbo jets. They are the largest heavier-than-air craft.

cloth for another's metal tools. For thousands of years trade was the single most important use of transport and, as new methods were found, trade routes were established across the oceans and continents of the world.

With the Industrial Revolution, improved transport was required to move raw materials to factories and finished products to markets at home and abroad. It was at this time—about 200 years ago—that passenger transport began to become available to large numbers of people. Previously, people would only travel long distances for special reasons. Merchants, scholars, diplomats, official messengers, explorers and so on would undertake long journeys, but most people stayed in, or close to, the place where they were born. Now it became

Below left: The Free State Interchange in Miami, Florida, showing a complex network of roads. As road traffic increases, elevated roads and highways are built to help solve the problem of traffic jams.

possible for people to move their homes more easily than ever before. Many people moved from the country to the cities, and many others moved across oceans seeking greater opportunities.

The development of railways in the 19th century both enabled more and more people to travel and reduced the time taken for journeys of hundreds of miles from days to hours. The railway was followed by the motor car in the early 20th century. Finally, passenger-carrying aircraft have made it possible to travel thousands of miles in a few hours.

The effect of this has been to change our way of life. Most people now travel at least a few miles to work or school. This has produced a new growth of public transport, with buses, trains, ships and aircraft provided by the community for anyone to use on journeys of all distances.

Many people now travel for pleasure. They may take holidays at special resorts in their own countries. Or they may go abroad to enjoy better weather, and to experience other ways of life.

Modern Milestones

Although new inventions have made it easier to transport goods, their main effect has been on passenger transport.

1681 The first steam-driven vehicle is built in Peking, China.

1783 The first steamship, *Pyroscaphe*, is launched in France.

1886 The first petrol-driven car is built in Germany.

1919 The first passenger aircraft services start in Europe.

Road Transport

Probably the single most important invention in the history of transport was the wheel. We do not know when the first wheel was made, but wheeled vehicles are described in the earliest known writings, which are dated around 3100 BC.

The first use of the wheel was on carts pulled by animals or by hand. These replaced the earlier sledges on which loads were simply dragged. And as the use of wheeled vehicles spread, roads began to be made for them.

The earliest roads were simple ruts in the ground made to guide cart wheels. But in China by 1500 BC a whole network of paved roads had appeared. The roads were graded according to their size, the biggest being wide enough for three carts to travel side by side. During the next 1,000 years the Chinese also developed the first traffic

Above: The wheel probably developed (about 3100 BC) from sledges or rollers which were used to transport heavy goods.

Below: Early steam vehicles were powered by stationary steam engines that had been adapted for use in carriages.

Bottom: Gottlieb Daimler's petrol car of 1886 was one of the first petrol-engined vehicles.

Roman Roads

The Romans began to build roads for reasons of trade, but then began to build them out into the areas which they had conquered so that the Roman armies could keep them under control. By the beginning of the 2nd century BC, so many roads radiated from the capital of the empire that it was said, 'All roads lead to Rome'.

The remarkable thing about Roman roads was their straightness, regardless of obstacles. The roads were made up of several layers, beginning with a layer of brown clay to act as mortar. Then came large flat stones, covered with broken-up stones and then sand or gravel to make a smooth surface. When suitable material wasn't available, large paving slabs of stone were used.

regulations. These were needed to control the increasing amount of traffic on the roads. Today, many countries have special police forces just to control the traffic.

In Europe the greatest early road-builders were the Romans. Between 300 BC and AD 200 the Romans built roads throughout western Europe and northern Africa for their armies to march quickly from place to place. The next great road-builders were the Incas in South America. Like the Romans, the Incas built roads to connect all parts of their empire to the capital. Their roads, however, were used only by foot soldiers and messengers because the Incas did not know about the wheel or the horse.

Until the end of the 19th century, many new types of road vehicles were produced. But they all depended on horses or other animals to pull them. The steam engine was later used to power some road vehicles, and, until quite recently, steam-driven traction engines were used as tractors and road

rollers. But steam engines were very heavy, and found their best use on the railways.

Then, at the end of the 19th century, the internal combustion engine was invented. This burnt diesel oil and petrol, and was more powerful for its size than any other previous type of engine. It proved to be the ideal way to power road vehicles.

The first motor cars began to be mass-produced in the United States in 1908. Since then, cars have become the most common type of road vehicle. They allow people to go anywhere where there is a road. And because of the enormous number of cars, buses and lorries a whole new road system has had to be developed. There are wide fast roads for long journeys, and smaller roads in towns connecting each street and house.

Below: The Harley Davidson motorbike has been developed with fast, long-distance travel in mind.

Above: The first Model T Ford was built in the United States in 1908. It made popular motoring possible.

Below: A Rolls-Royce Phantom II (1939). They were built for reliability, speed and comfort.

Los Angeles

Los Angeles, in California, is one of the world's biggest cities. In order to connect the different districts, a system of roads known as freeways has been built. The inhabitants of Los Angeles own an average of almost two cars each, and the car dominates life there. There are drive-in shops, banks and even churches so that people do not need to leave their cars. Unfortunately, this causes a great deal of pollution from exhaust fumes, and the city is often covered by smog.

Crossing the Seas

The first method people found of crossing water was probably to float on logs and to paddle with their hands. The next step was to hollow out the logs so that they would float better and loads could be carried inside them.

The dugout canoe was given built-up sides of planks, so that bigger loads could be carried. But for bigger vessels, carrying large loads across open seas, the most common form was a boat built up from a keel. Stem and stern posts at each end were joined by planks curved outwards in the middle. This meant that the typical boat was wide in the middle, tapering to a point at each end.

By 1000 BC the people of Crete and Carthage, in the Mediterranean, had begun to make long sea voyages. Usually warships were driven by large numbers of oars arranged in rows, one above the other. But the oarsmen left little room for cargo, and merchant ships were usually propelled by a sail. The next important development was the lateen sail, which could be positioned to take account of the wind's direction. By AD 1000 the triangular lateen sail was used on most European and Asian ships but in China a different form of ship had developed. This is called a junk, and has a flat bottom with square bow and stern.

Types of Ships

Ferries carry people across water too wide for a bridge.

Paddle steamers are river boats driven by flat boards turning on a big wheel.

Clippers were the fastest sailing ships, carrying perishable goods such as tea.

Packet boats are small ships carrying letters, a few passengers and light cargoes.

Oil tankers are the biggest cargo vessels. Some carry up to half a million tonnes of oil.

Passenger liners carry people long distances in great luxury.

Tugs are small, powerful boats which tow the bigger ships into harbour.

Above: An ancient Greek ship called a *trireme*. It had about 170 oarsmen.

Above: The *Mayflower*, the ship used by the Pilgrim Fathers in 1620 when they set off from Plymouth, England for Massachusetts in North America.

The Eskimo kayak is made from animal skins over a wooden frame.

Another Chinese invention was the stern rudder for steering. This was not used on European ships until AD 1200, more than 1,000 years after it was first used by the Chinese. The stern rudder greatly improved steering, and allowed ships to become much larger. As they grew in size, they were given more masts, each carrying a number of sails controlled by complicated arrangements of ropes and pulleys, known as rigging.

Improvements in navigation and the great voyages of discovery led to the opening of long-distance trade routes, with goods transported across the oceans. A great advance in worldwide trade came with the opening of the Suez Canal in 1869. This waterway joined the Mediterranean and the Indian Ocean and provided the shortest route from Europe to the Orient and the east coast of Africa. Its opening was followed, in 1914, by the Panama Canal which joined the Atlantic and Pacific

Top: The hovercraft, invented by Christopher Cockerell in 1955, glides over the surface of water supported by a cushion of air. It can also operate on land.

Above: Cunard's *Queen Elizabeth II,* one of the great transatlantic passenger liners, cruises at about 30 knots (56 km/h, or 35 mph).

Canals

One of the main advantages of water transport is that much heavier loads can be carried than is possible on land or by air. Rivers, therefore, became important routes. In more recent times the industrial nations have built networks of level waterways, called canals. Flat-bottomed boats called barges operate on canals. These are used to carry raw materials from the ports to the factories, and then to carry the finished goods from the factories to the customers. Canals have also opened new shipping routes and allow sea-going ships to reach inland ports. The biggest ships, however, must use special deep-water harbours.

Oceans. No longer was it necessary to make the long, dangerous journey around Cape Horn at the tip of South America.

By the beginning of the twentieth century, steam and oil-powered engines were being used to drive screw propellers, while metal construction allowed ships to become much bigger. Old sailing ships would simply anchor in a shallow bay or alongside a simple jetty, to load and unload their cargo, so that ports grew up around natural harbours or river mouths. For the largest modern ships, however, special docks have had to be built. These are designed for handling the large cargoes of oil tankers or container ships.

Railways

Railways existed long before the invention of the locomotive. People had known since the 1500s that carts run more easily along rails than on the rough ground. But these railway carts could move only as fast as men or horses could pull them.

The invention of the steam locomotive changed everything. Steam trains could travel much faster than any earlier vehicles. And they could carry very heavy loads. They helped the growth of industry. And they made it possible for people to build cities in places where hardly anyone had lived before—for example, in the western part of the United States.

The first steam railway to carry passengers on regular services opened in England in 1830. It was the London and Manchester Railway. But steam railways spread quickly. By the 1870s, many cities in Europe, North and South America, Australia, Asia and Africa had rail connections. Everywhere the 'iron horse' was taking over.

Steam, Electric, Diesel

Over the years, engineers developed faster and more powerful steam locomotives. But these were dirty, difficult to start, and had other faults. In the late 1800s, the first electric locomotives were built. They were extremely efficient, but they had to collect electric power from a third rail or an overhead cable. Later, locomotives driven by diesel engines were made. They were powerful, but ran less smoothly than electric locomotives. A further development has been the diesel-electric loco-

The first passenger coaches on the steam railways were modelled on the horse-drawn stage coaches that were still being used on the roads. They were uncomfortable, cold, and badly lit. Freight wagons, too, were based on horse-drawn vehicles.

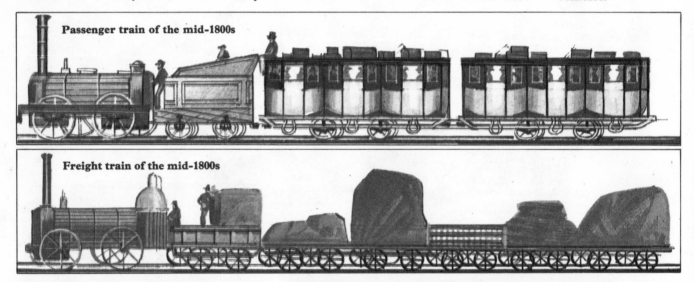

Passenger train of the mid-1800s

Freight train of the mid-1800s

City Railways

In industrial countries, special rail networks have been built in and around large cities. Each day, these are used by thousands of *commuters*—people who live in city suburbs but travel into the cities to work.

The trains on these networks are designed for short, fast journeys. Often, they carry more people than long-distance trains. Some of them are double-deck.

Within cities, railways are usually built underground, and run through tunnels. Modern underground systems are always electric, to avoid dirt and fumes in the tunnels.

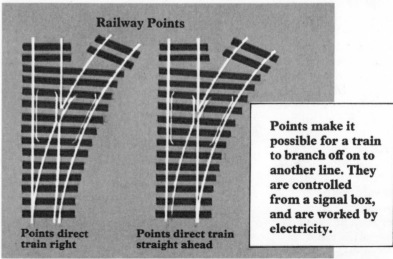

Railway Points

Points direct train right

Points direct train straight ahead

Points make it possible for a train to branch off on to another line. They are controlled from a signal box, and are worked by electricity.

motive. In this vehicle, a diesel engine drives a generator that provides power for the smooth electric motors that turn the wheels. Today, engineers are experimenting with various other forms of power.

Railway Words

bogie The carrier on which the wheels of a locomotive or carriage are mounted.

communication cord A cord that passengers can pull to stop a train in emergency.

cutting A valley cut through a small hill to keep a railway track level.

footplate The part of a steam locomotive in which the driver and fireman work.

freight train A train that carries goods.

gauge The distance between the rails of a railway track.

level crossing The place where a railway crosses a road on the level.

locomotive An engine that moves under its own power. Locomotives are used for pulling trains.

monorail A railway line with only a single track.

siding A line off the main track used for temporary accommodation of trains.

Top: New railways were not always welcomed. As they pushed farther west in the USA, the American Indians objected to the invasion of their lands.

Centre: A powerful diesel-electric freight locomotive of the Union Pacific Railway in the USA.

Left: A high-speed experimental train of the French Railways. It is known as the TGV, and has turbine engines.

169

Travel by Air

Although the first airplane did not fly until 1903, flying soon became the fastest method of transport. Today it is easily the most popular way of travelling long distances.

The first airplanes were not big or powerful enough to carry more than a pilot and perhaps a co-pilot, but during the First World War (1914–18) larger aircraft with up to four engines were developed to carry bombs. After the war some of these were converted to carry a few passengers. In 1919 the first regular passenger services were started between several cities in Europe.

Air transport was even then too expensive for most cargoes, but mail began to be carried by air at an early stage. This was partly because letters are small and light, and partly because businessmen, particularly, were prepared to pay more for their mail to be delivered by the fastest method. Especially in the United States, where

Above: The Canadair CL-215 is known as a flying boat. It takes off and lands on water.

Right: The Handley Page HP 42 was built in 1930. It flew mainly on the European routes.

Above: After World War II, commercial aircraft using various types of jet engines were soon in production. The Boeing 747 was built in 1968/69 and was the first of the jumbo jets. It is able to carry more than 400 passengers in lounges on two storeys.

Helicopters

While ordinary aircraft rely on air passing over curved wings to lift them into the air, helicopters are lifted by very narrow wings, or rotors, spinning round above them. This means they can take off straight up into the air instead of having to race along a runway to gain enough speed. They can, therefore, be used in very small spaces, such as in the middle of cities. Their use has increased considerably since 1945—they were first used in the Korean and Vietnam wars to carry troops and wounded soldiers. The largest helicopters can lift enormous loads and are used nowadays for many tasks including crop spraying, forest-fire fighting and traffic control. Helicopters have proven especially useful in rescue work after floods and earthquakes.

Air Speed Records

	Km/h	mph
1909 Wright biplane	54.77	34.04
1909 Curtiss biplane	69.75	43.35
1910 Blériot monoplane	109.73	68.18
1923 Curtiss R-2 C-1	429.96	267.16
1928 Macchi M-52 bis	512.69	318.57
1931 Supermarine S.6B	654.90	406.94
1939 Messerschmidt		
Me 209 V-1	754.97	469.12
1947 Lockheed P-80R	1,003.60	623.61
1958 Lockheed F-104A		
Starfighter	2,259.18	1,403.80
1961 McDonnell F4H-1F		
Phantom 2	2,585.43	1,606.51
1965 Lockheed YF-12A	3,331.51	2,070.10
1976 Lockheed SR-71A	3,529.56	2,193.17

The versatile helicopter is used by police, fire and rescue services all over the world. It is also used by farmers to spray their crops. Below: The layout of an airport. Every day thousands of passengers pass through its doors and hundreds of airlines use its runaways. There is a large staff to run the airport.

Flying Boats

The flying boat, which lands on and takes off from water, was first used for long-distance flights during the 1920s. One of the most notable was the Dornier DoX super flying boat of 1929 which could carry 170 people. It was 40 metres (131 feet 5 inches) long and had a span of 48 metres (157 feet 6 inches). They did not need special runways and in the early days of air travel were much safer for long journeys over the sea. But the airfields built all over the world during the Second World War meant that ordinary airplanes could go almost anywhere and so the main advantage of the flying boat disappeared.

letters could take over a week to cross the country by train, airmail services were the first regular transport flights.

The early passenger aircraft could carry only a dozen or so passengers, and only enough fuel for short journeys. For long distances, such as from Europe to the United States, airships, filled with very light gas and able to float through the air, began to be used in the 1930s. Unfortunately, the most common gas then used to fill airships, hydrogen, explodes very easily. A number of airships crashed and this type of transport was abandoned. More recently, new airships using the safe gas helium, have been built and airships may be used again to carry passengers and freight.

By the end of the Second World War in 1945, much larger airplanes had been produced. At the same time, military airfields had been built all over the world, and long-distance routes had been established. After the war, therefore, many military aircraft were bought by commercial airlines. The introduction of the jet engine, which provides much greater power than propellers, allowed even bigger and faster aircraft to be built. Today's wide-bodied airplanes can carry as many as 350 passengers.

Modern air transport passenger services are divided into two types. Scheduled services are regular flights, leaving for the same destination at the same time each day. Charter flights, on the other hand, are aircraft hired for one particular journey by a group of people. Air transport has allowed more people to travel abroad than ever before.

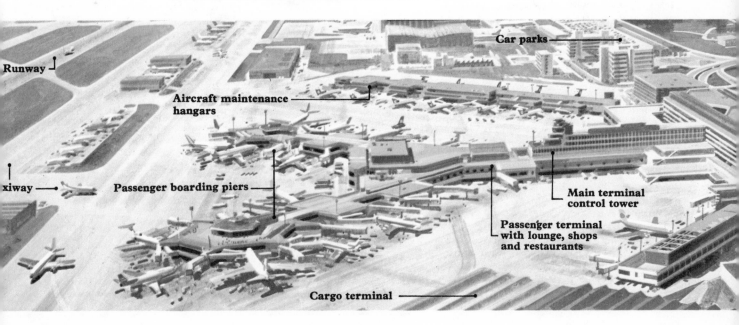

Runway

Car parks

Aircraft maintenance hangars

xiway

Passenger boarding piers

Main terminal control tower

Passenger terminal with lounge, shops and restaurants

Cargo terminal

12 THE BODY

The human body is one of nature's miracles. Consisting of millions of cells, it is more complex, better made, and more efficient than any machine invented by Man. It needs care and attention to keep it in good working order.

Anatomy and Physiology

The skeleton acts as the body's scaffolding or framework. Covered entirely with skin, the skeleton supports the body, gives it shape, and protects the vital organs inside the body such as the brain and heart. The spine, which consists of 26 interlocking bones or *vertebrae*, is the skeleton's central structure.

There are 206 bones in a normal adult skeleton. Bone consists mainly of minerals such as calcium and phosphorus which are essential for health and growth. The outer layer of bone is hard and rigid, but inside the bone there is a soft, fatty substance called *marrow*.

Where one bone meets another there is a joint. This can be movable or immovable. Movable joints include hinge joints such as knee and finger joints, and ball-and-socket joints like the hip joints. *Cartilage*, a tough elastic tissue, pads the joints. *Ligaments*, cords of stringy tissue, hold them together.

Muscles are the fleshy tissue of the body. There are about 650 muscles in the body and they consist of spindle-shaped bundles of fibres controlled by nerves. Together

Blood Groups

There are four main blood groups—A, B, AB, and O. The letters refer to the presence, or absence, of types of protein in the blood. These are known as A and B. Each person has blood which belongs to one of these four groups. Group A people have substance A in their blood; group B people have substance B. People in group AB have both and people in group O have neither. It is essential to know a person's blood group for a blood transfusion. The blood groups of the people giving and receiving blood must match each other.

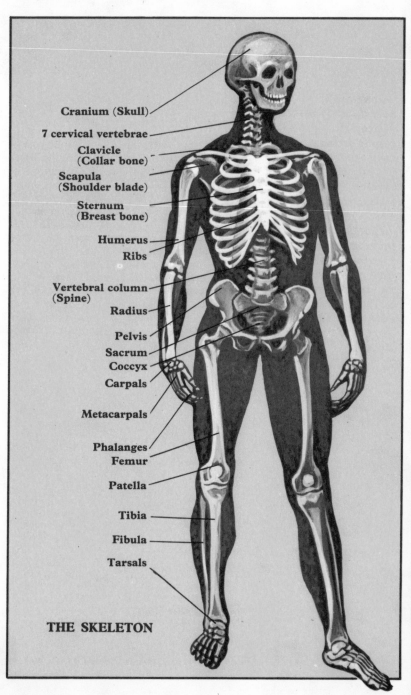

Cranium (Skull)
7 cervical vertebrae
Clavicle (Collar bone)
Scapula (Shoulder blade)
Sternum (Breast bone)
Humerus
Ribs
Vertebral column (Spine)
Radius
Pelvis
Sacrum
Coccyx
Carpals
Metacarpals
Phalanges
Femur
Patella
Tibia
Fibula
Tarsals

THE SKELETON

172

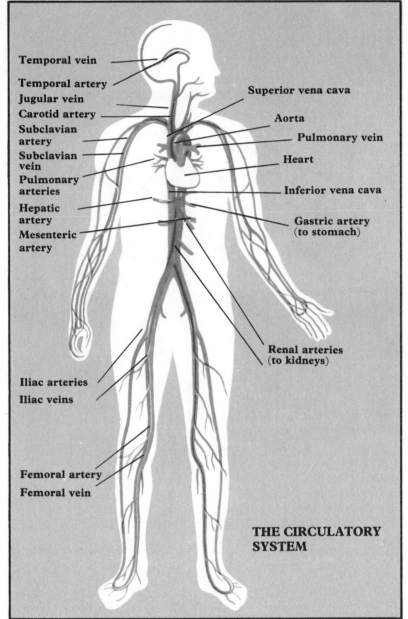

Temporal vein
Temporal artery
Jugular vein
Carotid artery
Subclavian artery
Subclavian vein
Pulmonary arteries
Hepatic artery
Mesenteric artery

Superior vena cava
Aorta
Pulmonary vein
Heart
Inferior vena cava
Gastric artery (to stomach)
Renal arteries (to kidneys)

Iliac arteries
Iliac veins

Femoral artery
Femoral vein

THE CIRCULATORY SYSTEM

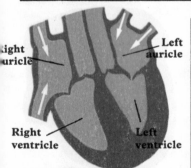

Right auricle
Left auricle
Right ventricle
Left ventricle

Right: Cells are the basic unit of life. The human body is composed of about 100 million million cells. They differ in type but each has the same basic structure.

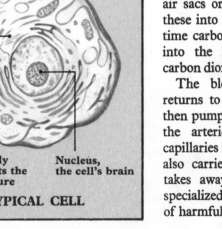

Centriole, plays a part in cell reproduction
Cell membrane, the cell's skin
Cytoplasm, a watery jelly that supports the cell's structure
Nucleus, the cell's brain

TYPICAL CELL

with the skeleton, muscles help the body to move. There are two kinds of muscles—voluntary and involuntary. *Voluntary* muscles are those that can be moved at will. They are attached to the bones by cords of tissue called *tendons*. When we move an arm, the brain sends a signal to the arm muscles. These contract or get shorter and pull on the bones of the forearm so that the arm moves up. When the muscles relax, the arm drops down. *Involuntary* muscles are those over which we have no conscious control. They are always at work and are found in the arteries, intestines, stomach, veins and many other organs. The lung and heart muscles are examples of involuntary muscles at work.

The heart and the lungs work together to supply the body with the oxygen that every cell needs to live. The heart (far left) consists of four chambers: two upper auricles and two lower ventricles. Large veins bring blood to the right side of the heart. From there it is pumped to the lungs.

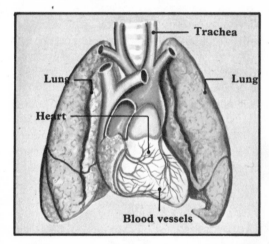

Trachea
Lung
Lung
Heart
Blood vessels

When we breathe in, oxygen passes into the lungs (above) through the trachea or windpipe. The lungs fill with air which enters a network of tubes ending in tiny air sacs or alveoli. Oxygen passes through these into the bloodstream and at the same time carbon dioxide moves from the blood into the lungs. When we breathe out, carbon dioxide is expelled.

The blood, now filled with oxygen, returns to the left side of the heart. It is then pumped out to the rest of the body by the arteries. Tiny blood vessels called capillaries link arteries and veins. The blood also carries food to the body's cells and takes away waste materials. In addition, specialized blood cells help to rid the body of harmful germs.

Anatomy and Physiology (2)

The brain is the body's control centre. It is sometimes compared to a computer but it is very much more complicated than any computer ever invented. The brain receives nerve impulses from sense organs in all parts of the body. In turn it sends signals to muscles and glands to take whatever action is necessary. In this way the brain controls all bodily functions and activities. It also controls our emotions, stores memory, and is where the thinking process occurs.

The brain consists of several parts. Each one is connected but each has its own specific job. The *cerebrum* is the top and largest part of the brain. It looks rather like a large walnut and is made up of two identical parts. Its surface is a mass of folds consisting of *grey matter*. Below is a mass of *white matter* consisting of bundles of nerve fibres. The cerebrum controls sensations such as seeing and hearing and activities such as movement and speech. Below is the *cerebellum*. This controls muscular movement and helps to maintain balance. The *medulla*, which lies on top of the spinal column, controls those functions of the body over which we have no control. The heart, lungs, stomach—all internal organs—are regulated through a system of

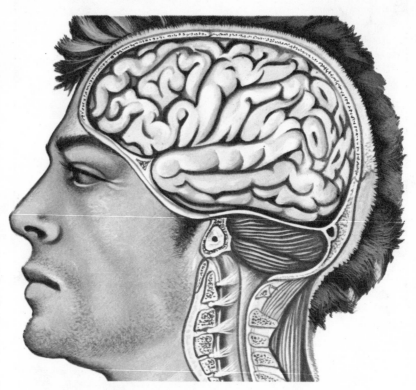

Above: The brain's soft mass is protected by the skull. The brain is made up of some 30,000 million nerve cells.

If we touch something hot a *reflex action* occurs. Nerve impulses travel as far as the spinal cord then back again.

nerves bundled together in groups called *ganglia*.

The nervous system co-ordinates all the body's activities. It consists of the brain, the spinal cord, and all the nerves that radiate from them. The nervous system works rather like a telephone network with the nerves acting like telephone wires. *Sensory* nerves react to various stimuli such as heat, cold, light or pressure. They send messages or impulses from the sense organs to the brain. The brain, like a switchboard, then sends instructions via the *motor* nerves to the muscles and glands to take the necessary action.

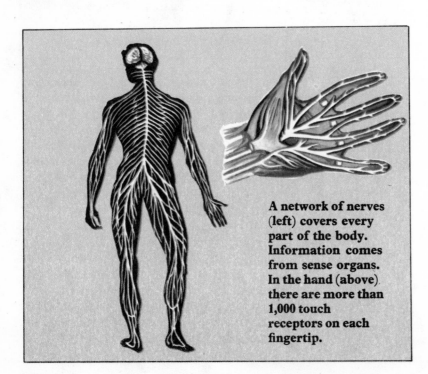

A network of nerves (left) covers every part of the body. Information comes from sense organs. In the hand (above) there are more than 1,000 touch receptors on each fingertip.

Dictionary

axons Nerve fibres that send impulses.

blind spot Point where optic nerve leaves the eye. It is not light sensitive.

central nervous system Consists of the brain and the spinal cord.

cortex The outer layer of the cerebrum.

dendrites Nerve fibres that receive impulses.

motor nerves Nerves that send instructions from the brain to muscles and glands.

neuron A nerve cell with fibres that connect with other nerve cells or organs.

olfactory nerves Nerves that deal with smell.

synapse The gap between nerve fibres over which nerve impulses must 'jump'.

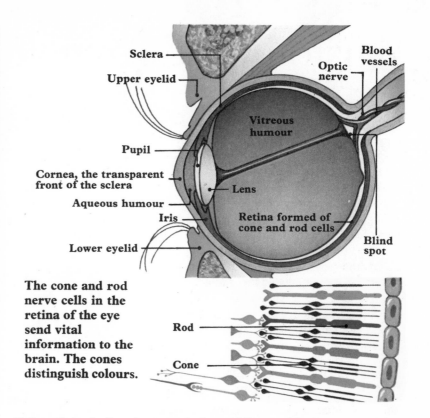

The cone and rod nerve cells in the retina of the eye send vital information to the brain. The cones distinguish colours.

Below: Sound vibrations reach the middle ear. The inner ear turns them into nerve impulses that travel to the brain.

OUTER EAR — MIDDLE EAR — INNER EAR

Auditory canal

Semicircular canals

Hammer

Anvil

Auditory nerve

Cochlea

Auricle

Eardrum   Stirrup   Oval window   Round window

Eustachian tube

Anatomy and Physiology (3)

The food we eat must be broken down into simple substances that can be absorbed by the blood. This process is called digestion. Digestion takes place in the alimentary canal, a long tube that runs from the mouth to the anus. Chemical substances known as *enzymes* break down the food.

Digestion begins in the mouth. The teeth chew food into small pieces and mix it with saliva. The food is swallowed and passes down the oesophagus into the stomach. Muscular movements of the stomach churn the food and mix it with gastric juices.

After some hours the now liquid food enters the small intestine. The top part of the small intestine is called the *duodenum*. It is here that several important substances join in the digestive process. First among these substances is *bile* which digests fats. Bile is produced in the liver and stored in the gall bladder. A system of ducts allows the right amount of bile to pass from the gall bladder into the duodenum where it mixes with juices from the pancreas. The pancreas supplies the digestive process with water, enzymes and bicarbonate. Tiny finger-like projections called *villi* line the walls of the small intestine. These absorb the digested food and it passes into tiny blood vessels. Once in the bloodstream much of the digested food goes to the liver

Diet and Health

For our bodies to work properly we must eat the right kinds of food. There are five main groups of food—carbohydrates, fats, proteins, minerals and vitamins. Fats and carbohydrates are the chief energy-giving foods. They include bread, butter, potatoes and sugar. Proteins are essential for health and growth and are found in cheese, eggs, fish, milk and meat. Only small quantities of vitamins and minerals are needed but they are vital. Vitamin sources include fresh fruit and vegetables, meat and milk. Calcium, for healthy bones and teeth, and iron are two of the most important minerals. Calcium is found in cheese, milk and fish, and iron in meats such as liver and in green, leafy vegetables like spinach.

Exercise is necessary to develop the muscles of the body, including the heart, and sufficient rest is also required.

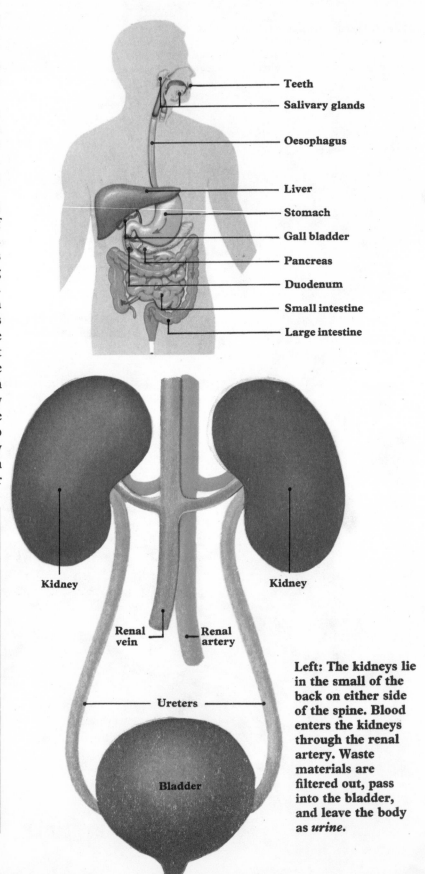

Teeth
Salivary glands
Oesophagus
Liver
Stomach
Gall bladder
Pancreas
Duodenum
Small intestine
Large intestine

Kidney
Kidney
Renal vein
Renal artery
Ureters
Bladder

Left: The kidneys lie in the small of the back on either side of the spine. Blood enters the kidneys through the renal artery. Waste materials are filtered out, pass into the bladder, and leave the body as *urine*.

where it is stored until needed. Undigested, or waste, food goes to the large intestine. It leaves the body through the anus as *faeces*.

Human Reproduction

Human life continues through the process of sexual reproduction. This involves the fertilization of a female egg cell by a male sperm cell.

Fertilization takes place inside a woman's body. The female egg cells or *ova* are stored inside the ovaries. Once a month an egg ripens and leaves the ovaries. During intercourse male sperm cells pass through a man's penis into a woman's vagina. If a sperm meets a ripened egg, fertilization occurs. One single cell is formed and attaches itself to the lining of the woman's uterus. There, during a period of nine months, it develops into a new human being. The fertilized egg divides first into two cells which in turn also divide, and so on. By this process the thousands of cells that form a human body are produced. In its earliest stages the bundle of cells is known as an *embryo;* after eight weeks the developing

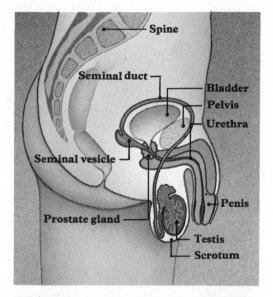

Spine
Seminal duct
Bladder
Pelvis
Urethra
Seminal vesicle
Penis
Prostate gland
Testis
Scrotum

Left: Sperms are produced in the testes, the male reproductive glands, and are passed to the urethra. During intercourse, millions of tiny sperm cells pass through the man's penis into the woman's vagina. When they reach the fallopian tubes one may unite with an egg from one of the female ovaries.

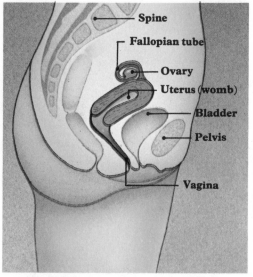

Spine
Fallopian tube
Ovary
Uterus (womb)
Bladder
Pelvis
Vagina

Left: The female reproductive glands are the ovaries. Each month an egg ripens and passes down to the uterus. If the egg is fertilized it forms a cell called a zygote. If not, the monthly menstruation takes place.

baby is called a *foetus*. The baby inherits characteristics from both parents.

The Chain of Life

Every human being starts life as one single cell. This divides time and time again to form thousands of other cells. Near its centre each cell contains a *nucleus,* the most important part of a cell. The nucleus contains minute thread-like *chromosomes.* Each cell in a woman's body contains 23 identical pairs of chromosomes including a pair known as X chromosomes; the cells in a man's body contain 22 pairs plus one X and one Y chromosome.

Chromosomes themselves contain long twisted strands of molecules known as DNA (deoxyribonucleic acid). Often called 'the chain of life', DNA contains all the *genetic* information needed to create a new individual. Among other things DNA determines a person's sex and body shape.

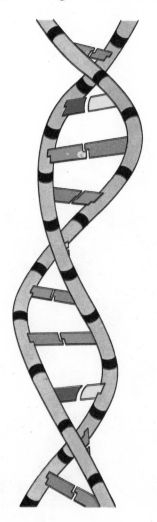

Left: DNA or deoxyribonucleic acid is the main chemical substance of which genes are made. They are located in the chromosomes of the cell nucleus. When the cell splits into two, DNA reproduces itself as well, and thus ensures that hereditary information is passed to new cells.

177

13 THE ARTS

'The arts' mean different things to so many people. This chapter traces the history and development of the arts and the contributions made to them by many cultures and individuals from nations all over the world.

What is Art?

Left: *Richmond Hill* by the English painter Joseph Mallord William Turner (1775-1851). He is renowned for his dramatic use of light and colour.

Below: By the end of the 12th century, the art of creating stained-glass windows had been perfected. One of the finest examples is this rose window of the Sainte Chapelle in Paris.

The word 'art' has two different meanings. It can mean drawing, painting and sculpture. When people say that they are interested in art, they usually mean that they enjoy painting and drawing or looking at paintings and drawings. But when we talk about 'the arts' we mean much more than this. 'The arts' include not only drawing, painting and sculpture, whose origins stretch back to ancient times but also music, literature, drama, dancing and more modern forms of art, such as photography, cinema and television.

Artists and Performers

An artist can be a painter, but a composer or author can also be called an artist because he works in one of the arts. Some of the arts, such as music, drama, cinema and television, need performers. They are often called the 'performing arts' and the performers (musicians and actors) can also be called artists.

Arts and Crafts

All the arts are concerned with creating things, but not everything that is made is a work of art. Some things are made to be used rather than just admired. For example, a man could make a wooden bowl and carve designs on the outside for decoration. He has made a bowl for people to eat out of, although it may be beautiful. Another wood-carver could carve a model of an animal, for example, which can only be used as an ornament. The wooden bowl is an example of a craft, as it is mainly a useful object, and the model animal is an example of an art. An artist makes beautiful things for people to admire but a craftsman makes things that can be used. Very often a craftsman makes something that is very beautiful, and is often considered a work of art, but this is not the main reason for making it. Some examples of craftsmen are potters, furniture makers, watchmakers and instrument makers.

Why do Artists Want to Create?

Artists write, paint and compose for many different reasons. The main reason is to communicate their ideas to other people. For example, when a painter sees a beautiful sunset, he may want other people to share the feelings he has about it. So, he might paint a picture of that sunset. Because the painting will not look exactly like the real sunset, the artist also tells us in his painting a little bit about what he feels about it. In

Right: The ancient Egyptians were skilled artists and craftsmen. This solid gold mask covered the head of King Tutankhamun's mummy.

Below: The Phillip Jones Brass Ensemble. Music is probably the oldest known art form for expressing people's thoughts and feelings.

Below: Ballroom dancing is one of the most popular forms of dance, especially in Great Britain.

the same way, writers can describe things in ways that let us know exactly what they think about them. Artists do not only describe things to us, but can also convey their ideas to us. A writer can, for example, tell us what he thinks life will be like in a hundred years' time, or even what he thinks is wrong with the world today. Poets are especially skilled in conveying feelings through their art, for the essence of poetry is the expression of emotions. In the dramatic arts, not only the playwright but also the actors want to communicate their thoughts and ideas through a play. Music, too, is a medium which can communicate a lot to us. In ancient times it was thought of as the gift of the gods. We all respond to music at some level—some pieces of music sound happy and gay, others sad and mournful. The composer of the music is telling us a little about how he felt when he was writing the music or is perhaps describing an experience he has had.

Drawing and Painting

Today, the easiest way to make a picture of something is to take a photograph, but before the camera was invented artists had to draw and paint pictures. Drawing is usually done with a pen or pencil on paper and makes a picture out of lines. Artists can indicate colour and shadow by shading.

Some pictures that look like drawings have not been made with a pen or pencil. They are engravings. They are made by cutting the picture on a flat block of wood or metal and then inking over the top of it. When the block is pressed on to paper it prints the picture in reverse. Another way of making line pictures is etching. It is like engraving but wax and acid are used to etch the picture on to a metal plate. With both etching and engraving, it is possible to make many prints.

Above: An Egyptian painting found on a tomb in Thebes. The Ancient Egyptians painted people in profile

Left: *Great Piece of Turf* by Albrecht Durer (1471-1528). Although a competent painter, he was famed for his woodcuts, engravings and drawings.

Painting

The first paints were made from natural substances, for example, soot and powdered earth. Later, artists painted on to the plaster of walls with colours mixed with egg white and vinegar. Artists then found that if colours were mixed with linseed oil they lasted much better and held their brightness longer. Another kind of paint is water colour. Water colour paints are used on paper, and oil paints on canvas.

Cave men decorated the walls of their caves with pictures of animals. The ancient Egyptians also covered their walls with pictures, as did the Romans and Greeks.

In the Middle Ages, most pictures were of religious subjects. After the Renaissance, or rebirth of art in Europe, artists began to paint other subjects, like scenes from history and portraits of people. Some artists painted scenes in the countryside, which we call landscapes, or pictures of flowers or objects, which we call still-life pictures.

After the invention of the camera, artists

Some Famous Artists

Leonardo da Vinci (1452-1519) Italian. One of the greatest artists of the Renaissance period. He was also an architect, engineer, musician and anatomist.

Albrecht Dürer (1471-1528) German. Dürer was a painter and engraver and invented the art of etching.

Michelangelo Buonarroti (1475-1564) Italian. Another great artist of the Italian Renaissance. He painted the ceiling of the Sistine Chapel in Rome.

Titian (1477-1576) Italian. A great oil painter famous for the rich colours in his pictures.

Rembrandt van Rijn (1606-1669) Dutch. Perhaps the most famous Dutch painter. He painted many portraits.

Pierre Renoir (1841-1919) French. Painted in a soft sensitive style that made him one of the leaders of the Impressionist school.

Paul Gauguin (1848-1903) French. He lived in Tahiti for a while and painted many Tahitian scenes in vivid colours.

Pablo Picasso (1881-1973) Spanish. One of the most famous 20th century artists. He led many modern movements, one of which was Cubism, where objects were transformed into geometric shapes.

Salvador Dali (1904-   ) Spanish. Dali's pictures are called 'surreal' because they appear realistic, but have a strange dream-like quality.

no longer had to draw or paint realistic pictures because they could just take a photograph. Many decided to paint things in a different way. The first artists to break with traditional painting were called Impressionists because their works gave only a quick, general impression of a scene, instead of a very realistic view. Many years before this, Arab artists had made pictures using geometrical shapes and patterns. Now modern artists also started to make patterns and shapes rather than pictures of things. We call this abstract art. Artists began to look at things in a new way and to communicate their vision in imaginative, new styles.

Above left: The *Mona Lisa* was the most famous portrait painted by Leonardo da Vinci.

Above: *Luncheon of Boating Party, Bougival* by the great Impressionist, Pierre Renoir.

Below: *Whaam!* by Roy Lichtenstein, an example of modern 'pop' art.

Sculpture

There are many ways of making sculptures. They can be modelled, using a soft material like clay, carved in stone or wood, or cast in a mould.

The first sculptures were pots and bowls made in clay, but very soon people began making clay models of their gods and sacred animals, and sculpture changed from being a craft into an art.

Carving of wood and stone soon became a popular method of sculpture. It is more difficult than modelling as pieces cannot be added and special tools are needed. In ancient Greece and Rome, sculpture in marble was very popular, but nowadays all kinds of materials are used.

To make a sculpture out of metal the sculptor first makes a mould out of clay and then pours in molten metal. This method uses a lot of metal, but the 'lost wax' method uses less. The sculptor makes a shape in clay, and then covers it with wax. After this he covers the wax with another layer of clay and heats the whole thing. As the wax melts and runs away, there is a gap left between the two layers of clay. When metal is then poured into this gap, it forms the shape that the wax had. When the metal is hard the clay can be taken off leaving a hollow metal sculpture.

The lost wax method of casting metal

Above: Portrait of Michelangelo, the famous Italian Renaissance sculptor.

Above right: Michelangelo's most moving sculpture, 'the Pieta', in Rome.

Right: Sir Henry Moore simplified human forms in this family group.

182

Some Famous Sculptors

Michelangelo Buonarroti (1475-1564) Italian. Specialized in marble sculptures of the human body, such as his 'David', his great statue of Moses, his pietas, and also figures for tombs.

Bernini, Gianlorenzo (1598-1680) Italian. Used interesting mixtures of materials, such as marble, bronze and glass. Fine examples of this are his 'Ecstasy of Saint Theresa' and his works in St. Peter's Cathedral, Rome.

Houdon, Jean-Antoine (1741-1823) French. Best-known for his portraits, such as statues of Molière and Washington. Also well-known is his 'Anatomical Man'.

Rodin, Auguste (1840-1917) French. Well-known for his figures 'Bronze Age', 'The Kiss', 'The Burghers of Calais', 'The Thinker' and his 'Gate of Hell', a huge bronze door.

Epstein, Sir Jacob (1880-1959) b. New York. Many of his sculptures are in public places, such as his 'Rima' in Hyde Park, London and a bronze group for Coventry Cathedral.

Calder, Alexander (1898-1976) American. An engineer and sculptor who invented mobiles.

Moore, Sir Henry (1898-   ) English. Mainly famous for abstract sculptures, such as 'The North Wind'.

Left: From earliest times, men have made figures of wood to represent their ancestors or gods. This African figure has a hornbill on his head.

sculpture was used very skilfully in Africa. In the kingdom of Benin (c.1100 to the early 1700s), in what is modern Nigeria, many fine bronze sculptures were produced. Benin artists created striking heads of family members to be used in ancestor worship. They also produced delightful pieces for decoration.

Subjects for Sculpture

The most common subject for sculpture is the human figure. There are statues of famous people in most towns and the best can be seen in art galleries all over the world. But statues are not the only form of sculpture. Some are like half statues attached to a background. These are often carved on stone walls and are called reliefs. If the sculpture is of somebody's head (or head and shoulders) we call it a bust. The ancient Greeks and Romans carved many beautiful statues and busts of their emperors and gods. Later, sculptors copied their graceful style, which we call the 'classical' style.

Recently, artists have made sculptures that are not so realistic. They have simplified, or complicated, and distorted the shapes of what they are carving, to make it more expressive. Other sculptors do not try to make realistic shapes at all. They are more interested in making unusual shapes out of wood, stone and metal, rather than models of people and animals.

Artists are now finding new ways of making sculptures. Instead of cutting or moulding materials, some sculptors stick things together or build sculptures out of many different parts. Using string, wire, pieces of wood, metal, and plastic, they can make very interesting shapes.

Perhaps the most interesting new idea is moving sculptures. Alexander Calder invented a kind of sculpture which he called a 'mobile'. In a mobile, pieces of wood, cardboard or plastic hang from pieces of wire and string. They are very carefully balanced and the slightest breeze makes them move.

Left: Chinese gilt dancing figures. They represent Bodhisattvas, or Buddhists who delay reaching nirvana in order to teach others.

Music

Music is the art of arranging sounds. The origin of music is lost in time, but we can imagine that it was a primitive form of communication or a part of man's earliest religious ceremonies. We do know, however, that music has always had the power to affect people's emotions. A stirring march, a lively dance, a song to share with friends or make a job go quickly—these were some uses of music in ancient civilizations, just as they are for us today.

Musical Instruments

The first musical instruments were probably invented by accident. When someone found that hitting a clay pot on the bottom produced an interesting sound, the first drum was born. Today, instruments that are struck—drums, cymbals or xylophones—are called percussion instruments.

Primitive man may also have discovered stringed instruments. Perhaps he heard the 'twang' of his bowstring. To play a harp or a guitar, you pluck the strings just like you pluck a bowstring. Later, somebody found

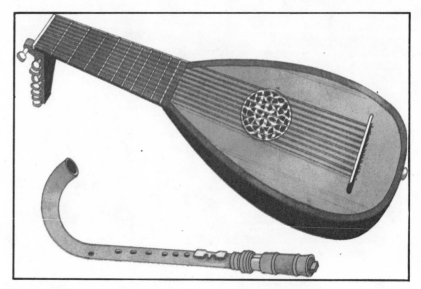

Above: The lute (top) is one of the earliest stringed instruments. It was very popular until the 17th century. The crumhorn (bottom) is a reed-cap instrument, popular in the Middle Ages.

Below: The Vienna Philharmonic Orchestra is one of the greatest symphony orchestras of today. It is just as happy playing Brahms as Stockhausen, and is famous for performing Strauss waltzes and marches.

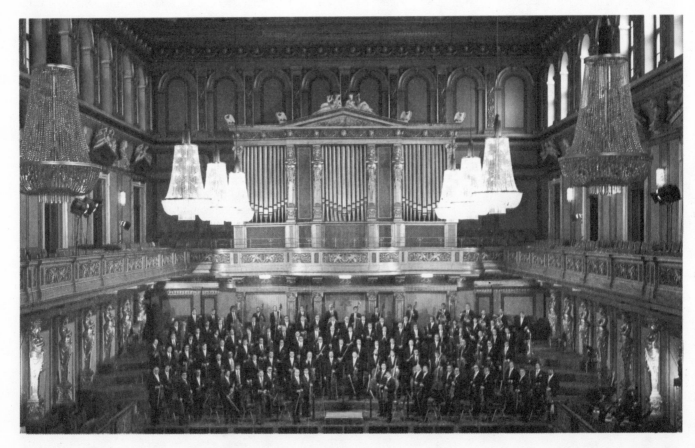

Some Famous Composers

Claudio Monteverdi (1567-1643) Italian. Wrote some of the first operas and a great deal of church music.

Johann Sebastian Bach (1685-1750) German. Wrote many pieces for orchestra, choirs, organ and harpsichord.

George Frederick Handel (1685-1759) German. The composer of the 'Messiah' and 'Water Music'.

Wolfgang Amadeus Mozart (1756-1791) Austrian. Began composing as a child. Wrote many operas, symphonies, and concertos.

Ludwig van Beethoven (1770-1827) German. Famous composer of symphonies. Started to go deaf at about the age of 30.

Johannes Brahms (1833-1897) German. Wrote symphonies and works for piano.

Johann Strauss (1825-1899) Austrian. Wrote the 'Blue Danube' waltz.

Peter Ilich Tchaikovsky (1840-1893) Russian. Wrote symphonies, operas and ballets, including the 'Nutcracker Suite'.

Edward Elgar (1857-1934) English. Wrote the 'Pomp and Circumstance' marches and the 'Enigma Variations'.

Benjamin Britten (1913-1976) English. Famous for his operas and music for young people, e.g. 'The Young Person's Guide to the Orchestra'.

Karlheinz Stockhausen (1928-   ) German. A modern composer who writes experimental music.

that the strings made a nice long sound when they were scraped rather than plucked. He had invented the musical bow, which violinists use today. The harpsichord and piano are also stringed instruments. Inside them is a mechanism that plucks or hits the strings when the keys are pushed down.

Another kind of musical instrument is the wind instrument. There are many different sorts, but they are all blown into to produce sounds. Reed instruments (oboe, clarinet, bassoon, and saxophone), whose notes are made by air vibrating a reed inside them, and flutes, are known as woodwind instruments because they used to be made entirely of wood. The brass horns of the orchestra are really only tubes made of brass. The most common are the trumpet, tuba, French horn and trombone.

Today, there are many kinds of electronic instruments such as synthesizers, and many ways to amplify instruments that would be very quiet on their own, for example, the electric guitar used in pop groups.

Above left: The greatest composer of his time, Ludwig van Beethoven. Many of his most famous pieces were composed after he had become deaf.

Above: Pop groups of the 1960s and 1970s revolutionized the musical scene. Amplified electric guitars and light shows added to the excitement of pop.

Below: A group of West Indians make their own music using empty metal oil drums, which are tuned and used as instruments. These groups are called steel bands.

Dancing

People dance for many reasons. Folk dancing and tribal dancing usually celebrate some special event. For example, African tribes often dance to celebrate the birth of a baby or a wedding, and even today in Europe people celebrate the beginning of summer by dancing round the maypole, or the success of the harvest with a barn dance. This kind of folk and country dancing is done for fun and for everyone to join in. People do not usually want to just watch this kind of dancing.

In the 17th century, these folk dances became quite popular with people other than the peasants who normally did them. The kings, queens and noblemen also wanted a kind of dance they could join in. They invented versions of the peasant dances that were stately and not so lively.

Right: This picture from a medieval manuscript shows early court dancing.

Below: Dame Margot Fonteyn and Nureyev in the ballet _Romeo and Juliet_.

Above: The Pirin Dance, danced standing on drums, comes from the mountains of south-west Bulgaria. Folk dancing is always done in the national costume of the dancers.

Right: The dancers of South-east Asia are very graceful and supple. Their dances tell stories and every movement of their arms, hands and eyes means something specific. This dancer comes from the island of Bali.

Above right: The Flamenco is danced in southern Spain to the sound of the classical guitar and the clack of castanets. It is a colourful and vivacious dance.

These dances included the minuet, allemande, gigue and gavotte. Then, in the 19th century, everyone wanted to dance in ballrooms like the nobility and the new dance, the waltz, became very popular.

Today, ballroom dancing is still popular. People not only like to dance the tango, waltz and cha-cha, but also enjoy watching other people dance. New dances are always being invented, and with jazz and pop music there are many dances for the ballroom and discotheque.

Most of this ballroom and disco dancing is not done in front of an audience. There is a kind of dancing, though, that is usually performed for an audience. It is called ballet. Ballet is a way of telling a story by

Choreography

Choreography is the art of writing dances. A choreographer must work out all the movements that he wants the dancers to make and then go through them with the dancers.

Folk dances have nearly always been passed from one dancer to another without being written down. The person who is learning the dance watches it and then copies. This system has not always been accurate enough, so dancers and choreographers invented ways of writing down the movements. At first they used little pictures like 'pin men' which were drawn under the music. Later a new system was invented which used dots to represent the hands, feet and head of the dancer on lines. This system looks rather like music. Choreography can be used for all kinds of dancing, from ballroom dancing to ballet.

In classical ballet, some of the best choreographers came from the traditional Russian companies. The ballets written in the early 1900s by Michel Fokine and by the famous dancer, Nijinsky, are still performed frequently. Some of the greatest living choreographers are Sir Frederick Ashton of Great Britain and the Americans George Balanchine and Martha Graham.

moving to a piece of music. In this way it is very much like opera or drama, but without the words. Classical ballet developed from the court dances of the 17th century. There is a large number of standard movements. Modern ballet is much freer in style, but it still tries to tell a story and express the feelings of the dancer through his or her movements with the music.

Dancing often plays a part in other dramatic forms such as operas and musicals, and variety shows often include scenes with a group of dancers dancing to a popular tune.

Literature

Literature is the written art. People write things down for several reasons. Text books and newspapers are examples of writing done to pass on information. Another example of this kind of writing is this encyclopedia. But this is not usually called art, as it is written to be useful rather than to entertain. Most literature is the art of telling a story, or describing thoughts and feelings.

Literature comes in two main forms, prose and poetry. Poetry is often written in verses with a regular rhythm and sometimes with rhymes at the end of lines. Prose is different from poetry as it does not use rhymes at all. Whether they write to inform or to entertain, prose writers do not write in verses. They divide their writing into sentences and paragraphs instead.

Story-telling is an art that began long before Man had discovered how to write. Most stories were first passed on by word of mouth. Literature began when a method of writing down these stories was discovered. Most of these stories are fiction. In fiction the people, or characters, in the story are imaginary, although the story may be based on real-life events. Sometimes an author (a writer of prose) writes a story about the future. We call this science fiction, 'sci-fi', or simply SF.

There are many different forms of fiction, but the two most common types are short stories and novels. A short story is exactly what it sounds like, a single story told in a short way. A novel usually has several stories told at the same time. These plots (stories) are connected together in the novel by the characters in them. Sometimes the plots get very complicated and the novels have many different characters all connected in some way.

Not all prose literature is pure fiction.

Right: One of the greatest French writers was Victor Hugo (1802-1885). He wrote drama and prose but his best works were thought to be his poems. Other French poets of the time were Alfred de Musset and Charles Baudelaire.

Below: Charles Dickens surrounded by the characters from some of his stories. He was probably the greatest English author of his time (1812-1870). His works tell of some of the dreadful social conditions of his age.

Some authors write historical novels which tell the reader a little bit about a period of history. These novels contain a certain amount of fact as well as fiction. For example, an author could write a novel set in the time of the First World War and describe events that really happened, but at the same time include in his novel characters that he has made up. An author can also write novels set in his own time which are partly fact and partly fiction.

Some literature can be completely true. This type of prose is called nonfiction. If an author writes the life story of a famous person, we call this a biography. When people write about their own lives, these stories are called autobiographies. Both are examples of nonfiction writing. Other examples are histories, scientific articles and books that teach new skills.

Poetry

Poetry can also tell a story. The poet Homer, who lived nearly 3,000 years ago, wrote long stories such as the 'Iliad' and the 'Odyssey' in verse. This kind of poetry which tells a story is known as an epic poem. There are as many different kinds of poetry as there are types of prose. Most do not tell a story, but express ideas or feelings.

The different kinds of poetry can be recognized by the number of lines in each verse, or by noticing which lines rhyme. The most important feature of poetry, though, is its rhythm and different forms of poem have different rhythms. For example, the sonnet, which is a form of poem used by many poets, has a completely different rhythm and rhyme scheme from the humorous limerick.

Below: A common theme in science fiction stories is that of the space ship that transports people backwards and forwards in time. One of the first science fiction writers was H. G. Wells. Others include C. S. Lewis and John Wyndham.

The Theatre

The art of acting in a theatre and writing plays for the theatre is known as drama. Most dramatic events take the form of actors acting out a story by a writer, called a playwright or dramatist.

Because this is usually done on a stage in a theatre, drama is also called theatre. The stories acted in the theatre are called plays. Drama is very much like literature, but is not written only to be read from books. In a way it is a kind of literature brought to life. Poetry too can be brought to life in the form of a play. The early plays were often written in verse, and Shakespeare's plays are in a form called blank verse. Blank verse is a kind of poetry where the lines have a regular rhythm, but there are not usually rhymes at the end of the lines. Most modern plays, though, are written in prose, which makes them more natural and realistic.

Some drama is not written down, but is made up by the actors as they go along. This is called improvisation. Another form of drama is mime. In mime, the actors do not say anything, but tell the story by their movements and facial expressions. In mime make-up and costume is important to show the kind of character that the actor is playing.

Early Drama

The first recorded play was performed by the ancient Egyptians around 2700 BC. The beginning of drama as we know it, however, was in ancient Greece, where it was origi-

nally part of a religious ceremony. The Greek plays were performed in semi-circular theatres built around an altar to the god Dionysus. These outdoor theatres could often hold over 20,000 people who came to see tragic and comic plays. The church in the Middle Ages also used drama as part of its worship, and the Bible stories used in the Christian Mass were later acted outside the church. These mystery and miracle plays became very popular and groups of actors went from town to town with a mobile stage to put these plays on.

Soon, actors and playwrights found new subjects for their plays. Towards the end of the 15th century, the Italians developed the

Above: The ancient Greek theatre at Ephesus. Western drama is said to have its beginnings in Greek theatre.

Below left: Mime (acting without speech) has been perfected by Marcel Marceau.

Below: David Garrick, (1717-1779) was an English actor, dramatist and theatre manager.

Above: William Shakespeare (1564-1616), probably the world's greatest playwright.

commedia dell'arte in which the actors made up their lines as they went along. A hundred years later, in England, William Shakespeare (1564-1616) was writing many plays on historical subjects. Nowadays, plays have as many different subjects as novels do and there are dramatists in many countries writing all kinds of plays.

Often there is some music in plays which we call incidental music. It helps to add atmosphere to the play. When a dramatist asks the actors to sing some songs as well as speak, we call the play a musical. If the actors do not speak at all, but sing all their lines and there is an orchestra playing with them, it is called opera.

Drama can also be found in places other than the theatre. At the end of the last century, cinematography was invented. Today there is a great deal of drama written for the cinema and it has become a popular art form. At first, the films were silent and the cinema was rather like mime on film. But when the 'talkies' were invented this gave dramatists a much more realistic atmosphere to work with.

Almost the exact opposite of mime and silent films is drama for the radio. Radio plays became popular soon after the invention of the radio in the 1920s. Dramatists had to change their style of writing to write radio plays as the audience could not see the movements or the expressions of the actors. The writers of radio plays have to make their stories clear by the words and sounds in their plays. They are still popular today, even though we have television, because people feel that they can use their imagination more when they listen to them.

Television, too, has changed drama. It has brought plays out of the theatre and cinema and into our homes. We can now see productions of all kinds of plays, from Shakespeare to detective stories, without leaving our homes.

Left: A Japanese kabuki play. These plays are full of colour, life and movement.

Below: Behind the scenes of a typical modern, Western theatre.

14 MAN THE BUILDER

From the time that Man moved out of his cave he has been a builder. First it was to provide a roof over his family. Then temples to glorify his gods, and castles to give protection against his enemies. Now, we have the marvels of modern architecture.

Housing

Houses provide a home and a place to keep belongings, but they also protect people from the weather. In hot climates, houses are built to be cool; in cold climates they keep off the rain and keep out the cold. Houses can be built of many different materials and there are almost as many different kinds of houses as people.

The First Houses
In early days houses protected people from wild beasts and enemy tribes. Caves were used because the entrance could be guarded and because, if you go deep enough, the temperature is always mild. Early men also built houses on stilts on lakes, where beasts could not reach them.

In the past, many people earned their living by working in their home. Farmers lived in the same building as the animals who gave them milk, eggs or meat. In Dutch towns, Venice and Hong Kong there are houseboats or houses by canals because people worked or traded on the water.

In most cities, people had their shops or offices on the ground floor of their houses, their living rooms on the first floor, and their bedrooms on the top. This system is as old as the Ancient Romans, and continues today, although now many more people leave their home each day to work elsewhere.

Ruling from Home
Rich and powerful men, whose job it was to rule, also worked from their houses. They needed strong buildings of stone in which the people they ruled and protected could take shelter when enemies attacked. These

Above: Prehistoric cavemen did not build houses. They simply selected a suitable cave, probably near a good hunting ground, and moved in with their few belongings.

Below: In many parts of the world people still lead a wandering life. Their homes must be easy to erect and dismantle like these Bedouin tents in the Negev Desert of Israel.

Building Terms

beam Horizontal support for floor or wall resting on at least two columns.

brickwork A wall made of equal-sized blocks of hard baked clay. Bricks are laid in a pattern to make the wall strong.

column Vertical support used for holding up a roof or floor.

girder A beam, often made of iron or steel, used to support the framework of a building or a bridge.

masonry Natural stone blocks cut to a shape and fitted together to form walls.

mortar A mixture of sand, cement and water used to bind bricks together.

timber frame Heavy timber beams and columns make up a skeleton of a house and the outside walls are built on to it using bricks.

Left: During the Middle Ages the rich nobles of Europe built fortified castles. This imposing castle stands on the edge of the River Rhine in Germany.

Below: The modern trend in housing is to build blocks of flats, usually made from concrete.

Bottom: The crowded waterfront of Hong Kong. Much of the population lives in tall blocks of flats or tenements. Many people live in boats such as these Chinese junks.

were castles. Poor people usually lived in hovels which could easily be knocked down or set on fire.

From Castle to Palace

After the Middle Ages, when law and order was established, rulers turned their castles into palaces. Palaces are unfortified houses where kings and princes ruled and had offices for their court—the people who served them. Many palaces and grand houses survive in Europe. An early and beautiful palace was built by the Duke of Urbino in Italy, and the great French king Louis XIV built a number of palaces, of which Versailles, near Paris, is the largest— the size of a small city.

Even today, heads of government live in special houses. The British Prime Minister rules from a house, No. 10 Downing Street in London, and the President of the United States lives and works in the White House in Washington, D.C. Most people, however, have houses just to sleep and relax in.

Ancient Monuments and Buildings

The first buildings men constructed were probably houses, but from very earliest times people made other kinds of buildings, too.

Some monuments, like Stonehenge in England and similar groups of stones in Malta, Africa and China are difficult to understand. Why did people drag huge stones over miles of ground to arrange them in complicated circles? Was it to make a place to gather for a religious ceremony? Was it to build a temple for worship of the sun? What was its importance to its builders? The usual theory today is that Stonehenge was a primitive clock and calendar.

In order to have Stonehenge built, the priests must have been able to command hundreds of people. In the same way, the Pharaohs of Egypt must have needed thousands of people to build the pyramids for them. The pyramids were built as tombs for the Pharaohs. A Pharaoh would put into his tomb everything he thought he would want in his life after death. The pyramid had to be strong and thief-proof, for he believed that if his goods were stolen his spirit would suffer.

Another reason why people built huge structures was the need for protection. The Romans built two walls in the north of England, Hadrian's Wall and the Antonine Wall, many miles long, to protect them from Scottish invaders. The Great Wall of China was also used for defence.

Above: The ruins of Stonehenge near Salisbury in southern England. It is the best-preserved structure which remains from the New Stone Age.

Below: The Great Wall of China, built as a monument to Shih Huang-ti, the founder of the Ch'in Dynasty. It took many years to build.

Above: The Great Pyramid, showing the entrance to the inner chambers. The pyramids were built by the ancient Egyptians as tombs for their pharaohs.

The Pyramids

There are 70 pyramids in Egypt, some of which are made of stone blocks and others of large clay bricks.

The largest—the Pyramid of Cheops—was 147 metres (482 feet) tall, and 230 metres (756 feet) along the sides.

Many of the stone blocks were cut from local stone which splits fairly easily in good straight faces. If the quarry for the stone was too far away the blocks would be transported by river in special boats and then rolled on logs by slaves because the wheel had not been invented. Ramps built up the side of the pyramid were used to haul the stones to the top. The ramps were afterwards removed.

The Beginning of Architecture

The Greeks and Romans also had buildings of stone—temples for worship, stadiums for contests, theatres, gymnasiums and palaces. They discovered that to make a building beautiful the balance between the different parts that make up the building, or its proportions, must be just right.

Until recently, many Europeans and Americans took their idea of what made a building beautiful from the Romans and Greeks. There are other languages or 'styles' of building, but it was the Greeks who first mastered the art of 'architecture' rather than just building. The Parthenon in Athens is a perfect example of this. The architects of the Parthenon knew exactly how to balance the height and circumference of the columns to achieve a pleasing design. The

shape of the columns also contributes to the light effect that was achieved, even in solid stone.

Many buildings built before the 20th century have columns and domes and many other 'classical' parts, in imitation of the great buildings of the past.

The largest church in the world, St Peter's in Rome, was built in the 15th and 16th centuries to rival the great architecture of the Romans. The architects of St Peter's had studied the Roman Colosseum, which had been built to hold thousands of people. In stone, St Peter's speaks the same language—it is made up of carefully proportioned and beautifully carved columns. Even modern buildings, which are not built in the 'classical' way, need good proportions if they are not to be ugly.

Top: The Colosseum was the largest and most famous amphitheatre to be built by the Romans. Beast hunts and battles between gladiators were held there regularly.

Above: The Parthenon, the temple of Athena on the Acropolis of Athens. Its beautiful proportions have been an inspiration to many architects since it was built in the 5th century BC.

Modern Marvels

Using iron and concrete, modern engineers have made bridges, towers, dams and other buildings of an enormous height and size. But nobody would want tall structures like the Eiffel tower, or the huge blocks of flats or offices that are now in every city, without lifts. Lifts (or elevators) made today's enormous buildings possible. In 1852 an American called Elisha Otis invented the safety lift—not just a lift with a motor to haul people up and let them down, but a lift with a patent safety device to prevent the lift falling if the cable holding it broke.

Before the 18th century, if people wanted a large building, they had to build it in wood and stone. During the Industrial Revolution, however, they learnt how to make iron girders, which are stronger than wooden beams, and so they could make larger buildings.

In the 20th century people discovered that by putting steel girders inside concrete ('reinforced concrete') they had something even stronger than stone. Large modern buildings are built of steel and concrete—they are really huge steel and concrete skeletons clothed with walls. Architects often disguise the bulk of the building's construction by using glass to cover the exterior of skyscrapers.

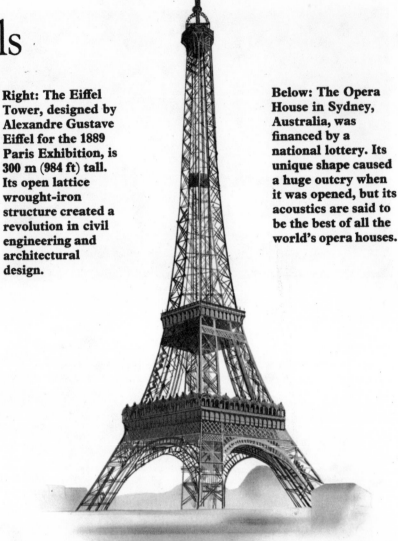

Right: The Eiffel Tower, designed by Alexandre Gustave Eiffel for the 1889 Paris Exhibition, is 300 m (984 ft) tall. Its open lattice wrought-iron structure created a revolution in civil engineering and architectural design.

Below: The Opera House in Sydney, Australia, was financed by a national lottery. Its unique shape caused a huge outcry when it was opened, but its acoustics are said to be the best of all the world's opera houses.

Tallest Structures

The tallest structures in the world are radio masts. They are made of steel with cables called 'guy ropes' to keep them up. The tallest, the Warszawa mast, is in Poland. It is 645 metres (2,110 feet) tall.

The second tallest group of structures is broadcasting towers. The tallest is the Canadian National in Toronto. It is 553 metres (1,815 feet) tall, and it was built in one continuous operation. The main part of the tower is built of concrete and this was poured day after day into a special mould which climbed up the tower as the core grew taller. This special method is called slipforming and when the weather permitted the special moulding apparatus was climbing at a top speed of 6 metres (20 feet) a day.

The tallest office building is the Sears Tower in Chicago. It is 442 metres (1,975 feet) high.

Britain's tallest structure is the Post Office tower—189 metres (613 feet) tall.

Top: The Olympic Stadium built for the 1972 Games used modern materials to create a splendid venue for the athletic events.

Above: The two towers of the World Trade Centre in New York dominate the skyline of lower Manhattan.

Left: The tallest tower in the world is the CN Tower in Toronto, Canada. It is 553 m (1,815 ft) high.

High Rise

Even with a lift to go up in, most people prefer to live close to the ground, so that they can come in and go out without a journey. The reason why blocks of flats and offices are built so tall is that there is so little space on the ground in the centre of cities. If you spread out Manhattan, the centre of New York, into ordinary buildings of three or four floors, it would make the city at least five times wider—and this is impossible, since Manhattan is an island.

When buildings were made of stone, there was a limited number of shapes they could take. With reinforced concrete, architects can design buildings in almost any shape they like. The Sydney Opera House is a good example of the new trend in modern architecture.

Bridges

Bridges are platforms crossing empty spaces, and they need to be supported. Through history engineers have found better means of supporting their platforms and of making them longer.

The simplest sort of bridge is a log bridge. The Romans supported their bridges on arches. They built bridges several miles long with hundreds of arches to carry water from the mountains to the cities—these bridges are called aqueducts.

Another way to cross space is to support the platform on a kind of scaffolding. Both wooden and iron bridges have been built with various kinds of scaffolding. The ancestor of the huge modern bridges was the first bridge built of metal girders, at Coalbrookdale in Shropshire in 1779. There are two main types of scaffolding bridges: those with scaffolding underneath which supports the platform by pushing and those with scaffolding above (suspension bridges) which supports it by pulling.

Left: The first bridges were probably built by early man to overcome the problem of getting from one side of a river to the other. They simply placed a tree trunk over the water so that an.end rested on each bank.

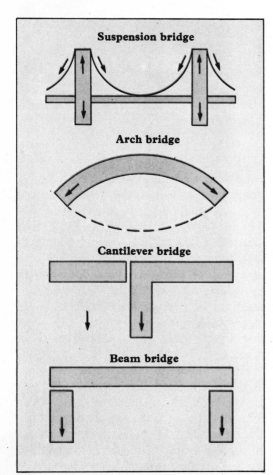

Suspension bridge

Arch bridge

Cantilever bridge

Beam bridge

Above: Tower Bridge, across London's River Thames, is a famous example of a *bascule* bridge—it moves up and down rather like a drawbridge.

Below: Suspension bridges, such as the George Washington bridge in New York, are very graceful structures which can easily span a gap of 1000 metres.

198

Dams

The first reason why men built dams was to control the watering of their crops. The ancient Egyptians built small dams to control the way the Nile River flowed into their fields, and Asian farmers do the same today in their paddy fields.

Later, dams were built to control rivers, to prevent them flooding or to keep them deep enough for boats to travel on. These dams, called locks, had gates which opened to let the boats go by, and openings called sluices which let the water through the gate when the level of water behind it was high enough.

Then people found that water passing through a sluice could turn a wheel and produce power. Before electricity was invented, watermills provided power all over Europe and Asia.

Water is still used today to provide power, and this is the chief reason why dams are built. 'Hydroelectric' dams build up a store of water which escapes through sluices and turns dynamos that produce electricity. The largest hydroelectric dams can provide electricity for domestic and industrial use over a wide region. Scientists are now experimenting with ways of damming the waves of the sea to make power.

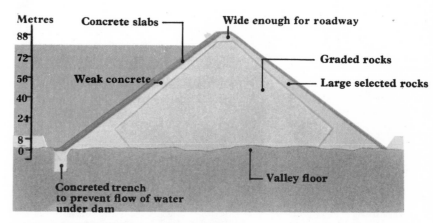

The Largest Dam in the World

The tallest dam in the world is the giant Nurek embankment dam in Russia. It stands 317 metres (1,040 feet) high and is 730 metres (2,400 feet) long.

But the largest dam in the world, if you go by the amount of material taken to form the embankment, is the Tarbela Dam in Pakistan. This dam rises to a height of 143 metres (470 feet) and stretches 3 kilometres (nearly 2 miles) in length.

The biggest reservoir in the world is in Russia. It holds enough water to cover the state of Texas 300 millimetres (1 foot) deep in water.

Above: A cross-section of a rock-fill dam showing the various materials used in its construction. The choice of site depends upon the purpose of the dam.

Below: The Kariba dam, on the Zimbabwe/Zambian border, is 128 m (420 ft) high and 618 m (2025 ft) long. A road runs along the top of the dam.

15 SPORTS

Games and sports are exciting and colourful features in the lives of many people. Sporting events and personalities have created traditions which have played a strong part in the social history of many nations all over the world.

Glossary of Sports

Archery A sport in which competitors use bows and arrows. The main variations of archery are target shooting, flight, field and cross-bow. In target shooting, archers are awarded points for shooting a given number of arrows at a target made up of five circles, within one another.

Baseball Outdoor bat-and-ball game played by two teams of nine players each, on a diamond-shaped pitch. Teams take it in turn to bat and field. Each team tries to score more runs than the other. A player scores a run when he circles all the bases round the pitch without being put out.

Basketball Indoor or outdoor ball game played on a marked court between two teams of five players each. The object is to hold on to the ball by bouncing it and passing it by hand to team mates, and finally throw it into the other team's basket and thus score a goal. *Baskets* are small bottomless nets, one of which hangs three metres (ten feet) above the ground at each end of the court.

Above: A young archer aims for the innermost circle.

Below: Baseball in San Francisco —Giants v Dodgers.

Above: Bicycle road racing is run on public roads.

Above: Fishing is one of the world's most popular sports.

Below: The Oakland Raiders, an American football team.

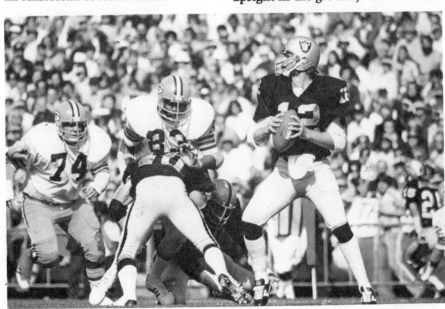

Billiards games Indoor ball games played on a long table covered with green felt with six pockets around the edges. Players drive coloured plastic balls against other balls and into the pockets with a long stick called a *cue*.

Boxing Ancient sport in which two fighters in a roped square and wearing special boxing gloves, punch each other on the face and on the body above the waist. A fighter wins by scoring most points for good punching or by knocking the other man down for more than ten seconds (*a knock-out*).

Cricket Outdoor bat-and-ball game played on grass between two 11-man teams. The bowler bowls a ball at the *wicket* (three wooden sticks stuck upright in the ground). The batsman defends the wicket and tries to hit the ball with a bat and score runs.

Cycling Bicycle racing between individual people or teams.
Track races are run on oval tracks that slope inward at a steep angle at each end.
Road races are run on public roads, and may be 80 kilometres (50 miles) or more long.

Fishing The catching of various kinds of fish for sport, using rods, lines, hooks, and bait; also called *angling*. Freshwater fishing is carried out in inland waters such as rivers and lakes; sea fishing is done in the sea, either from land or from boats.

Football Outdoor ball game in which two teams of eleven players each try to carry, throw or kick an egg-shaped ball across the other team's goal-line. Played almost wholly in the United States, it is often called *American Football*.

Golf Outdoor club-and-ball game in which the player knocks a small white ball over a long grass course into a small hole. He uses sticks with bent or shaped heads and tries to hit the ball as few times as possible. A golf course has nine or 18 holes.

Gymnastics Indoor sport of strength, grace and speed, using special equipment. Set exercises for men are floor exercises, vault, pommel-horse, parallel bars, horizontal bars, and rings. Women do floor exercises, vault, beam and asymmetrical bars.

Hockey Stick-and-ball game of two main kinds: *ice hockey* and *field hockey*. Ice hockey is played on an ice rink by two six-man teams wearing skates. They try to drive a hard wooden disc, called a *puck*, with long wooden sticks along the ice and into a goal cage at each end of the rink. Field hockey is played by two teams of eleven players each on a grass pitch. They use curved sticks to try and hit a small ball into one of the goals at each end of the pitch.

Glossary of Sports (2)

Above: HRH Princess Anne on her event horse, Goodwill.

Below: Unarmed combat is practised for self-defence.

Horse-riding events Competitions to test the speed, strength and ability of horse and rider. They include *dressage* (a series of special movements) and *show jumping*. The *three-day* event includes a cross-country test.

Japanese martial arts Forms of competitive sport based on self-defence and unarmed combat.

Judo developed from a form of self-defence called *jujitsu*. An opponent could be crippled or killed using only bare hands and feet. Judo means 'the gentle way'. A judo fighter yields to his opponent's attack until the right moment to counter-attack. He then tries to unbalance his opponent, throw him, and pin him to the floor.

Karate is another form of unarmed combat in which the hands, feet, elbows and knees are all used to strike an opponent. Karate means 'empty hand'. Blows are aimed at the softest parts of the body, such as the throat and stomach. In sport, contestants stop short of actually hitting each other or, at most, just touch each other lightly.

Kendo is the Japanese art of sword fighting. The word means 'sword way'. Contestants wear protective clothing or armour and usually fight with bamboo sticks. Real swords are sometimes used by experts. The object is to land two scoring blows on the opponent's target area.

Rugby football Outdoor game played with an egg-shaped ball by two teams. The ball is passed backwards, or kicked, or carried until a player can kick it over the other team's goal crossbar or touch it down behind the goal line, for points. Amateur teams play *Rugby Union* (15 players), professionals play *Rugby League* (13 players).

Soccer Football game played with a round ball between two teams of eleven players. Players try to kick or head the ball through the other team's goal. When in play, the ball may be handled only by the goalkeepers, in their own area. Also called *football* or *assocation football*.

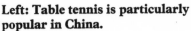

shot-put, discus, and hammer. Also called *athletics*.

Water sports Sports that can be divided into two main groups: swimming and diving, and boating.

Pool swimming includes races over 100, 200, 400, and 1,500 metres, using either free-style or some other predetermined stroke such as butter-fly, breast stroke, or back stroke; or a mixture of strokes.

Water polo is a team water sport with seven strong swimmers in each team. The object is to throw or head a large inflated ball into the opponents' goal.

Diving takes place in pools. High diving is from platforms at 5, 7.5 and 10 metres above the water. Springboard diving is from springboards fixed at heights of 1 and 3 metres.

Boating covers rowing, canoeing, sailing and powerboat racing. Rowing is divided into *sculling* and *sweep-oar* racing. In sculling, each oarsman uses two oars. Such boats include single sculls, double sculls and quadruple sculls. In sweep-oar racing each member of the crew handles one much bigger and heavier oar. Such crafts hold two, four, or eight men. Eights, and sometimes fours, hold an extra man—the *coxswain* or *cox*—who steers the boat.

Canoeing is a sport in which one or more people sit in a small craft facing forwards, and paddle through the water. The craft may be a *canoe*, which is pointed at both ends and is propelled with a single-bladed paddle; or a *kayak*, in which the paddler uses a double-bladed paddle.

Sailing or yachting can be carried out in many different types of sailing boats. Boats in the same class compete against each other.

Wrestling Form of unarmed combat using arms and legs to grasp and throw, and usually hold, an opponent on the floor. *Sumo* wrestling takes place mainly in Japan; *free-style* and *Graeco-Roman* are practised in many parts of the world.

Squash Indoor game played by two or four players in a special four-walled court. Players hit a small, hard ball with long-handled rackets so that it bounces off walls and floor.

Table tennis Speedy indoor game for two or four players, played on a long table. Players face each other and, with a rubber-covered paddle, hit a small plastic ball so that it passes over a net stretched midway across the table. The ball must bounce once each time before being hit.

Tennis Game for two or four players played with rackets and a ball on a specially marked indoor or outdoor court. Players hit the ball to and fro over a net across the middle of the court. Each player tries to hit the ball so that the opponent cannot hit it back over the net within the court. Also called *lawn tennis*.

Track and field General name for running, jumping and throwing competitions. *Track* events are races over various distances, usually from 100 to 10,000 metres. *Field* events include long jump, high jump, pole vault and triple jump; and throwing competitions such as the javelin,

Above left: Sir Francis Chichester, lone yachtsman.

Left: Undersea diving is a fascinating sport.

203

Olympic Games

The Olympic Games are the greatest celebrations of sport in the world. They are held every four years. Nearly all the nations of the world take part. Thousands of athletes gather to compete in all kinds of sports, from athletics and swimming to archery and weightlifting.

Team sports include soccer and hockey outdoors and basketball and volleyball indoors. Combat sports include fencing, boxing, and wrestling. There are also water sports, such as sailing and rowing. Horse-riding, gymnastics and cycling are other major Olympic sports.

A separate festival is held in the same year for winter sports. These include skating, skiing, tobogganing, bobsledding and ice hockey.

The Olympics are for amateurs—that is, the competitors do not get paid. The winners receive gold medals, the seconds silver, and the thirds bronze. It is considered a great honour by many sportsmen and women to compete in the Games.

Far left: Baron Pierre de Coubertin, the Frenchman who pioneered the modern Olympics. He modelled them on the ancient Greek Olympics.

Below: Speed skating, one of the winter sports, which are held as a separate games at a different venue.

Bottom: Nadia Comaneci, the young Romanian gymnast who won 3 gold medals in the 1976 Olympics at the age of 14.

Olympic Games		Winter Olympics
1896	Athens, Greece	*The first separate Winter Olympics were held in 1924. But previous to that, figure skating and ice hockey had been included in the main Games.*
1900	Paris, France	
1904	St. Louis, USA	
1908	London, England	
1912	Stockholm, Sweden	
1920	Antwerp, Belgium	
1924	Paris, France	Chamonix, France
1928	Amsterdam, Holland	St. Moritz, Switzerland
1932	Los Angeles, USA	Lake Placid, USA
1936	Berlin, Germany	Garmisch-Partenkirchen, Germany
1948	London, England	St. Moritz, Switzerland
1952	Helsinki, Finland	Oslo, Norway
1956	Melbourne, Australia	Cortina, Italy
1960	Rome, Italy	Squaw Valley, USA
1964	Tokyo, Japan	Innsbruck, Austria
1968	Mexico City, Mexico	Grenoble, France
1972	Munich, W. Germany	Sapporo, Japan
1976	Montreal, Canada	Innsbruck, Austria
1980	Moscow, USSR	Lake Placid, USA

World Cup

The World Cup rivals the Olympics as the greatest event in international sport. All the world's soccer-playing nations compete in groups over a period of nearly two years. The winners of these groups go forward to the finals, which are held every four years. Most of the finalists are from Europe and South America.

The sixteen teams that reach the finals are divided into four groups, in which the four teams play each other. The top two teams in each group then go forward to two semi-final groups of four. The winners of these meet in the final, which is watched on television by hundreds of millions of viewers in all parts of the world.

Brazil have been the most successful team in the World Cup. When they won it in 1970 for the third time, they kept the famous Jules Rimet Trophy, named after the Frenchman who was president of FIFA, Soccer's international governing body, from 1920 to 1954. The new trophy is the FIFA World Cup, presented by FIFA. Uruguay, Italy and West Germany have each won the World Cup twice. England and Argentina have won it once each.

World Cup Finals

Year	Where held	Winners		Runners-up	
1930	Montevideo, Uruguay	Uruguay	4	Argentina	2
1934	Rome, Italy	Italy	2	Czechoslovakia	1
1938	Paris, France	Italy	4	Hungary	2
1950	*Rio de Janeiro, Brazil	Uruguay	2	Brazil	1
1954	Berne, Switzerland	West Germany	3	Hungary	2
1958	Stockholm, Sweden	Brazil	5	Sweden	2
1962	Santiago, Chile	Brazil	3	Czechoslovakia	1
1966	Wembley, England	England	4	West Germany	2
1970	Mexico City, Mexico	Brazil	4	Italy	1
1974	Munich, West Germany	West Germany	2	Netherlands	1
1978	Buenos Aires, Argentina	Argentina	3	Netherlands	1

*Deciding match of final group.

Top: The colourful scene at the opening ceremony of the 1970 World Cup, at the Aztec Stadium in Mexico City.

Left: Tostão of Brazil in action during the 1970 World Cup. With Jairzinho and the great Pelé, he was one of the exciting stars who helped Brazil to win the trophy for the third time.

Famous Sporting Figures

Muhammad Ali stands scowling in triumph over Sonny Liston after knocking him down in the first round of their second fight in 1964. Liston did not get up, and Ali was still champion.

ALI, Muhammad
American boxer, world heavyweight champion. As Cassius Clay, he first won the title in 1964, from the ferocious Sonny Liston. He forfeited the title for refusing, for religious reasons, to join the armed forces, but regained it in 1974 from George Foreman. Remarkably quick for a heavyweight, he also became known for his fast talking. After losing to Leon Spink in 1978, he won the return fight the same year to take the championship for a record third time.

BANNISTER, Sir Roger
British athlete, the first man to run a mile in under 4 minutes. His time of 3 minutes 59.4 seconds at Oxford in 1954 was a great milestone in athletics.

BEAMON, Bob
American athlete, Olympic long jump champion in 1968. His leap of 8.90 metres (29 feet 2½ inches) in Mexico City beat the world record by 55 centimetres (1 foot 9½ inches).

BORG, Bjorn
Swedish tennis player, Wimbledon champion for the third consecutive time in 1978. Only 22 at the time, he was the first man to accomplish this feat for over 40 years.

BRADMAN, Sir Donald
Australian cricketer, widely regarded as the finest batsman of all time. He captained Australia in 5 Test series and averaged 99.94 runs per innings in his 52 Test matches from 1928 to 1948.

EVERT-LLOYD, Chris
American tennis player, the outstanding

Right: Chris Evert-Lloyd, outstanding tennis star of the 1970s.

Centre: Roger Bannister breaks the tape in his historic mile.

Bottom: Babe Ruth, the man who brought the crowds to baseball.

figure in the women's game from the mid-1970s. She first won the Wimbledon singles titles in 1974, at the age of 19.

FRASER, Dawn
Australian swimmer, the first woman to break 60 seconds for the 100 metres freestyle. She won her third successive Olympic gold medal at this event in the 1964 Games

LAVER, Rod
Australian tennis player, the only man to win the 'Grand Slam' twice. This involves winning the world's four major traditional titles (Wimbledon, US, Australian, and French) in one year. He did it as an amateur in 1962 and then as a professional in 1969.

MEADS, Colin
New Zealand ruby union lock-forward. He won 55 international caps, and captained the All Blacks.

MOORE, Bobby
English soccer player, and captain of the side that won the World Cup in 1966. A wing-half at first and then a central defender, he won 108 international caps.

NICKLAUS, Jack
American golfer, one of the biggest hitters in the game, consistently the world's leading golfer since the late 1960s, he set numerous records in the major tournaments.

PELÉ
Brazilian soccer player, the star of the 1958 and 1970 World Cups. He scored over 1,200 goals for Brazil and his club Santos. He helped to make soccer popular in the United States when he played for the New York Cosmos in 1977 before retiring. His name was Edson Arantes do Nascimento.

PLAYER, Gary
South African golfer, the first non-American to win the world's four major titles (including the British and US Open Championships). He was a consistent big tournament winner from the mid-1960s.

RUTH, 'Babe'
American baseball player. He set numerous batting records with the New York Yankees, including 60 home runs in a season (1927) and 714 in his career. His big hitting brought huge crowds flocking to watch baseball in the 1920s.

SOBERS, Sir Gary
West Indian cricketer, from Barbados. The outstanding all-rounder in the game, he scored a world record 8,032 runs in 93 Tests, including a record 365 not out against Pakistan in 1958. He also took 235 Test wickets. He once hit 6 sixes in an over when playing against Glamorgan (1968).

SPITZ, Mark
American swimmer, winner of a record 7 gold medals at the 1972 Olympic Games. Four were for individual events (freestyle and butterfly) and all were won in new world record times.

SURTEES, John
The only man to win the world championship in both motorcyling and motor racing. An Englishman, he won all his titles with Italian machines—MV Agusta motorcycles (late 1930s) and Ferrari cars (1964).

VIREN, Lasse
Finnish athlete, the leading middle-distance runner of the 1970s. He won the 5,000 and 10,000 metres Olympic titles at the 1972 and the 1976 Games in Munich and Montreal.

FAMOUS LIVES

There are a great many people who have made history through various actions and achievements. Whether through a spirit of adventure, curiosity or a deeply-felt cause, these people played an important part in shaping our world.

Mighty Conquerors

ALEXANDER THE GREAT (356-323 BC) was one of the greatest generals of all time. At 20 he was crowned king of Macedonia, a mountainous region in south-east Europe.

In 334 BC he invaded Persia with an army of 35,000 men and little money. But he won a quick victory and stormed on into Asia Minor. A year later, when King Darius of Persia had raised another large army to fight him, Alexander defeated the Persians again with his newly-formed *phalanx* (a solid square of soldiers with long spears).

He freed Egypt from the Persians and built the great city of Alexandria there, naming it after himself. He conquered the whole of Asia Minor, and marched eastwards to Afghanistan and India. Eventually his men refused to go any further, and he had to turn back. He died of a mosquito bite at the age of 32.

HANNIBAL (247-183 BC) was the greatest general of Carthage, an ancient North African city. When the Romans declared war on Carthage in 218 BC, Hannibal decided to invade Italy from Spain.

It was a bold and risky adventure, and was quite unexpected by the Romans. Hannibal led 60,000 men, 6,000 horses, and 37 elephants across the Pyrenees and the Alps.

In 216 BC he defeated a large army at Cannae in southern Italy. It was the worst defeat ever suffered by a Roman army, but because of poor support from Carthage Hannibal never did capture Rome. He spent his last years helping other rulers to fight the Romans in Syria and what is now Turkey. When he was faced with capture by his old enemies the Romans, Hannibal ended his life by swallowing poison.

Above: Alexander defeating the Persians at Issus.

Below: Hannibal and his elephants in the Alps.

CAESAR, JULIUS (*c.* 100-44 BC) was a Roman soldier and statesman, and one of the great rulers of his time. He became one of the rulers of Rome in 60 BC together with Marcus Licinius Crassus and Gnaeus Pompey.

In order to gain more power, Caesar invaded Gaul (France) and Britain. But Pompey became alarmed and jealous at Caesar's success and popularity and in 49 BC ordered him to give up his army. Caesar refused and launched a civil war. Pompey fled and Caesar conquered Italy in less than 50 days.

He was made absolute ruler for life, but some Romans feared that he would crown himself king. They plotted to prevent this and stabbed him to death.

ATTILA (*c.* 406-453) was king of the Huns, a mongoloid tribe centred in what is now Hungary. The rulers of the eastern Roman Empire paid him a lot of money each year to keep him from invading their land. But if dues were late thousands of fierce warriors on horseback would attack. He was referred to as 'the scourge of God'.

He attacked Germany and Gaul (France) but in 451 the Romans managed to force him back over the Rhine. In 452 he invaded Italy but his army was hungry and sick and he had to return to his homeland. He died on his wedding night and shortly afterwards his kingdom was split up.

NAPOLEON I (**Bonaparte**) (1769-1821) was born in Corsica. He became a soldier and was soon promoted to major and then brigadier general.

In 1796 he was sent to Italy to drive out the Austrians. He succeeded brilliantly and

Above: Caesar was a proud and ambitious man.

Above: Attila was much feared by the Romans.

Right: Hitler salutes his armies in 1941.

Below: Napoleon at the battle of Austerlitz.

returned to Paris a hero.

In 1804 Napoleon was made emperor. He defeated the Austrian and Russian armies at Austerlitz, but was beaten by the British under Lord Nelson in a sea battle at Trafalgar in 1805.

He invaded Russia in 1812 and fought his way to Moscow, but he had to retreat when the Russian winter set in.

In 1814 he gave up his throne and was exiled to Elba. He escaped and raised an army but was beaten by Wellington at Waterloo. He died in exile on St. Helena.

HITLER, ADOLF (1889-1945) was born in Austria and during his early years he was very poor. He built up a hatred of all Jewish people because he blamed them for his wretched state. During the First World War he fought bravely in the German army and after the war he became leader of the 'Nationalist Socialist Workers' (Nazi) Party.

Within a few years he became master of all Germany. He carried out cruel acts against the Jews and other groups of people, and re-armed the German forces. He believed that the Germans were a master race and he invaded neighbouring lands to gain more territory for the German nation. His invasion of Poland in 1939 sparked off the Second World War. After nearly six years of fighting Germany was defeated in 1945. In the last days of the war Hitler was thought to have shot himself.

Bold Adventurers

RALEIGH, SIR WALTER (*c.* 1552-1618) was an adventurous English soldier, and a favourite of Queen Elizabeth I.

Raleigh explored parts of North America from North Carolina to Florida and tried more than once to establish an English colony there, but failed. He called the whole region Virginia, after Queen Elizabeth, who was known as the Virgin Queen.

Raleigh helped to introduce the potato and tobacco into Ireland from America. He helped to defeat the Spanish Armada in 1588. But he lost the Queen's favour when he married one of her maids-of-honour.

Elizabeth died in 1603, and the new king, James I, did not like or trust Raleigh. He eventually had Raleigh beheaded for disobeying orders.

LAWRENCE, THOMAS EDWARD (1888-1935) was a British soldier, secret agent, and author who so greatly helped the Arab cause in the First World War that he became known as Lawrence of Arabia.

When war broke out in 1914 Lawrence was sent to Egypt and found himself helping the Arabs free themselves from Turkish rule. Promoted to the rank of colonel, and

Above: Sir Walter Raleigh.

Below: Lawrence of Arabia.

often dressed and disguised as an Arab himself, he led many daring and successful raids across the desert against the Turks.

But after the war Lawrence was not able to do much for his Arab friends. Disappointed, he left his government job and joined the Royal Air Force. In 1926 he published a book, *Seven Pillars of Wisdom*, which recounts his experiences in fighting for the Arab cause. He was killed some years later while riding a powerful motorcycle.

EARHART, AMELIA (1897-1937?) was an American airwoman. She was the first woman passenger to cross the Atlantic Ocean by air and the first woman to fly it alone.

Miss Earhart set up a number of other records, including the first flight made by a woman from Honolulu to the United States mainland, and the first flight by a woman across the United States in both directions.

Her colourful career was suddenly cut short when she vanished mysteriously in 1937 near Howland Island in the Pacific, during an attempt to fly around the world. No trace of her or her airplane was ever found.

STANLEY, SIR HENRY MORTON (1841-1904) was a British journalist and explorer who will always be remembered for his journey to find the Scottish explorer and missionary **DR DAVID LIVINGSTONE** (1813-73).

Livingstone was sent out to Bechuanaland in Africa (now Botswana) by the London Missionary Society in 1841. He wanted to convert people to Christianity, and he hoped to end the slave trade by replacing it with legitimate commerce. He also wanted to explore the largely unknown continent of Africa. He discovered Victoria Falls in 1855 and explored the eastern Zambezi River from 1858 to 1864 and in 1866 set off on an unsuccessful journey to find where the Nile River began.

Nobody heard from him for some years. Because of fears for his safety, Henry Morton Stanley, a British journalist working for the New York *Herald*, was sent out to look for him. After many exciting adventures he found him in the town of Ujiji on the shores of Lake Tanganyika. On seeing this gaunt white man in the jungle, Stanley,

ever polite, is reported to have said: 'Dr Livingstone, I presume!' Livingstone refused to go back to the coast with Stanley, and died a year later at Lake Bangweulu. The local people had loved this old doctor for his courage and healing touch, and they mourned his death.

On hearing of Livingstone's death, Stanley returned to Africa to continue his friend's work. He led a number of daring expeditions, made important discoveries, and established the Congo Free State for Belgium, after the British had showed no interest in the region.

Top: Amelia Earhart, American airwoman.

Middle: Stanley went in search of Livingstone.

Above: Livingstone went to Africa as a missionary.

Right: Hillary and Tenzing on top of the world.

HILLARY, SIR EDMUND PERCIVAL (1919-) and **TENZING NORGAY** (c. 1914-) were the first mountaineers to reach the top of Mount Everest, the world's highest mountain. Hillary, a New Zealander, had already climbed part of the way up Mount Everest in 1951 and 1952. In 1953 he reached the top with Tenzing Norgay, the Sherpa guide to the expedition. Queen Elizabeth II later knighted Hillary for this feat.

Hillary wrote the story of this wonderful climb in a book called *High Adventure* (1955). In 1957 and 1958 he set up base camps for Sir Vivian Fuchs' famous expedition across Antarctica from McMurdo Sound to the South Pole.

In 1960 he led an expedition that climbed the Himalayan peak, Mount Makalu I (8,480 metres, 27,824 feet). This was in order to test man's ability to live at great heights without using oxygen. The expedition also looked for a creature called the Abominable Snowman. Hillary described this climb in a book called *High in the Thin Cold Air* (1962).

Valiant Crusaders

BOOTH, WILLIAM (1829-1912) was the founder of the Salvation Army. As a Methodist minister he became unhappy with his work and in 1861 he left the church and devoted the rest of his life to working among the poor.

In 1865 he and his wife started holding open-air meetings in the poorest parts of London. They formed their followers into a mission band, and in 1878 named it the Salvation Army. It was a semi-military organization formed to declare war on the devil and all his works. Booth was tireless in organizing meetings and encouraging effort and self-denial among the workers. His courage and sincerity gained him respect throughout the world and turned the Salvation Army into the vast and honoured movement it is today.

JOAN OF ARC (1412-31) was a French heroine. When still very young she said she saw visions which she believed were messages from heaven telling her to lead the French armies. At the time, much of northern France was held by England. Joan believed it was her mission to free her country from the English.

At 17 she persuaded King Charles VII of France to let her command the French soldiers against the English at Orleans, which was under siege, or blockaded. By the clever use of her armies and her own bravery she defeated the enemy and lifted the siege of the city. She went on to free Reims and saw the coronation there of Charles VII as king of all France. Joan defeated the English wherever she met them. But she failed to take Paris. Badly wounded, she was captured by the Burgundians who sold her to their English allies.

The English accused her of being a witch and of being disobedient to the Church. They sentenced her to death, and on 30 May 1431 she was cruelly burnt to death tied to a stake in the city of Rouen.

Because of Joan's victories, however, the French gained a dominant position over the English armies and by 1453 had turned them out of France. In 1456 Joan was found innocent and in 1920 the Roman Catholic Church declared her a saint.

Above: William Booth (1829-1912), founder and first general of the Christian Mission, later renamed the Salvation Army.

Below: Joan of Arc (1412-1431) who, after performing many valiant deeds for her country, was burned as a witch.

Above: Saint Paul was blinded by a vision and heard the word of God on the road to Damascus.

Below: Brigham Young (1801-1877), the second president of the Mormon church which is still based in Salt Lake City, Utah.

SAINT PAUL (*c.* AD 3- *c.* 68) was the most important of the early Christian leaders. His story is told in the Bible.

Paul was at first called Saul, and he was a well-educated, very religious Jew. He had never met Jesus, but he hated all Christians and whenever he found them he had them thrown into prison.

One day, on his way from Jerusalem to Damascus to arrest more Christians, Saul was suddenly surrounded by a dazzling bright light and fell to the ground, blinded.

He claimed he heard Jesus saying: 'Saul, Saul, why do you persecute me?' Saul immediately saw the wrong he had been doing, humbly changed his name to Paul, and soon recovered his sight.

The rest of his life was spent preaching Christianity in much of Asia Minor. He had many hair-raising adventures. He was stoned, flogged, and shipwrecked, but his faith in God never failed. He was finally imprisoned in Rome and executed.

YOUNG, BRIGHAM (1801-77) was the second president of the Church of Jesus Christ of Latter-Day Saints, better known as the Mormons.

Joseph Smith, the founder of the church, was shot and killed by unbelievers in Illinois in 1844. To avoid further trouble, Brigham Young led the little band of Mormons on a long trek to the Great Salt Lake valley in Utah.

The desert all round was barren and the settlers were faced with many problems, but under Young's leadership they made the desert bud and blossom. Young is credited with leading 100,000 persons to the mountain valleys.

Revolutionary Thinkers

BUDDHA (*c.* 563-483 BC) was the title given to Siddhartha Gautama, the Indian who founded the Buddhist religion.

When he was a young man he left home to look for an answer to life's problems. He finally found the answer, or enlightenment, while sitting under a bodhi tree in Gaya. He realized that *nirvana,* a state of absolute peace and happiness, could bring release from the pressures of life. This state could only be reached by giving up all desires for worldly things.

ARISTOTLE (384-322 BC) was a Greek thinker, educator, and scientist. His ideas have had more influence on the thinking of the western world than those of almost any other person. He was a pupil of the philosopher Plato for 20 years and these two men are regarded as the most important of the ancient Greek thinkers. Aristotle was the tutor of Alexander the Great.

In 334 BC Aristotle founded a school in Athens called the Lyceum. He wrote and taught deeply on many subjects, including science, religion, astronomy, logic and politics. Aristotle's philosophy is characterized by its emphasis on reason and practicality. But the people of Athens accused him of not worshipping their gods properly and he left Athens to avoid a sentence of death.

Above: Buddha, the Enlightened One.

Right: Aristotle, a great scholar.

Below: Darwin, and HMS *Beagle.*

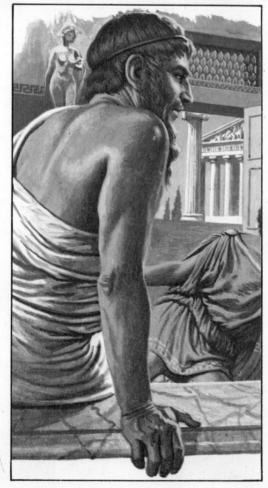

DARWIN, CHARLES (1809-82) was an English scientist who worked out the *theory of evolution by natural selection.* In *The Origin of Species,* Darwin showed that living things evolve, or develop, because some individuals are produced with characteristics that make them better able to adapt to their environment. These plants and animals are more likely to survive to pass on their special characteristics than those that are not so well adapted.

Darwin worked out his ideas after a long expedition in HMS *Beagle* to South America and the Galapagos Islands in the eastern Pacific Ocean.

Top: Karl Marx lived and studied in England for many years.

Above: Gandhi walked barefoot around India preaching peace and love.

Left: Martin Luther King spoke out against the injustices to black people.

MARX, KARL (1818-83) was a notable German thinker. His ideas were published in three long books called *Das Kapital.*

Marx believed that there was a constant struggle between what he called the ruling, and the working classes. He preached that *capitalism,* or free enterprise, was doomed, and that *socialism,* which means that land, money, and other means of production should be owned and controlled by the workers, was bound to take its place through revolution.

Today Marx is regarded as the founder of the Communist movement.

GANDHI, MOHANDAS KARAM-CHAND (1869-1948) was one of India's greatest men. He lived for many years in South Africa where he led strikes and protests against the unjust treatment by whites of non-whites. Back in India he used totally non-violent methods—fasting, marches, non-payment of taxes—to assist in freeing his country from the rule of the British. He believed in the brotherhood of all men and tried to unite India's Muslims and Hindus, its rich and its poor.

KING, MARTIN LUTHER, Jr (1929-68) was an American Negro who led the fight for fair treatment for his fellow Negroes. King first gained national attention in 1955 when he organized a boycott of segregated buses in Montgomery, Alabama. Like Gandhi, he used non-violent methods. He made an inspired speech during a massive demonstration in Washington. This was a turning point: soon laws were passed to give Negroes equal rights with whites. He received the Nobel peace prize for his efforts. Like Gandhi, King was killed by someone who opposed his ideas.

Pioneers and Inventors

The Archimedean screw

ARCHIMEDES (*c.* 287-212 BC) was a Greek mathematician and inventor who discovered a scientific law by proving that the King of Syracuse had been cheated. The king wanted to know if his crown was made of pure gold or not. Archimedes solved the problem while sitting in his bath and watching some of the water spill out. He was so excited that he rushed into the street, dripping wet and naked, shouting 'Eureka' (which means 'I have found it' in Greek).

Archimedes realized that all he had to do was to plunge the crown into a bucketful of water and measure the overflow. He then did the same with an equal weight of gold. The amounts of spilled water were not the same, so Archimedes sadly told the king that the gold in his crown must have been mixed with some other metal.

Archimedes had discovered the scientific rule of specific gravity. He also discovered the principle of buoyancy. He found that an object becomes lighter when it is submerged in water. The weight it loses is equal to the weight of the water it displaces.

One of his most useful inventions was the Archimedean screw. This is a long spiral screw that is turned by a handle and raises water from a lower to a higher level.

Archimedes was killed by the Romans when they captured Syracuse in 212 BC.

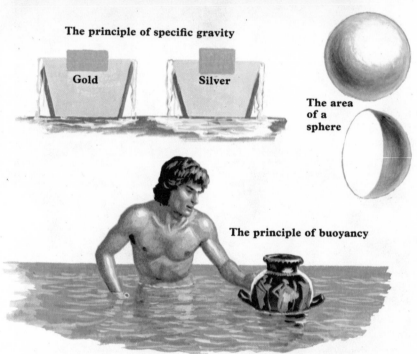

The principle of specific gravity

Gold

Silver

The area of a sphere

The principle of buoyancy

EDISON, THOMAS ALVA (1847-1931) was a famous American inventor, whose inventions have had a dramatic effect on modern life.

As a boy he sold newspapers at railroad stations and learnt how to use the telegraph machines for sending messages. During several years in Boston as a telegraphist, he invented many electrical gadgets.

People began to pay for his inventions and his fame spread. In 1876 he moved to Menlo Park, New Jersey, and the world came to know him as 'the Wizard of Menlo Park'. A year later he invented the phonograph or record player.

His most famous and useful invention was the electric light bulb in 1879. Altogether he filed more than 1,100 inventions under his name.

WRIGHT BROTHERS, Wilbur (1867-1912) and Orville (1871-1948) were the inventors and builders of the first truly successful airplane.

They developed their interest in the science of flying at the end of the 1800s. In those days flying meant balloons, kites and gliders. The Wright Brothers concluded that one could make a flying machine by attaching an engine and a propeller to a glider.

In their bicycle shop they began to develop their first gliders between 1900 and 1902. Each autumn they built and flew the gliders at Kitty Hawk, North Carolina, where the sand dunes and wind conditions made an ideal test ground. After successfully

Top: Archimedes' discoveries. The Archimedean screw was used to irrigate land. Middle left: The law of specific gravity. Because silver is lighter than gold, 1 kg of silver displaces more water than 1 kg of gold. Middle right: The area of a sphere equals four times the area of the half circle when the sphere is halved.

flying these, they planned their first powered airplane. By the fall of 1903 it was ready. It cost less than $1,000 to build, had wings that were 12 metres (40½ feet) long, and weighed 340 kilos (750 lbs) with pilot. The plane was powered by a lightweight gasoline engine specially built for it by the brothers.

They tossed a coin to see who should pilot it first, and Orville won. He flew 37 metres (120 feet) and stayed in the air for 12 seconds. The brothers had made history.

FLEMING, SIR ALEXANDER (1881-1955) was a British scientist who discovered the germ-killing power of penicillin.

In 1928, he was preparing some common germs for an experiment when he noticed a mould growing in the middle of them. It had accidently fallen into the germs from another plate. A mould is a tiny, simple plant of the fungus family that is related to mushrooms, rusts and mildews. Fleming could see that all around this mould the

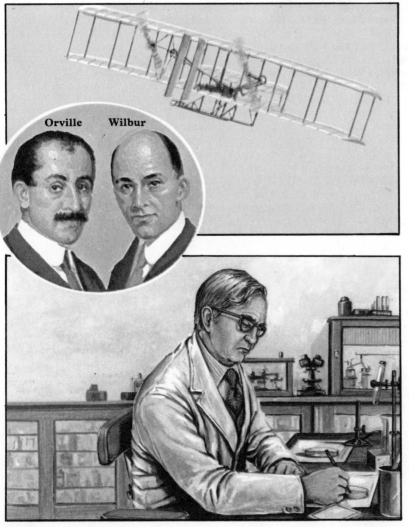

Orville   Wilbur

Above: Thomas Edison's best-known invention was the electric light bulb.

Left: The Wright brothers made the first engine-powered flight.

Below: Sir Alexander Fleming discovered the power of penicillin.

germs were unable to grow.

Fleming realized what this could mean. He decided on a simple experiment. He grew the same mould on broth. Then he took some test tubes that contained disease germs and put some of the prepared broth into the test tubes. As he had suspected would happen, the living germs were destroyed.

Fleming called the broth penicillin, but later that name was applied only to the chemical substance in the broth.

Penicillin was eventually purified for practical use as a medicine in 1940 by two other scientists, Howard W. Florey of Australia and Ernst Chain of Great Britain. All three shared the 1945 Nobel prize for medicine for their work.

The discovery of penicillin started a new age of medicine. It is used in the treatment of many common illnesses such as pneumonia, and has led to the making of many more equally useful drugs.

Index

ACKNOWLEDGEMENTS

The Publishers would like to thank the following individuals and organizations for their kind permission to reproduce the photographs in this book.

All-Sport 197 above, 200 below, 201 below, 202, 203; Heather Angel/Biofotos 29, 30, 34, 37, 111 above; Anglo Chinese Educational Institute 90 below, 91 left; Associated Press 207 centre; Australian News & Information Service 48; Clive Bardon 179; Norman Barrett 200 above; B.B.C. 159; B.P. Photographic Library 98 above; Paul Brierley 132; Peter Clayton 71 below; Colorpix 92 centre, 93, 96 below, 101 above, 105 centre and below, 199; Colorsport 204 below, 205 below, 207 above; Cooper-Bridgeman Library 71 above, 78 above, 180 below, 181 right, 182 above, 183, 190 below right; G. & P. Corrigan 92 below; Council of Christians and Jews 130, 131 above; Decca 184; Douglas Dickins 187, 190 above; A. M. Ehrlich 64 above, 103 below, 156, 158, 167, 186 above, 188, 189; E. T. Archive 79 below; Geoslides 104 below; Giraudon 181 left; Robert Harding 70; M. Holford 64 below, 65, 74, 180 above; Hong Kong Tourist Office 193 below; Alan Hutchison Library 84 left, 89 centre, 102 below, 103 above, 104 above, 105 above, 112, 113 above and centre; Illustrated London News 81; Japan Information Centre 91 right; Japan National Tourist Organisation 204 centre; H. R. Lewis 73 below; Mansell Collection 76; MEPhA 131 below; Henry Moore Foundation 182 below; National Portrait Gallery 78-79; New Zealand House 115 centre; The Patent Office 154; Popperfoto 82, 83, 90 above; Publicare 204 above; Salvation Army 212; Satour 102 above and centre, 103 centre; Solar Films 99 centre; Tate Gallery 181 below; UKAEA 84 right; U.P.I. 205 above, 207 below; U.S. Travel Service 32, 107 above, 108 below; John Watney 85; Werner Forman Archive 73 above; Reg Wilson 186 below, 190 below left; ZEFA 18, 19, 23, 25, 27, 33, 45, 51, 66, 68, 72, 88, 89 above and below, 94, 95, 96 above, 97, 98 centre and below, 99 above and below, 100, 101 below, 107 centre and below, 108 above, 109, 110, 111 below, 113 below, 114, 115 above, 117, 155, 163, 178 below, 192, 193 above and centre, 194, 195, 196, 197 centre and below, 198.